A CURE FOR
SERPENTS

THE DUKE OF PIRAJNO

An Italian doctor in North Africa

WITH A NEW PREFACE BY
DERVLA MURPHY

TRANSLATED BY
KATHLEEN NAYLOR

ELAND BOOKS, LONDON
&
HIPPOCRENE BOOKS, INC., NEW YORK

Published by
ELAND BOOKS
53 Eland Road London SW11 5JX
&
HIPPOCRENE BOOKS, INC.,
171 Madison Avenue, New York, NY 10016

First published by Andre Deutsch 1955
© Andre Deutsch

First issued in this paperback edition 1985
Reprinted 1986, 1987

British Library Cataloguing in Publication Data

Denti di Pirajno, Alberto
    A cure for serpents: an Italian doctor in North Africa.
    I. Medicine—Africa, North—History
    I. Title
    610′.92′4   R652

ISBN 0-907871-16-X

Printed and bound in Great Britain
by Redwood Burn Ltd, Trowbridge, Wiltshire

Cover Illustration © *Tony Ansell*
Cover Design © *Patrick Frean*
Map © *Reginald Piggott*

CONTENTS

Maps are to be found on pp. 12, 13 and 14

ILLUSTRATIONS

Publisher's Note

The photographs used in the first edition are lost. The present reissue uses imperfect reproductions in the belief that readers will prefer them to none at all.

NEW PREFACE

Sixty years ago King Victor Emmanuel III of Italy posted four men to Tripoli, to the remote coastal station of Buerat el Hsun on the Gulf of Sirte. The group was led by a very, very tall young man, a cousin of the King, later to become the Duke of Aosta. His medical officer was Alberto Denti, later to become the Duke of Pirajno. The first Duke of Pirajno had been created in 1642, by King Philip IV of Spain and Sicily, and Alberto Denti didn't believe that 'all men are equal' – he only behaved towards them as if he did. This makes a nice change from some modern do-gooders who fervently preach Equality but quite often fail to act accordingly.

A Cure for Serpents is about the "inestimable satisfactions known only to those who have lived in Africa". It is a happy, uncomplicated, unpretentious book and the author comes through as unassuming, kindly, humorous. He valued what are now alarmingly known as "the old-fashioned virtues" of courage, honesty and loyalty. He was apparently untroubled by inner doubts and conflicts about the role of the white man in Africa and he approvingly quotes Kipling's reference to the sons of those who conquered India "possessing that territory by right of birth". He goes on: "I would like on a humbler note to sing the praises of the unknown Italian women born and bred in our colonies. White or half-caste, they added savour to success when it smiled upon their men, and rallied their spirits when they were felled by adversity".

That allusion to 'half-castes' is revealing. It marks a fundamental difference between the Italians (or French or Portuguese) as colonisers and the British in that role. India's large population of Anglo-Indians is witness to the fact that many British males allowed colour-prejudice to be cancelled out by more urgent emotions. But then, in relation to their

5

offspring, master-race attitudes – convenient to justify one's 'civilizing' mission – sternly reasserted themselves. Few British colonial administrators would have written in praise of India's Eurasians as the Duke of Pirajno wrote of half-castes in the Italian colonies.

The Duke spent several of his African years in Ethiopia, eventually becoming Chef de Cabinet to the Duke of Aosta when he was appointed Viceroy of what was then called Abyssinia. The Ethiopian chapters in this book are scarcely less hilarious than Evelyn Waugh's recollections of that country, though they are much more tolerant and affection-ate. In general, the Italians were not condescending to those they conquered. This must partly explain something which greatly surprised me when I trekked through Ethiopia's highlands in 1967. Nowhere did I encounter the anti-Italian bitterness my reading had led me to expect. In Asmara – capital of the Italian colony of Eritrea, to which the Duke of Pirajno was posted in 1930 – there remained a few thousand Italians, most of whom had been born in the rather dreary Italian-built town. After the union of Eritrea with Haile Selassie's Empire, in 1952, they had chosen to "stay on" because to them Eritrea was *home* as nowhere else could be. Their relations with the Eritreans seemed to be excellent, and all the locals with whom I spoke declared emphatically that Italians were their favourite foreigners. Further south, in the town of Gondar – Ethiopia's ancient capital – my Amhara host remarked that any Ethiopian government would have taken a century to build the roads and bridges and establish the telephone communications that were pro-vided by the Italians in five years. People rarely referred to the Italians' motives for this development of their country; having got rid of the occupying forces, the Ethiopians seemed to have amiably chosen to view the Italian era as an unmixed blessing.

Many recently reprinted travel books have heightened our awareness of the pace of change – political, technologi-cal, ecological – during the past fifteen or twenty years. The

Ethiopia I knew in 1967 had scarcely changed since the Duke of Pirajno travelled by mule "in caravans with hoardes of Gallas and packs of negroes, sleeping very often under the stars with a pack-saddle for a pillow". It was not then a poor country, as the Indian subcontinent is poor. The peasants were indeed exploited in many areas by the land-owning Coptic Church, but they were adequately clothed and fed. I shared their diet for months and it was sustaining, though monotonous. Yet already, because of deforestation and erosion, there were identifiable "starvation danger zones" along my route through Tigre, Begemdir, Gojjam and Wollo provinces. I wrote at the time – "All over Addis Ababa, extravagant, meaningless new buildings rise at random from amidst a huddle of mud shacks, to offend both the eye and the reason of the beholder . . . Evidently these architectural frolics are inspired by a desire to create an impression of imminent prosperity. Much suffering might have been avoided by the spending of this money in drought areas. Addis is used as a screen behind which the Ethiopians themselves hide from the facts of their national life. In the 1960's the simplest way to gratify the old Amharic blind pride is by building a spectacular capital: to lessen trachoma or forestall famine in remote areas would be unobtrusive achievements, giving no impression of Instant Progress . . The formidable communication problem presented by the highland terrain is sometimes given as an excuse for this governmental flight from reality. Yet, unlike many other undeveloped countries, Northern Ethiopia is fortunate in having a uniquely healthy climate and a generally self-sufficient population . . . An energetic and responsible government could bring prosperity to most parts of the region". But already, though I didn't realise it, disaster was too close to be averted. Within seven years a Marxist military régime had replaced the Emperor and had attempted land-reform, following the famine of the early 1970s. They seemed however to lack the will, the resources and the know-how to cope with the combined effects of erosion and recurrent drought. It may be some small comfort to the Pirajno ghost that without the roads built by his country-men the situation now would be even worse than it is.

One of the Duke of Pirajno's most attractive character-istics was his skill at vaulting cultural barriers and finding a friend on the other side – or a tribal ideal with which he could enthusiastically identify. He rejoiced to discover that the aristocratic louse-infested warriors of the Azdjer Tuaregs were "blood brothers to that Roland who, at Ronce-valles, overpowered by the Moors and with the icy hand of death already gripping his heart, refused to retreat by so much as a step".

The Duke himself was frequently louse-infested; being superbly adaptable, he didn't find it necessary to travel with a posse of servants bearing home-comforts. He relished his many opportunities to share in the hardships of his patients' daily lives – in nomad desert encampments, on rugged mountainsides, in remote oases. He was less happy when called upon to serve in large towns, but his years in Asmara were redeemed by a pet lioness, reared from a tiny cub. The story of Neghesti records what must be one of the most remarkable leonine/human relationships ever to have devel-oped.

Being Dr Alberto Denti, as well as Duke of Pirajno, our hero had uncommon opportunities for entering harems. And being an Italian he had few inhibitions about recalling, vividly but decorously, what was revealed when some of his women patients disrobed. He frankly enjoyed describing the bodies of naked tribeswomen, paying special tribute to their breasts. These descriptions are neither scientific nor salacious. The Duke appreciated beauty: beautiful carpets, beautiful landscapes, beautiful buildings, beautiful women. Modern readers, coarsened by years of exposure to the vulgar exploitation of sex, will find these passages bland – almost coy. Yet when *A Cure for Serpents* was first published, in 1955 – just before the hectic dawn of the Per-missive Society – it shocked some of the author's British contemporaries. Certain retired pillars of the Raj, then in their seventies, thought it both unseemly and unprofessional – "No better than that Burton fella!"

In his opening chapter, the Duke of Pirajno describes the Duke of Aosta as "grave or gay as his mood or the occasion demanded . . . his humanity caused him to be interested in everything and everyone . . . he was intolerant only of complacency, meanness and pomposity". By the end of this book, readers will have recognised that these two dukes had many virtues in common.

Dervla Murphy © 1985

Chapter One

A DOCTOR AMONG THE JINNS

ONCE upon a time there was a King.

When I was presented to him I felt sorry for him; he seemed to me to be a prisoner of the surroundings into which he was born, to be humiliated by the tallness of his guards, resigned to the rascality of his servants and wearied by the vanity of his court.

Those admitted to his inner circle knew him as a man of keen intelligence and wide culture, a natural sceptic with a pungent sense of humour tinged with pessimism.

He was very short – but he had some extremely tall cousins.

One of them – even taller than the rest – would have filled the role of a demigod had he lived in pagan times; in the heroic Christian era he would have been a crusader or a knight errant. But in this greedy age, when knights are no longer brave, when cowardice mocks at valour, when ideals perish, done to death by ignoble expediency, and the ambitious frog puffs itself up but acquires none of the attributes of the ox except its presumptuous and stubborn obtuseness, this goodly young man was out of place.

He had an extraordinary quality – a radiance seemed to emanate from him and he had the gift of infusing into those around him something of the vitality of his own happy nature, which expanded in the glow of warm, human contacts and withered in the shadow of conventionality and compromise. He was grave or gay as his mood or the occasion demanded, and his humanity caused him to be interested in everything and everyone; he was sensitive to both the joys and sorrows of others, intolerant only of complacency, meanness and pomposity – which last he knew how to deflate with a single biting remark.

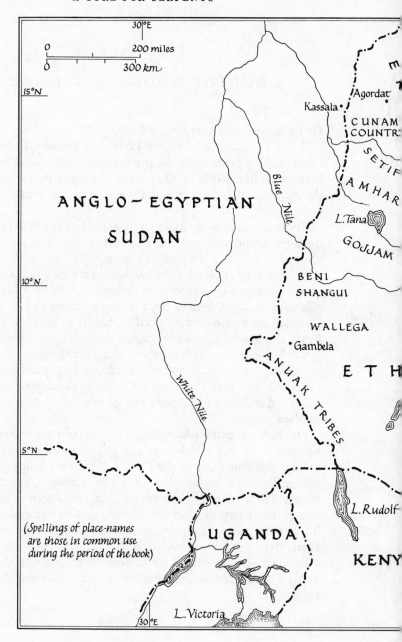

30°E

0 _____ 200 miles
0 _____ 300 km

15°N

E

Agordat

Kassala •

CUNAM
COUNTR

SETIF

AMHAR

Blue Nile

L. Tana

GOJJAM

ANGLO — EGYPTIAN

SUDAN

10°N

BENI
SHANGUI

WALLEGA

• Gambela

ETH

White Nile

ANUAK TRIBES

5°N

L. Rudolf

(Spellings of place-names
are those in common use
during the period of the book)

UGANDA

KENY

30°E

L. Victoria

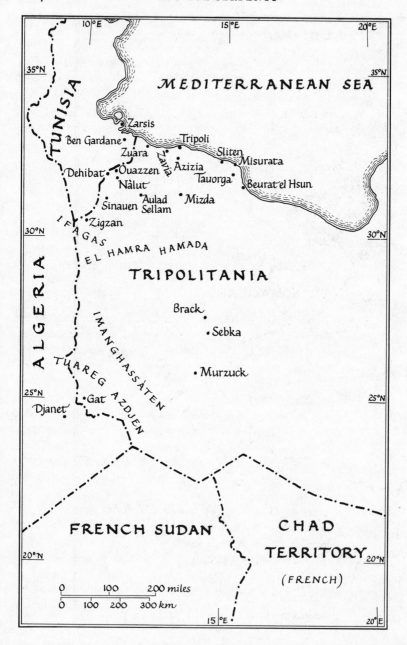

One such remark was repeated to the King.

Probably His Majesty – who was King Victor Emmanuel III of Italy – had no desire to become angry with the cousin he loved, but he lacked the energy to resist the zeal of some of his more realistic courtiers.

Perhaps, too, he thought that the punishment would be acceptable rather than otherwise to this Tall Young Man – who later became the Duke of Aosta – and who was always ready to engage enthusiastically in activities in distant lands. Or perhaps it was merely that at that particular moment the King found it impossible to forgive him his enormous height.

Whatever the reason, the cousin was posted to Tripoli, and on an August day which now seems fabulously remote he found himself in exile at Buerat el Hsun, in the Gulf of Sirte, with three officers, one of whom was a physician.

Thus it was that in Buerat el Hsun I opened my first African dispensary.

★   ★   ★

The time was 1924. In those days our colonies were interesting places – either because Rome had not yet made any attempt to regulate the lives of those who lived in them, or because, seeing that there were no prospects of easy and rapid enrichment, the Italians who went there were few, and endowed with unusual qualities and singular defects.

There were few colonial civil servants, for bureaucratic inflation had not yet extended to the colonial service. In general, officials were drawn from other departments and from the armed forces, and to a large extent they were men of undeniable worth and of an unimpeachable honesty which today would be regarded as quixotic.

The younger officials were trained in the school of men to whom honesty was as the breath of life, who took their responsibilities seriously and were imbued with a high sense of duty which nowadays seems to belong to the realm of make-believe. Labouring as they did for an ungrateful country, which at that time seemed to have a definite aversion for those who served her with loyalty and enthusiasm in places where everything was hostile, they found their recompense in those inward and inestimable satisfactions known only to those who have lived in Africa.

During the last war most civil servants in the African colonies were withdrawn to the towns, but many remained in the outlying districts, and many lost their lives there. In Tripoli, after the Italian and German troops had retreated into Tunisia, all the civilian officials remained at their posts pending the arrival of the British. These officials, with the help of a quantitatively negligible but qualitatively invaluable police force, succeeded in maintaining order and preventing outbreaks of violence even in those areas where the withdrawing military authorities lightheartedly abandoned shops and stores bursting with food, equipment, arms and ammunition.

Many of those whom the regular civil servants and the Army called 'civilians' were at that time pioneers in the real sense of the word. Later, owing to the undue multiplication of this category, the term 'pioneer' was used ironically, but those early adventurers were pioneers indeed – concessionaires, professional men, tradesmen, artisans, who succeeded in making a life for themselves on the desert shores of Libya and formed the nucleus of the Italian population. There was also, of course, the usual proportion of disappointed men who, impelled by native restlessness or by life's delusions, sought to forget the past and to build themselves a new life under a strange sky.

All these types were represented in microcosm at Buerat el Hsun.

There was the camel corps officer – a horseman of European fame who, fascinated by the desert, renounced the future international triumphs which certainly awaited him; there was the young second-lieutenant who 'disembarked with joy and exultation' in the hope of passing into the regulars, the seasoned and taciturn colonial veteran, the unfrocked monk who made a living as a photographer, the centurion with the immortal wife. This last likeable and unhappy youngster had surprised his wife *in flagrante delicto* and had riddled her with bullets, one of which entered the nape of her neck and emerged through her mouth after splitting her tongue. Three months later this imperishable lady, completely recovered, gave evidence in court without the slightest impediment in her speech.

Buerat el Hsun was a coastal station, caught between deserts of sea and sand. There was no local population and the nearest Bedouin tents were about eighty miles away. But although we were isolated we were certainly not lonely.

Along the shore stretched the tents of the married quarters of a desert unit; a hundred Blackshirts and a company of Eritrean Askaris constituted the military garrison. Occasionally a troop of *sawārī* in transit halted for a while; less often, the 'Gina', an ancient little steamer and relic of the Ottoman Navy, dropped anchor off shore, bringing us provisions, letters from Italy and gossip from Tripoli.

In Arabic, Buerat el Hsun means the 'wells of the Hsun', but no one knew who these Hsun were, and all trace of them had long since vanished. Our little world which for a time had its being in that remote corner of the Sirte has also disappeared and gone the way of the Hsun. The Very Tall Young Man died a prisoner in the hands of the British; the intrepid horseman who commanded the camel corps was treacherously struck down in an ambush; the centurion preceded his tenacious consort into the next world; the second-lieutenant sleeps beneath the cross planted by his comrades – and even the photographer-monk is lost among the shadows of a monastery which offered peace and forgiveness to a repentant sinner.

When the few survivors meet and talk of those far-off days and of that little world which has vanished, they are perpetually astonished to discover that it was not all a dream.

★ ★ ★

So there we were, in the family encampment stretched out along the shore. There was no lack of patients, and the various aspects of native life provided me with ample material for study. I was, moreover, forced to learn Arabic, and an old, half-paralysed non-commissioned officer named Dimadima initiated me, with the aid of a rapidly disintegrating spelling book, into the art of writing from right to left.

The camp was composed of people from every corner of Libya – for the most part women and children. They lived in the camp as in a large village, under the supervision of an old *shumbāshī* whose many wounds entitled him to a period of rest while the unit was away in the south, on the edge of still un-occupied territory, endeavouring to cut off the caravans which supplied the rebels. The women sighed and said resignedly that it would be a long war, unconscious of how much may be con-densed into the words: a long war, a soft-hearted government, a wily rebel.

Practically the whole gamut of tropical pathology was repre-sented in the camp, and the work was intensely interesting because of the very diverse origins of the subjects. All the various forms of malaria were present; the whole range of intestinal parasitology was covered; tuberculosis, very prevalent among people transferred from the desert or from the mountains to the coast, was rife; we had all the endemic-ophthalmias of the East, venereal disease in all its most florid manifestations, and children's and women's complaints in plenty.

I was the official medical officer of this human conglomeration, and the *shumbāshī* Busnina el Fituri was the mayor, or civil authority – a mayor, be it said, who wisely confined himself to the administrative field, because he knew full well that it would be difficult to attempt to impose his authority on his young and capricious wife, on his shrewd and sagacious mother-in-law, or on the Sanhedrin of older women who were the real rulers of the camp. Most of these dowagers were under forty-five, and only two were nearing sixty. In Europe they would have been considered still comparatively young. But these women, married as soon as they reached the age of puberty, exhausted by early and repeated confinements, often obliged to perform tasks beyond their strength, lost their youth and beauty early. In some of them there still lingered a vivacious smile, a certain spontaneity as a reminder of what they once had been. The Berber women in particular retained some semblance of youth, their slim, lithe bodies being preserved by their plain diet, which consisted largely of ground barley.

To compensate for their premature physical decay, however, these women enjoyed the authority and prestige which the Moslem world confers on those to whom years have added wisdom. They had, in fact, imposed a matriarchal regime upon the camp.

One of the most respected of these matrons was the mother of a non-commissioned officer called et-Turk because of his Ottoman origin. The old woman still insisted on her title of *lālla* which is Berber for 'Mrs', for although it was forty years since Lalla Saida had abandoned Southern Algeria to follow her husband, a *bashi-bazouk* sergeant, she still remained obstinately Berber, and even at that date could hardly conceal a certain disdain when speaking of an Arab.

Another attribute of her race which Lalla Saida possessed in marked degree was that unfortunate passion for the supernatural which has gained for the Moslems of the west – of the Maghreb – that solid reputation for witchcraft and sorcery, which causes them to be abhorred by all other followers of the Prophet.

I had been treating Lalla Saida for some time for sciatica, and when this cleared up she regarded me with high esteem and even benevolence. One day when I was drinking tea in her tent she honoured me with all kinds of compliments for, as she said, it was seldom that Allah conceded to mortal man – and especially to an infidel – the power to expel *Tab'a*.

Charmed to receive the benediction of Allah and honoured by so much favour, I was nevertheless obliged to confess that I had not the pleasure of *Tab'a's* acquaintance. Lalla Saida shook her head sadly at my ignorance and handed me a third cup of tea full of roasted peanuts.

It was clear, she said, that I had not lived at Laghūat or at Ghardai, where every Berber child knew things which were hidden from even the oldest and wisest Arabs and other profane persons. In the Mzab, everyone knew that *Tab'a*, the Persecutrix, was the embodiment of all the malevolence of all the evil spirits that had ever troubled the seed of Adam, from the spiteful fairies to the pitiless, relentless fiends; that she was the cause of every misfortune, every disaster.

As far as I could gather, this monstrous incarnation of evil combined the cheerful malice of the Neapolitan *munaciello* – who amuses himself by upsetting saucepans, hiding the careful housewife's knitting needles, tormenting lovelorn girls during the long, languid summer afternoons – with the limitless ferocity of Eblis, the prince of demons.

In any case, Lalla Saida assured me that *Tab'a* was no laughing matter; that she was indeed a most terrible being; sometimes she took pleasure in calling the timid and fearful by name, haunting them invisibly, so that when they turned round to look they found no one. But that was nothing: *Tab'a* also troubled people's sleep and induced horrible nightmares. She might, for example, appear in the dreams of a respectable matron, taking the form of a negress or a witch, and, having insulted her, beaten her and thrown her down a ravine, she would disappear in smoke, carrying off with her the woman's gold and silver ornaments, her sons and her husband. Lovers, said Lalla Saida, lived in terror of *Tab'a*, who was capable of rendering a bridegroom impotent on his wedding night; she had a particular predilection for deflowering maidens, implanting lacerating pains in the bones of older women, blinding adulterers, and covering the faces of the vain with horrid spots. There was no remedy in the ordinary sense of the word against *Tab'a:* you could only say prayers, have a spell cast over you, and hope to find ways of escaping the demon's notice.

But I, continued Lalla Saida, had practised no exorcism – and yet *Tab'a* had definitely removed her attentions from her leg. At this point she slipped off one trouser leg and offered for my inspection a limb which thirty years ago must have provided considerable food for the imagination. 'Perhaps there is magic in the injections?' she suggested, still amazed at the success of my treatment. Well, however that might be, there was no doubt that I was one of Allah's chosen vessels, since he had deigned to give me power over evil spirits; perhaps one day he might even permit me to talk with the genii who guarded the subterranean treasure. It would be a sign of great favour, leading to untold riches. 'Allah's will be done,' said Lalla Saida hopefully.

Unfortunately, Allah has not yet seen fit to grant me that boon.

★ ★ ★

'Whence come disease and healing?' asked the Prophet Moses of God.

'From me,' was the reply.

'What purpose then do doctors serve?'

'They earn their living and cultivate hope in the heart of the patient until I either take away his life or give him back his health.'

Thus it was written in Nozhat el Majalis some centuries before Ambroise Paré said to the King of France, with superb humility: '*Je t'ai pansé, Dieu t'a guéri . . .*'

To the Moslem the physician is Allah's instrument, and it is Allah who allows him to cure a patient when he, Allah, has decided that he shall recover. It is this, of course, that gives the physician his privileged status in Islamic society.

Nevertheless, without in any way questioning the Divine will, the believer may still enquire into the origin of the diseases to which he is subject and ask the reason for his suffering.

Disease, he is told, is sent from God for the expiation of sins, and it may also be taken into account in the final reckoning after death. But Allah does not always act directly, and the believer knows that sickness may be caused by one of three agents through which the Divine power may work: the stars, mortals, and the jinns. Heavenly bodies, it seems, have a great influence on the onset and course of disease; particular importance is attached to the phases of the moon and to its eclipses, and certain constellations – the Pleiads, for example – may bring sickness and death to your house. But man too can adversely affect his neighbour's health. He may have the 'evil eye' and the power to invoke misfortune, or he may be able to summon up evil spirits and jinns and obtain the help of supernatural beings for the accomplishment of his malevolent designs. The good Moslem fears and worships the jinn and his consort the jinniyah; they, it seems, were the first inhabitants of the world, long before the appearance of man, and the sons of Adam are still under their occult influence. They abound in lonely places and are the cause of all phenomena for which natural laws provide no other explanation. The universe is so full of them that Ibn el Hajj Ettlemsêni affirms that if a needle fell from the heavens it could not fail to fall upon the head of a jinn or a jinniyah.

From the medical point of view it appears that there are three categories of jinn: the itinerant type, who cause epidemics, the stationary type, who cause endemic diseases, and the personal type who cause individual sickness and disorders.

Tab'a belongs to the last category; in her, I was told, all the powers of hell are united.

★   ★   ★

It was not until a month after I had ceased to treat little Selima bent Nuri et-Turk that I discovered that she was the grandchild of Lalla Saida. There was no reason to suppose they were related, as I had always visited the old woman in her tent, whereas the child, accompanied by a servant, came regularly to the dispensary for the injections which cured her of the Jacksonian epilepsy from which she suffered.

One day, however, on entering her grandmother's tent I found Selima there, and Lalla Saida spoke to me with pride of this grandchild, daughter of her son Nuri et-Turk, who at that time was with his unit in the Mizda territory. The grandmother admitted to spoiling the child shamelessly; at the age of six she already possessed all the grace and coquetry of a woman.

Selima's elegance when she presented herself at the dispensary was quite breath-taking; she was always adorned with such an array of harmonious colours that she looked like some wondrous, exotic bird. There were pale blue trousers embroidered with darker blue, puffed *sirwāl* clasped into gold anklets, spotless white blouse under a *stambulina*, a long green velvet jacket embroidered with silver and reaching to the knees – all this finery beneath a pink and yellow *holy* which covered her from head to foot. A touch of rouge at the level of her cheek bones gave warmth to her amber skin, and her grandmother told me that the child had given them no rest until she had been allowed to wear her mother's own necklace of gold coins and to spray herself with perfume when she visited the Christian doctor, for she was a little nervous of the *tebīb* and wished to make a good impression.

On entering the dispensary the six-years-old Selima would pause ceremoniously on the threshold and make a low bow, to which I replied with equal solemnity, subsequently inviting her to climb on to the bed. While I busied myself removing the pieces of the syringe from the sterilizer and unwinding the gauze in which they were wrapped, she would remove her *hāik*, loosen her trousers with the utmost dignity, and clamber on to the bed, dropping her sandals with a curious sound like the beating of a bird's wing. If the old negress who accompanied her attempted to help her, Selima, with the proud and fretful air of a weary sultana, would dismiss her with the words: 'Leave me, creature!'

By the time I approached the bed the sultana would be lying face downwards with a minute triangle of skin visible between the folds of the green velvet *stambulina* and the silver belt of the lowered trousers. She did not flinch as the needle penetrated the flesh or as the syringe emptied: only a convulsive contraction of the bare feet betrayed the pain.

She was completely dressed again almost before I had finished washing the syringe, standing before me enveloped once more in her pink and yellow *holy*.

'May God be with you, my father.'

'Allah's blessing on you, O princess.'

As she reached the threshold, she paused in answer to my last ceremonial salutation, drew a corner of her *hāik* across her face, looked over her shoulder at me, and with great dignity murmured a word which unfortunately happened to be one of those used by accessible women to curb the enthusiasm of too audacious admirers. The servant clapped her hand to her mouth in horror, but nevertheless gave me a broad smile of pride in her prodigious charge, who was now proceeding gravely down the footpath between the tents, stepping over the stones as if she were executing a ritual dance.

Selima's mother had been one of the most beautiful prostitutes in Benghazi. During an excursion to Tripoli she met Nuri et-Turk, fell in love with him, and married him.

In the Moslem world such marriages are not considered shocking, and they are no more unsuccessful than marriages to which the bride brings her virginity intact. Neither is a man who makes such a marriage cut by his friends. Women in this category are pitied rather than despised, for has not Allah, who orders all things, ordained that they shall follow that profession?

This fatalism with regard to individual destiny makes it unnecessary for the mother of a family who has been a prostitute before her marriage to conceal her past, and if she refers to it she does so without any false shame. A princess of the House of Savoy, when visiting the family encampment of a battalion of Libyan Askaris near Tripoli, once asked the sergeant's wife who was acting as hostess how she came to speak such good Italian. The woman replied with a touch of pride: 'Oh, your Highness, I went to bed with so many officers!'

It was certainly not these women who created problems for the excellent Busnina, whose task it was to maintain order and harmony in this harem of husbandless wives.

There were times when a wave of madness seemed to sweep through the camp, when Busnina cursed his fate and gesticulated with his great tattooed hands and called on Heaven to witness that he had never done anything to deserve this. On these black days the spirit of discord popped up from the infernal regions to sow trouble, and any slight and stupid question of precedence at the well, or a donkey which overturned a saucepan as it careered round the camp, or a slap given to a neighbour's child by a woman tired of being pestered by it, was sufficient to fan the smouldering flames and to start savage fights which obviously served as an outlet after too much abstinence.

There might be a period of idyllic calm undisturbed by any incident – two or three weeks perhaps, when no invective was heard, when all was sisterly amiability, with endearments and respectful forms of address on everyone's lips (*ukhaytī, yummī* – little sister, mother mine); and then the arrival of an Askari to spend a short leave with his wife would be sufficient to upset everyone and disrupt the whole camp.

When it was known that the husband of Fatma was arriving, her happy excitement was taken as shameless provocation; and when she braided her hair anew and applied fresh colour to her eyes, or shut herself in her tent and stopped up every little hole, or crouched over a brazier for hours at a time to impregnate herself with the perfume of *lubān* and of *bhur* for the greater delight of her husband, all this was too much. Every poisonous epithet to which the other women could lay their tongues was flung at her, defaming Fatma herself, her family and her whole race.

Was it not a crying shame that Ahmed ben Aissa was coming on leave when much more deserving husbands who had been longer away could not obtain so much as one day off? Had not even Hassuna el Jammâli, who had been awarded the bronze medal, written to his wife, saying that he would not be able to come to her until the autumn? Such injustice and favouritism were not to be borne.

Fatma's bosom friends naturally had their own contributions to make. Had her husband not been a batman once? That explained it, of course; dear Fatma had obviously known how to obtain favours from the officer; was she not a woman of the Zintan? It really was hard – in this world, prostitutes had all the luck.

And so on.

But with her husband's arrival the storm subsided. All the women welcomed the soldier with little shrieks of joy and clustered round him excitedly; his wife's friends pressed hard upon him with the excuse of obtaining news of their husbands. They talked to him in low voices, their breath coming quickly, and they stretched their faces towards his like hounds on the trail. They blocked his way into the tent and commented indignantly on the shamelessness of Fatma, who refused to relinquish his arm for a moment and devoured him with the eyes of a bride fresh from her marriage bed.

'Look at them!' Busnina said to me. 'Do you see how they smile at Fatma? And if they could, they would throttle her. The mere sight of a male is enough to make them lose their senses. Would you believe it – when they go to Dimadima Eshebâni on the pretext of dictating letters to their husbands they stand before him as petrified as owls in daylight? They scent the male even in that paralysed old scarecrow! May Allah curdle their blood!'

★ ★ ★

When the younger women wished to consult me at the dispensary they had to bring someone with them – either their children or their mother or mother-in-law or a woman friend. 'You can't be too careful with those she-devils,' Busnina explained. So far as women were concerned, Busnina trusted only his wife and his mother-in-law.

So, when the women came to see me, they arrived in groups, chattering and pushing their children in front of them. They entered, murmured a greeting to those who had arrived earlier, and sat on the floor in the waiting-room, their *hāiks* drawn across their faces, leaving only one eye visible – but missing nothing of what went on.

In the early days I knew too little Arabic to be able to manage by myself, and in any case in dealing with women I thought it advisable to use an interpreter. One of the older women in the camp had been employed in the hospital at Tripoli when she was young and had learned Italian. She was a fairly good nurse, and would have been useful as an interpreter if she could have been persuaded to refrain from embellishing her translation with interjections of her own which bore no relation to what the patient said. Also, after every few words, she would throw in a few phrases such as, 'Just imagine that!' or 'Allah's curse upon it!' or 'Would you believe it?' and other irrelevancies which made the whole thing unintelligible to me. The patient, always with her face covered, would describe her symptoms in a low voice, occasionally throwing me a glance to make sure I was following. Eventually, the old woman would interrupt the monologue with

an authoritative gesture, turn towards me, stand to attention, and
in stentorian tones begin her translation, which might run something like this: 'As you know, this woman has the liver of a
camel, Allah's curse upon it, and, would you believe it?—her
belly hangs down to her very thighs and if she breathes, why,
without more ado she spits and dies on the very day of your
lordship's feast – and that's the truth!'

With these delightfully accurate and lucid descriptions of the
patient's symptoms at my disposal, I was often obliged, with the
little Arabic I could muster, to try to understand something of
the torrent of words which the woman, pleased to be able to
speak to me directly, let loose upon me.

They all started by being reluctant to undress. When I asked
them to remove their clothes they looked appealingly at the
nurse, their mother or their mother-in-law, as though calling
upon them to witness that the sacrifice of their modesty was
being forced upon them. However, once their virtue had been
properly affirmed they offered no further resistance, and after
undressing lay naked on the bed, covering their faces (that last
defence of the virtuous woman) with hands enmeshed in a
chemise.

When a gynæcological examination was necessary they protested more vigorously, but they submitted in the end, and were
often convulsed with laughter at some remark made by the nurse.
On one occasion I had to examine the wife of the unit's bugler.
She was a superb creature from the Ulad Mahmud; her skin was
like polished bronze and she leaned against the wall in the attitude
of the Medici Venus, staring wide-eyed at the speculum I held
in my hand. 'For the love of God,' she stammered, 'surely you
are not going to look inside me with a telescope?' She was
trembling from head to foot, but when the old nurse, wagging
her head, croaked at her, 'You are beautiful, very beautiful,
Khadigia, but even you won't have stars in your belly,' she
laughed and lay down on the bed with her arms over her face,
and went on laughing behind them throughout my examination.

They had great respect for medicines and drugs. Pills,
powders and decoctions possessed for them a magic which could

not fail to cure them. But their greatest veneration was reserved for the scalpel which 'cut out the pain' and for the syringe which immediately 'put the lost health back into the blood'.

Accustomed to being treated with fire-balls, scarifications and blood-letting, they found modern medical methods exceedingly tame, and were astonished at the results. In fact, having had so little recourse to modern drugs, very little resistance had been created, so that amazing cures were obtained. The strength and rapidity of the reactions were such that the manifestations of advanced syphilis and painful arthritic symptoms cleared up on a second injection of bismuth and after the first doses of salicylate, and it was necessary to insist with great firmness on the continuation of the treatment, since the patients, believing themselves cured, naturally saw no further need for it.

The unexpected cures it was possible to obtain engendered a blind faith which sometimes tore at the heartstrings. Once I was at the bedside of an old woman who was dying. The eyes of her daughters were fixed on me, expecting a miracle, and when I repeated to them the words of the Koran: 'All is sent from God', they calmly replied: 'And healing also' – meaning that, as the physician is Allah's instrument, healing can be bestowed however grave the malady.

There was also the mother who, on a night of *Ramadān*, held out to me in mute appeal the body of her dead son, expecting me to bring him to life again.

On another night, also during *Ramadān*, while the women were busy preparing the meal which would make up for the day-long fast a child of two fell into one of the fires. When I reached the tent I found the mother, in the light of the flames, rocking the dying child to and fro with the rhythmic movement of an automaton. She was only a child herself. As I ran my fingers lightly over the frightful burns with which the child was covered, the mother's eyes – terrified and imploring – never left my face. She said nothing, but at every moan from the child's lips her eyebrows twitched spasmodically. Busnina was beside me, interpreting my gestures, and when he saw that the child had died, and muttered the usual words of resignation, the child-mother broke into such frightful, sickening laughter that the little crowd around us instinctively drew back.

She went on laughing, and, pressing the body of the child against her breast, began in a gay voice to talk to it rapidly, feverishly, in a way that made one's blood run cold. She called the child by name, asked why it was sleeping, promised it a sweet, a new embroidered vest. She bent close over it, and her talk ran on and on. Her *hāik* had slipped from her head, and the pierced silver pieces on her forehead jangled together. In the crook of her arm the little head lolled inert, the dull, unseeing eyes wide open to the stars. Suddenly she stopped rocking the child and looked closely into the little face, which death had turned into a dark mask. Then her voice began to falter; she looked again, and her speech became slower, until at last it died away in a dry sob which escaped through lips which still smiled into the face of her son.

The women had withdrawn into their tents; the men had gone away. In the midst of the now neglected and dying fires the child-mother sat alone, crouching low like a wounded animal, rocking her dead child to and fro.

★ ★ ★

All the women of the camp doted on their children and illustrated to perfection the old Arab proverb which says that in the eyes of its mother a cockroach is a gazelle. The children were dirty, unkempt, and ragged, and the most elementary rules of hygiene were neglected – but nevertheless their mothers were their most humble, willing slaves. I never detected any difference between the treatment of boys and of girls; their mothers worshipped them irrespective of their sex, and were as worried over the girls as over the boys when they were ill, though in their attitude to the latter there was perhaps already something of that subjection to the male which Islam imposes on its women. They were proud of their daughters' beauty, and would talk of how the men would fight for them in later years; and in the precocious exploits of their sons they detected with satisfaction the future bandit, the terror of the caravans.

B

One young mother of the Magharba tribe whom I had treated became exultant when she thought she had discovered the mark of a brigand in the son at her breast. Shut in a tent in the vast encampment, with the Sirte wind blowing furiously outside, she held up her naked son before her, supporting him under the armpits and, ignoring his whimpering, kicking and writhing, she danced him up and down on her lap to the accompaniment of endearments and shrill exclamations of delight. – 'Ah! . . . you will be taller than them all; Sef en-Nàsser will pay you tribute; the arms of your women will be weighed down with bracelets; you will raid all the tents from the mountains to the Fezzan! O *tebīb*, this man will make off with the camels and leave no trace! . . .'

In general the Arab woman judges a man by primitive standards. It is the strong man to whom she gives her unstinted admiration – the man who tolerates no injury, rebels against authority, takes savage revenge upon his enemies and fearlessly commits robbery and murder. I was therefore not surprised at the pride with which an old woman of the camp informed me one day that she had five sons, and that all were in gaol – three in Tunisia and two in Tripoli. 'So you see,' she confided to me, 'all my sons are true Rogebans. Do you know what happens when we Rogeban women give birth? When the pains begin, they remove our ear-rings, bracelets, rings and necklaces – otherwise the child would make off with them as soon as he was born! Our lads are strong. Ask anyone. Anyone will tell you about the Rogebans!'

The warrior spirit and courage of their sons is the women's pride, and Hamîda Fargiani, who had two sons serving as Askaris with the unit and two others among the Salem el Atayoush rebels, was not at all disturbed at the thought that they might meet in battle on opposite sides and slaughter one another. She felt only pride and satisfaction in the knowledge that her sons were warriors. 'My sons are born with a gun in their hands,' she told me, 'and they shoot in whatever direction they choose.'

In addition to the great love which Moslem parents have for their children they also believe that children who have acquired merit in the eyes of Allah and die professing their faith can save their parents from eternal damnation.

The Arabs tell a story of a twelve-year-old orphan who fell ill and died. He had recited the Koran so well and had praised Allah with such fervour that he was received into heaven and acclaimed with joy by all the angels.

Seeing himself so honoured and glorified, the boy became proud; he paraded up and down the pathways of the celestial gardens, compared himself with the unfading flowers of paradise, and gazed at his reflection in the crystal fountains, murmuring to himself, 'Is there anyone in paradise as beautiful as I?'

An angel surprised him at this vainglorious amusement and said to him, 'How can you be so self-satisfied while your parents burn in hell?'

At these words the boy was smitten with remorse, and realised that in his exclusive concern with his own eternal bliss, he had not taken the trouble to discover what had become of the souls of his parents.

'Oh God,' he prayed, 'if you cannot give me back my father and mother, let me at least go and suffer with them.'

God sent the Archangel Gabriel to him with the reply, 'Seek your parents throughout the infernal regions, and when you have found them bring back with you to paradise whichever one of them you will.'

The boy immediately set off to the regions of the damned. He searched the whole gehenna in which Moslems burn, but found neither father nor mother; and in the Christian and the Jewish hells he had no better fortune. He descended into the *Saqar* where sorcerers purge their sins and picked his way among the dark holes inhabited by worshippers of the stars; he combed the abyss where the polytheists groan, and continued his way down until, in the lowest pit of all, the *hāwīya*, he found his mother.

But when he asked her to leave with him she refused. 'I was disobedient,' she said. 'I did not recite the prayers. I drank wine. I did not observe the fast of *Ramadān*. I did not keep myself pure. It is your father you must save; he worked in the sun and the rain to earn us bread.'

The boy was beside himself with grief at these words, and when at last he found his father he cast himself into his arms, weeping.

But his father also refused to be saved by his son. 'Go back to your mother,' he said. 'It is she you must redeem. She bore you for nine months in the womb, gave you milk from her breast for two years, cradled you upon her knees, kept watch against vipers and scorpions, lay awake at night to warm you with her body. I am too great a sinner; I have offended too much against Allah; I am unworthy to enter paradise.'

Then the son threw himself to the ground, and wept, and tore his face with his finger-nails. 'Oh God,' he cried, 'what shall I do? Let me remain here, I beseech Thee, in the fire with my father and mother.'

And at that moment he heard the voice of Allah saying, 'Take your father and your mother and seventy of their companions, and bring them with you into the kingdom of the blessed.'

The heretical Berbers also believe that a dead child can gain eternal salvation for its parents, but the form of their belief differs slightly from that of the four orthodox sects. They do not believe, for instance, that dead children can save parents who have wept at their death, or even those who have continued in their hearts to mourn their loss. This stern rule is interpreted as a punishment for believers who have not learnt to submit to the divine will and lack the courage to purge their hearts of sorrow which Allah sends to test the piety of good Moslems.

A flute-player had a little daughter who died. He was an ignorant man, a poor sinner who drank wine and committed adultery, but he never rebelled against the will of God, and accepted with humility the trials that were inflicted upon him. He therefore did not weep when his child slept her last sleep, but uttered the words of resignation and continued quietly playing his flute. Some years later, when he was playing at a wedding, death overtook him suddenly, and the angel Israfil received his soul.

He found himself on the dry and stony bed of a river, and as he walked among the stones he became aware that an enormous serpent was following him. He tried to run, but his legs were as heavy as lead. At the edge of the river-bed he saw a little old man walking slowly along. 'O my father,' he cried, 'save me from this monster!' The old man replied, 'I cannot; I am too weak', and went on his way.

The serpent was gaining upon him, and when it had almost reached him he suddenly came upon a man with a body all covered in feathers and with two enormous wings attached to his shoulders, who said to him, 'Climb that mountain.' And in fact there was a mountain, the peak of which was shrouded in golden mist, and the flute-player made a supreme effort to scramble up it, with the serpent still at his heels. At last he reached the summit, and there the mist cleared and the sky was blue, and the sinner found himself in the midst of thousands and thousands of children. Some were throwing rosebuds at each other, some were twining themselves wreaths of stars, others were running races with young stags or playing with snow-white doves. A chorus of young boys sang the praises of Allah, while others wrote lines from the Koran on sheets of silver at the dictation of old men with shining faces.

And here the flute-player was greeted by his daughter, who dismissed the serpent with a gesture of her hand. Overcome with emotion, he embraced his child and told her of his adventure with the serpent; and she, being versed in the secrets of the realms beyond, explained its meaning. 'The serpent you feared so much represented your sins; the old man was the embodiment of your good actions, which were too negative to overcome your faults; the bird-man was Israfil in one of his many forms – and this is our children's paradise, where God allows us to intercede for our parents when they have not wept for our death.'

★　★　★

As for the Arabs' attitude to women: Giâmi in his *Spring Garden* warns men to be on their guard against them – 'even if they belong to the right tribe'. He asserts that their intelligence is deficient, and that they are faithless: 'Do not trust her; if she is bad, show her no respect, but even if she is good, do not trust her.' However, this cynicism does not extend to a man's mother. The most rascally Arab respects his mother, and even a man of mature age, usually proud and overbearing, will become meek and timid in her presence.

Great respect is also paid to a man's mother-in-law, whom, as if to strengthen the family connection, he calls 'aunt'. Busnina el Fituri had an enormous respect for his mother-in-law, and when he spoke of her it was with the utmost awe and reverence; when he said 'my aunt, Khalti' he pursed his lips and lifted his eyebrows as though to say, 'What a woman!'

Busnina's mother-in-law was indeed a most exceptional person. She was, of course, no longer young and had lost all pretensions to beauty. She dressed differently from the other women. Her face was nearly always uncovered and she wore a silk shift which was not the traditional *surīya*. Her small mouth was set in a fixed smile, her florid, though not obese, features were set off by heavy gold ear-rings; and she waved her arms a great deal to show off her bracelets and her beautiful, henna-tinted hands. Her skin was as white as that of a European and this made her dark eyes, with their heavy brows joined together by a brush stroke, even more remarkable.

When she talked it was immediately apparent that she was somebody; in fact, to her family, relatives and friends she was the 'chief', the *shekka*. She served tea with an unusual lack of formality, laughing and talking freely, and she did not hesitate to offer me a cigarette, lighted at the brazier on which the tea-kettle was singing.

She belonged to the Karughla people. Two centuries ago, in order to get rid of them the Turks sent a number of janissaries to defend their North African territories. The janissaries married native women, and their descendants in Tripolitania, the Karughla, still follow the Hanefite rite of their country of origin. Even today they still display certain physical and psychological characteristics which distinguish them from the pure Arabs.

When this woman of the Karughla spoke of her daughter Farha, wife of the *shumbāshī*, she lifted her shoulders and sighed to indicate how unkind fate had been to that lovely young creature. 'A flower in the hands of a monkey,' she whispered to me in a confidential moment.

One day Busnina informed me that his wife was unwell, and asked if I would go and see her in her tent after dispensary hours.

The *shumbāshī's* tent was one of the 'plundered' variety, a military bell-type, sustained by a single central pole and high enough to stand up in. Being of double material and lined with green fustian, it also offered protection against cold in winter and heat in summer.

In the tent, with her mother, I found Farha – completely covered in her *ḥāik*, huddled on the floor with her back to the central pole and looking more like a bundle of old clothes than anything else. Her husband sat in front of her, and between them was a cushion for me.

The three ritual cups of tea having been consumed, some camp gossip exchanged, and a cigarette smoked, the formal part of my visit was accomplished and it was time to pass on to professional matters. But the patient did not wish the Christian *tebīb* to touch her, and she refused categorically to uncover her face.

Farha was a fanatical Moslem and, although she uttered no word, the gestures of a hand through the folds of her *ḥāik* made abundantly clear her refusal to have anything to do with me.

In vain her mother tried to persuade her to allow herself to be examined. 'O Farha, my daughter, here is the doctor come especially for you, and you do not wish him to see you. But why? Do you not wish to be cured? Must your mother continue to weep for your lost health, my treasure?'

The husband added his exhortations. He had been secretly delighted with his wife's exemplary modesty, but now her continued refusal to obey him seemed like an affront to his marital prestige.

'But this is the *tebīb*,' he insisted. 'The *tebīb* is our father. Do you not see how many white hairs he has? Allah has given him wisdom and the years have brought him experience. He will certainly cure you.'

But even the allusions to my physical deterioration were

powerless to move the woman. By this time she had hidden herself completely in her garments and confined herself to obstinately shaking her head.

'But how can he cure you if he does not see you?' cried Busnina, beginning to lose his temper. 'I am your husband, and it is I who command you to uncover yourself. God grant me patience!'

Farha only shrugged her shoulders disdainfully, and then, leaning suddenly towards her husband, she hissed through her veil, 'And how much did the Nazarene give you to see my face?'

Busnina was sitting next to me and was a head taller; some slight admixture of Negro blood gave him an already darker skin, but when he grasped his wife's meaning his face turned quite black. For a moment he remained as if turned to stone, and then, raising his enormous hand, he aimed a blow at his wife that would certainly have broken her neck if it had reached her. But Farha was quicker than he; she ducked, and her husband's hand passed over her head and caught the tent pole fair and square just where one section fitted into the next. Before we realised what was happening the whole structure was about our ears and we were buried in a mountain of tent cloth.

After frantic efforts to extricate myself from the enveloping canvas, to disentangle my feet from the ropes, and find a way out over cases, cushions, water bottles, mats, saddles, carpets, etc., without burning myself on the cinders from the overturned stove, I eventually emerged into the open.

People came running from all corners of the camp. The *shumbāshī*, raving and shouting that he would strangle his wife, was being held back by the men, while the women shepherded the mother and daughter into an empty tent, where I joined them.

The mother still retained her autocratic air, but was unable completely to control her amusement. Farha, her *hāik* gone, and dressed now only in a very low-necked shift, with her hair tumbling over her forehead and neck, was helpless with laughter.

'Busnina is so jealous,' her mother whispered. 'You can't imagine what trouble there would have been if the poor girl had acted otherwise!' Then she raised her voice, cast a tender look at her daughter, and said, 'There, now you can examine her in peace. And you will give her some medicine, will you not? Look at her, *tebīb* – is she not a true daughter of the Karughli?'

She produced a packet of cigarettes, offered me one, put one in her own mouth, lighted both, and began to talk. Busnina, it seemed, was as strong as a bull – 'but in the arms only', added his mother-in-law with a sigh. He was thirty years older than Farha, poor child, and, as if that were not sufficient, when the unit was camping at Tiji he had had the misfortune to sit on a chameleon – one of the large kind – and everyone knew what happened to the man who touched one of those. She would admit, however, that he had a heart of gold; he shouted and threatened, but would not hurt a fly. Now she would go and soothe him; her tiresome daughter had really been too insolent . . .

Farha, half-naked, huddled on the mat, kept her eyes downcast. But she was watching me out of the corner of her eye, and the shadow of a smile flitted across her mouth.

★ ★ ★

The seasons change in the Gulf of Sirte according to the prevailing winds, which bring in turn humidity, the infrequent rains, cold weather, and finally the warmth of spring, when the desert rats emerge from their holes, leaping like kangaroos, and the dunes are covered with grass which soon withers in the scorching sun.

The only unchanging element in the course of the year is the sea, and the rare appearances of the ship 'Gina' seemed something of an anachronism; it seemed out of place on those ancient waters, where the sails of Ulysses had spread and over which the purple and saffron-painted galleys of the Phoenicians had once passed.

The months slipped by. The Very Tall Young Man worked hard and astonished everyone by his prodigious memory; the camel corps officer was silent and spent his time shooting at empty tomato-sauce tins; the young aide-de-camp waited impatiently for the arrival of the 'Gina' with letters from the object

of his affections and meanwhile gazed at the full moon thinking
how many full moons had been wasted. On the whole we forgot
our personal problems during interminable camel excursions to
Tmed Hassan or into the salt plain of Taworga.

'Know ye that this world's life is only a sport, and pastime,
and show,' says the *Sūra* of Iron in the Koran, and we all had the
feeling that the wheel of fate which had brought us together
was about to give another turn which would separate us.

Before it broke up, however, our unit was transferred to
Mizda, deep in the desert, where the men of the Mishasha tribe
were arriving to make their act of submission to the Government. At that time Mizda was the extreme limit of the area
under our control beyond the mountains, and the submission
of such a large body of Arabs as the Mishasha meant that the
policy of the Southern Territory command had been eminently
successful.

The fort of Mizda stood isolated in the empty plain. Around
its massive towers a group of huts, built of earthern bricks, straw
and dung, formed a village famous in Tripolitania because it
contained the house sacred to the Sunni and a Senussite *zāwiya*.

An Eritrean battalion was encamped round the fort; headquarters were installed in the tower, as was also the commander's
wife, a quiet, docile woman who did not dream that her legs
fired the imagination of the young officers, so that they took it
in turns to go and stand where they could contemplate them
while this amiable and unsuspecting creature sat taking the air
on her balcony.

But to return to the Mishasha – drawn up and patiently waiting in front of the fort. They inhabited a part of the desert
called Ghebla, south of Tripolitania, and they had given a lot
of trouble. It might be said that their submission was the result
of the persevering and intelligent work of a Christian, a Jew and
a Mohammedan, each of whom contributed to the successful
outcome according to the measure of his responsibility, his
personal ability and his native sagacity. The resistance of the
whole area had been undermined by General Graziani's military
action, which had made possible Colonel Carrara's peaceful

penetration and Captain Khalifa's direct contacts with the tribal authorities.

The Mishasha listened respectfully to the act of submission read by their chief, Mohammed Shushan. He was a man of small stature, with the pointed features of a ferret, and he read slowly in a voice unsteady with emotion; from time to time he cast a furtive glance from the Prince (the Tall Young Man) to the General, from Colonel Carrara to Captain Khalifa. The minor chiefs then stepped forward and recited the first line of the *fatha*, the first chapter of the Koran, to consecrate the oath. They stood erect, their arms outstretched at shoulder level, palms upturned as though they carried the sacred book, their eyes following the lines of the imaginary page.

At the time the whole thing seemed to me a hypocritical farce – and perhaps even a trap set for the ingenuous Christians – seeing that no oath can bind a Moslem to keep faith with an infidel. In theory I was right, but in practice events proved me wrong. The Mishasha kept their oath, made possible the reconquest of the Fezzan, and fifteen years later, when French armed columns from the Sahara advanced to the coast, they behaved no worse than a great many Italians.

Mizda is reputed to be a country of sorcerers, weavers of spells, and holy men. It was perhaps this tendency towards the supernatural which gave that inscrutable expression to the faces of the Mishasha drawn up in front of the fort and caused the voice of Mohammed Shushan to tremble. The Arabs call Mizda *blād el asrar*, the land of mysteries. This is probably in part due to the existence of the Senussite *zāwiya* and to the presence of Negro families who brought with them superstitions and tribal practices from equatorial Africa.

It was Mahdi, the fort's medical orderly, who first told me about the scorpions. Mahdi could read and write and he talked to me about scorpions with something of the air of a specialist. However, he was inclined sometimes to get a little out of his depth, and it was obvious that he was repeating fragments he had heard from someone else who had studied the subject.

In any case, it was from Mahdi that I learned that although

many fanatical Moslems condemn the use of magic because it involves diabolical intervention, nevertheless the Prophet himself permits the use of spells to protect the faithful against the stings of scorpions – on condition that the spell, the *roqia*, is pronounced in comprehensible language and contains the sacred name of Allah.

When I expressed some doubt about the existence of magicians nowadays, Mahdi assured me that they did exist. He told me about Fusúda, a negress who handled the most poisonous scorpions as though they were harmless crickets. When therefore he offered one evening to take me to see Fusúda, so that I might witness her extraordinary powers for myself, curiosity got the better of me and I agreed to go.

The *zāwiya* is in the lower Gontar district and behind it, hidden in a labyrinth of narrow, earth-coloured walls, under a few ragged palm trees battered by unceasing winds, we came upon a hovel with crumbling walls, discoloured by smoke.

The only light in the interior, which was without windows, came from a brazier; people and objects were only vaguely discernible, and the darkness magnified the sound of whispering and the shuffling of bare feet on mats, so that when an invisible hand lit a lamp in a niche on the wall I was surprised to find that there were only four of us: Mahdi, two old black women from the Fezzan, and myself.

The negresses were perfectly aware of the object of my visit, but they insisted on Mahdi's explaining all over again that the *tebīb* had come because he wanted to see Fusúda. The sly smile of the brothel-keeper sat firmly on each wrinkled, ape-like countenance; they pressed around me and seized me by the arms to force me to sit down. Tea had to be taken with solemn ritual before Fusúda appeared before us.

The hut had a low roof made of palm trunks; the wind whistled outside, and from a distance came the sound of boys' chanting in the *zāwiya* – young voices which trailed off into a confused murmur when the teacher began in a nasal voice to intone a new verse.

The teapot was now singing on the brazier and the tea was

poured first into the cups and then back again into the pot to obtain the right infusion of bitter tea and sugar. I was required to drink three cups – the first only slightly sweetened, the second flavoured with mint, and the third full of roasted peanuts.

The Arabs say that tea-drinking was introduced among them only two centuries ago. A Moroccan, while on a journey to Mecca, was given some of the precious leaves by a Chinese pilgrim, and on his return he taught his countrymen how to make the infusion. It chanced that a sultan's son, whose system had been poisoned by alcohol, was cured by tea, and the sultan straightway decided that this innocent drink, which revives and stimulates the intellectual faculties, should become the popular beverage throughout the Moslem countries of Africa.

When I had emptied the third cup the old woman threw some *bhur*, dear to the nostrils of negroes, on the fire, and as its perfume began to fill the hut Fusúda entered like a shadow, enveloped from head to foot in a *hāik* so dark in colour that it was almost invisible.

She sat herself in front of me and looked me over with the one eye which the *hāik*, twisted over her head and drawn across the face, left uncovered.

'God save you. You are the *tebīb?*'

The chanting from the *zāwiya* rose and fell, and Fusúda swayed to and fro to the obsessive rhythm.

'You have come to see the scorpions?'

Her voice was slow and a little husky, and she spoke with an accent that distorted the words.

'Do you know the spell that charms the scorpions?' she asked.

'No.'

A malicious smile played round her mouth, and there was a passing light of mischief in the one visible eye.

'You know many things, *tebīb*, yet you do not know how to charm scorpions.'

She shook her head and continued musing.

'I think you wish to see the scorpions because you do not know the medicine for them.'

She became silent and relaxed her posture, closing her eyes; she seemed to fall asleep, but her shoulders continued to move to the rhythm of the distant chanting. On the brazier the *bhur* continued to smoke and made a slight sizzling sound. Suddenly, the girl shook herself and with a slow movement of head, breast and hips threw off her *hāik*. Seated cross-legged, erect from the hips, she remained covered by the *surīya*, the sleeveless, low-cut Arab shift.

She was a young negress with thick, purplish lips and a short, only slightly flattened, nose. She must have been a native of the Wadhai, or perhaps of some more distant region. Her forehead was strongly convex, her eyes coffee-coloured with yellowish whites; her tight black curls clung closely to her head and left her ringless ears uncovered; her arms and hands were bare of bracelets or rings. Beside her the ugliness of the two old Fezzanese women was repulsive.

She took a wicker basket which they handed to her and lifted the multi-coloured lid. In the bottom of the basket a large scorpion was lashing about in a fury, its tail erect like a sword.

Fusúda looked at it, her lips half-open, her eyes half-closed, and then took it between two fingers and placed it on her shoulder. The creature stumbled there, scrabbling upon the buckle of her chemise, then lost its foothold and slipped down into the hollow of her collar-bone. She threw back her head and the scorpion climbed up her neck, across her lower jaw and made its way slowly along her cheek. She closed an eye and it passed over her eyelid on to her forehead and attached itself to her woolly hair.

Fusúda took it in her hand again, stroked it, murmured some words I could not catch, tickled its belly and suddenly popped it in her mouth. Only its tail, quivering and lashing out in every direction, protuded from between her thick lips, its poisonous sting striking the girl's chin and nostrils. A moment later the scorpion, covered in saliva, was frantically twisting about, wild with excitement, in the palm of her hand; she smiled at the little monster, and laid it in her armpit. Then with a swift movement she unfastened her shoulder buckle and let fall her *surīya* so that she was naked to the thighs. She thrust the scorpion between her legs, leaving only the tail obscenely protruding.

Fusúda threw back her head and laughed – with silent, ghoulish laughter, her mouth wide open, her glazed eyes nearly closed.

Meanwhile she started playing with another, yellow-striped scorpion, smaller but more poisonous than the other. She poked it with her finger-nail and blew on its head, and when it lashed out in fury she put out her tongue and used it to fence with the deadly tail, which struck but did not wound her. Both scorpions were now on Fusúda's crossed arms. She watched them. Antediluvian monsters in miniature, they faced each other with all their members and weapons ready. Slowly and clumsily they approached each other; they grappled each other by the legs, their tails lashing and quivering in a frenzy which communicated itself to the girl, who shivered as if she were suffering from a tertian fever. Her lips were drawn back from her teeth and her eyes converged on the combatants in a ferocious squint.

Suddenly she emitted the shrill, piercing notes of the *zaghārīt*, the war-cry which incites men to battle, and the two monsters in miniature seemed to understand and to respond. Locked together, they wrestled and struggled, clawing at each other, their arched tails waving, seeking the adversary's vulnerable spot; their stings beat against each other's backs as they had beaten against Fusúda's face and tongue and lips. All at once they were still. The thrusts had gone home; the poison had struck them motionless. There was a spasm or two in the tails still inserted in the wounds; a pincer let go, slowly, painfully; a leg stretched out in a last spasm, and the two reptiles, still interlocked, rolled dead on to the mat.

Fusúda's body slumped forward, and she clasped her hands round her knees, shuddering; she was foaming at the mouth, and her breasts and belly were running with sweat.

By this time the room was full of *bhur* smoke. The two old women crouching in the corner began coughing. The faces seemed distorted through the perfumed smoke; Mahdi's was a livid yellow, as though swollen with pus, and his eye-sockets seemed empty. Fusúda's face was lifeless; she remained motionless, with closed eyes. The only sign of life was a quiver that now and then mounted across her abdomen. I touched her arm; it was cold, like that of a corpse.

'Truly this woman knows the Koran,' said Mahdi, this being apparently the only conclusion he had been able to arrive at. For myself, I could draw no conclusion at all.

When we emerged into the darkness the *zāwiya* was asleep; night had fallen, the wind had ceased, the silence was complete.

★   ★   ★

It was Mahdi, too, who introduced me to the *faqīh* Hajj Belgassem ben Said.

The title *faqīh* no longer means a lawyer, a student of canonical law; it has become more modest in its claims, and in Libyan Arabic may signify a student of the Koran, a schoolmaster, or even a good calligraphist. But to ordinary people the *faqīh* was also a magician with the power to command spirits, so that Mahdi, when speaking to me of Belgassem, told me that he was *wāhed sahhār men assahhārá* – a king among sorcerers.

In appearance he was a dried-up little old man with crossed and rheumy eyes and a sharp, protruding chin covered with a curly beard – a creature with nothing whatever of the necromancer about him. He spoke in an idiotic, high-pitched voice and, presumably from nervousness, never ceased from smoothing a crease in the corner of his *hāik*.

When I met him, being under the impression that a *faqīh* of Misda must be connected with the Senussite institution, I introduced a serious topic of conversation and asked him how long he had worked at the *zāwiya*. This was a most unfortunate opening. He fixed me with his cross-eyes and asked angrily if I took him for a dog, and without giving me time to reply began abusing and cursing all sects, founders of sects, followers of sects, and all their works. Sidi Hajj Belgassem, he informed me, belonged to no sect, but he knew the mysteries and could command spirits.

He used a great many words I did not know and was so upset

by my opening question that he gabbled incoherently and at a great rate and, what with this and his lack of teeth, I found it quite impossible to follow him.

Mahdi explained to me that the *faqīh* was a physician in his way – a physician who cured without medicine by provoking curative convulsions in sick people; Hajj Belgassem, moreover, only treated women. When I asked him if the reverend gentleman was a gynæcologist he said he was nothing of that sort: the *faqīh* cured the souls of women by liberating them from the spirits that caused disease.

One Friday after the mid-day prayer Mahdi came for me and took me into the courtyard of the magician's house. According to him I was going to witness the cure of a girl suffering from what I suppose we would call extreme melancholia, a condition, said Mahdi, caused by some dark and evil spirit.

We crept in and placed ourselves behind the boards of a disused storeroom so as to see without being seen. About seventy women were crouching on the ground in a wide circle, in the middle of which was a tub full of water. A woman's voice was chanting – such low notes that they seemed to come from a ventriloquist – to the accompaniment of a dull beating of drums and ringing of invisible bells.

The women swayed from their hips to the rhythm of the drums, their heads falling now on to one shoulder, now on to the other, as though blown by the wind. A continual murmur of prayer rose from the congregation, and at times swelled into groans and cries which dominated the singing and the beating of the drums.

This had been going on for some considerable time. It was hot, and what with the monotony of the voices and the hypnotising effect of the rhythmically waving heads, my eyes became heavy and, seated as I was on the ground with my back to a wall still warm from the sun, I must have fallen asleep when a sudden silence woke me with a start.

Hajj Belgassem had appeared in the doorway and was standing at the top of the six steps leading down into the courtyard. He seemed to me more insignificant than ever as he slowly descended, followed by an old woman with a bundle tied in a coloured handkerchief.

He sat down in the front row between two women who hastened to make room for him. The old woman untied the knots in the handkerchief and took out a large frog with henna-tinted legs which she set down reverently in front of the *faqīh*. 'That is his spirit,' whispered Mahdi in my ear, adding that it was the jinn which gave him his thaumaturgic power.

All eyes were fixed on the frog. The singing had stopped and the drums and bells were silent. I became aware that I too was staring stupidly at the creature. It lay there with legs outspread and eyes closed – so torpid and motionless that, except for the perceptible beat under its jaw, it might have been stuffed.

The old man made a sign with his hand and the women again began swaying and crying out, the drums began to beat furiously and the singer resumed her singing with renewed vigour.

The whole crowd was now shrieking invocations, and the singer was doing her best to hold her own against the combined racket of the women and the drums.

This hellish din had continued for an hour or so and my head was beginning to ache when suddenly a girl sprang to her feet in the corner of the courtyard. Her eyes were open wide in an expression of stark tragedy. She stepped quickly over the women in front of her, flung herself into the open space and began to throw herself about in the most savage manner, stamping her feet, jerking her shoulders, agitating her arms and shaking her head so violently that the braids of her hair broke loose, and silver ornaments and bangles, amulets and little red woollen tassels flew in all directions. Gasping and panting, she took great leaps into the air; she drew her head into her shoulders, thrust it forward and then flung it back with such force that it seemed she must dislocate her neck. She had progressively dispensed with *hāik*, bodice and trousers, and was now covered only in her shift, tied at the hips with a coloured scarf.

These contortions continued for an hour; the girl became soaking wet; her shift clung to her body, her hair stuck to her face and lips, and a stream of foam and sweat ran down from the corners of her mouth.

Suddenly she stopped in front of the *faqīh* and fixed her eyes on him, wrinkling her forehead as if she were trying to remember something. Then, with a piercing shriek, she flung herself on to the ground. The dust clung to her wet arms and legs as she writhed and twisted, dragging herself on her stomach along the ground which was strewn with beads from her broken necklace. At this point, two powerful and bony negresses picked her up and removed the last remnants of the tattered shift which hung from her shoulders. Naked, the girl seemed to be made of ivory as she hung between the smoke-black arms of the negresses who carried her towards the tub. For a moment my view was obstructed by the crowd and I only heard the sound of a body plunged repeatedly into the water. When I saw the girl again, she was wrapped in a blanket and her expression was completely altered. As the women flocked around her she smiled ecstatically and cast her eyes heavenwards; she kissed the singer on the head and smilingly received the congratulations of her friends, as they led her to the magician's feet.

The *faqīh* had not moved at all throughout the séance, except to take on to his lap the frog with the henna-tinted legs. The girl knelt before him and asked his blessing, his *baraka*. As Belgassem placed his hands upon her head, Mahdi and I slipped out of the courtyard: we had been there several hours, and the evening shadows were already falling.

Chapter Two

A CURE FOR SERPENTS

In 1926 I left Buerat el Hsun and set up a dispensary in Misurata, further along the coast. In those days Misurata was almost entirely cut off from its hinterland. The revolt of the Arabs was recent and still smouldering, and only a few miles away there were tribes which had not yet submitted to the Government and were sitting on the fence wondering which way to jump.

In Misurata there were bullet marks on the walls of many of the houses; the regular clients of the town's only bar recalled days not so very long ago when they were obliged to enter the premises on all fours to avoid the attentions of the solitary sniper perched on the top of a palm tree in the oasis.

A few at a time, the scattered inhabitants returned to the town and the number of patients presenting themselves at the dispensary grew daily. It was quite a different clientele from that at Buerat el Hsun: it was composed for the most part of men – nearly all Arabs – either from the town, or belonging to wandering tribes. There were no Berbers, but a good many negroes.

In the family encampment at Buerat, which had consisted almost entirely of women, a kind of military discipline had been imposed by the older matrons among them. Here in my dispensary it was I who ruled. I represented that magical figure which holds sway over all primitive communities: the Possessor of Knowledge, raised on high and supported by those two columns upon which any self-respecting dictatorship rests: ignorance and fear.

However, as I had no need to curry popular favour, it was not necessary for me to behave like a tyrant and I could permit myself the luxury of a fatherly affection for my subjects. They turned to me believing that I could free them from pains of whose nature they were ignorant, and cure diseases caused by they knew not what, so that they might perhaps postpone the day fixed by Allah when he would call them, his creatures, to himself again.

In my small realm I had two 'ministers' and a kind of female public health officer to assist me – and a 'chief of police' to maintain order. My two 'ministers' were the two male nurses, Mohamed ed Dernàwi and Aissa ben Jahia. Mohamed had attended a native school for nurses and had worked for several years in the hospital at Tripoli. He was a native of Cyrenaica and considered himself very advanced; he regarded the ignorance of his co-religionists with condescension, smiled pityingly at their superstitions and spoke with benevolent indulgence of bigots who believed in marabouts and holy men. One day when he was suffering from a mild bronchitis which made him cough like an old asthmatical horse, I told him to undress so that I could examine him. Tied under his armpit I found a very small leather case containing a strip of paper on which was written in a pains-taking hand a line of the Koran to keep away malignant spirits. Mohamed was extremely mortified and for several days turned his head away whenever I looked at him.

Aissa was less capable and less intelligent than his colleague and his pretensions were not nearly so lofty. He was as ugly as an ape, with a pock-marked face, and his conversation was always of what he had just eaten or of what he was about to eat; he laughed uproariously on the slightest provocation, exposing the decayed remains of a deplorable set of teeth, and when he spoke of an attractive and not too virtuous woman he clicked his tongue and exclaimed 'mashi' – untranslatable into Italian and therefore certainly not to be rendered in English, but approxi-mating to a more colourful version of 'oh boy!'

My 'chief of police' was Mahmud Ferjiani, nicknamed Burâs, meaning 'big head'. He was as massive and obtuse as an ox and he acted as porter, watchman and odd-job man in the dispensary. On crowded days he kept order by rolling his eyes ferociously and hurling fearful threats at offenders: 'Hi! you, snubnose; do you want to be strung up by your guts?'

Lastly there was Ehlia, a stockily built and ageless Jewess who took charge three times a week when we checked up on the girls of the local brothel.

Complete calm reigned now in the area immediately surrounding the town. Our military commander was an old colonial of vast experience who had passed most of his life in Africa and had served at one time in the Belgian Congo. This man was working, without haste and with great good sense, to win over some of the uncertain, dissident and rebellious elements that roamed the hinterland. Like the old African fox that he was, he neglected no opportunity, left no stone unturned, despised no stratagem which might bring over to the Government's side the neutral tribes in the pastures of the no-man's land. He knew, among other things, how to turn the work of the medical officer to good account in this operation of slow persuasion.

In the territory where declared rebels dared not penetrate and where it was undesirable that the Government should intervene until the time was ripe, roamed the Seraxa, a tribe which had previously given a lot of trouble. They no longer supplied the rebels with arms but they had not yet decided to submit to the Government. The men of the tribe came to Misurata to sell their goat hair mats and leather belts in the market, and those who were sick but able to walk came to the dispensary – which harassed Mahmud Burâs not a little, for to him they were all bloodthirsty bandits.

In fact, these fearful brigands gave me no trouble at all; they waited their turn patiently and when I questioned them they answered timidly; keeping a wary eye on the stethoscope or on the apparatus for taking their blood pressure. When they asked me to visit the women and children in their encampment, the military authorities gave me every facility and I was usually accompanied by one of the two male nurses.

One evening I arrived at the wells of Dufan, where the Seraxa were encamped, and was led to a tent in which a strong, massively built man was crying out from the pains in his legs. He was lame as the result of a gunshot wound which many years before had splintered his shin-bone, but it was not this that was causing the pain. Neither did there seem any reason to suspect the machinations of *Tab'a*, the lady who had treated Lalla Saida so roughly. The trouble was that an old syphilitic infection had suddenly reappeared and was nightly giving him a foretaste of the punishment that probably awaited him in hell.

This sturdy cast-iron specimen was Abdullah es-Salahi Belhajj, the tribal chief. I stayed with him ten days and when I left I promised him a safe-conduct pass so that he could come to Misurata and follow a course of treatment which – if it was God's will – would cure him.

During my stay in his tent I had noticed an old carpet which much impressed me. It had a graceful, multi-coloured, lozenge-shaped design woven on a white ground, and the chief explained to me that it was an authentic example of the old Misurata carpet – vastly different from the vulgarised products which were now being made to satisfy modern taste. I asked him if the women of his tribe could make me a carpet like it, about six yards square, and after a moment's thought he said he would speak to his mother about it.

A week later, when he arrived with his entourage at the dispensary to begin a course of injections, he brought me the reply. They had made the most meticulous calculations: they would need so many *okka* of sheep's wool, so many of goat's wool; for the colours, so much of this plant, so much of that. The estimated price would be three hundred lire and the work could be finished in about fifty days. I remarked that fifty days seemed to me very little for so much work, but Abdullah raised his shoulders and assured me that if his mother had said fifty days, fifty days it would be.

Two months later, the promised carpet was unloaded off a camel at my door. When I unrolled it, there in the centre, pinned by a palm needle, was a twenty-five lira note. It was the amount left unspent from the three hundred lire I had advanced and the chief's mother had therefore returned it to me.

During my earlier visits to the tents of the Seraxa I had made the acquaintance of this magnificent old woman. She was tall, very thin, with a delicate profile, and her air of authority, her bearing and movements and the tone of her voice, all made it clear that she was the chief's mother. It was obvious, too, that all the members of the tribe, not least her son, were her devoted subjects. She rarely smiled; her commands were given more by gesture than by word, and she had eyes like gimlets that penetrated one through and through.

My first encounter with her was when her son had taken me to her tent so that I might examine a grandchild suffering from conjunctivitis. I had hardly recognised Abdullah: in his mother's presence he was dumb and moved about in a timid and self-effacing manner: when his mother spoke to him, he bowed his head as a sign of reverence before replying.

On that first occasion my visit was short: after I had treated the child's eyes we withdrew and I returned to Misurata. On subsequent visits, however, I was nearly always pressed to stay to dinner. During these banquets, at which kids stuffed with aromatic herbs and roasted whole over braziers were placed before us, I noticed that the old mother never took her eyes off me. She followed the conversation in an absent-minded way and kept watching my hands; sometimes she stopped eating altogether and turned right round the better to observe me.

One evening after coffee it seemed she could no longer contain herself. She spoke in a low voice, and in order to make the pill more palatable, she called me 'my son' instead of addressing me by my professional title.

'Listen, my son: has no one ever told you that you eat like a camel-herd? You use both hands, and look what a mess you are in. Your mouth is covered with grease – and even your nose. And you have stained your shirt. My son, whoever taught you your table manners?'

She was as shocked and pained as an old duchess who, having invited the bailiff of her estate to dinner, sees him eat his peas with a knife.

So it was from her that I learned to take my food with the right hand only (at table the left hand is non-existent, since it performs the 'secret ablutions') and not to use more than three fingers. I learnt how to make little balls of semolina, rice or meat of the right size using only my thumb and first and second fingers, without dirtying the other fingers or the palm of my hand. From her I learnt (seated cross-legged on the carpet) how to lean from the hips towards the central dish, just close enough to take a mouthful, without dropping grease either on the mat or on my clothes. I also achieved the art of two-finger feeding, of popping the ball of food into my mouth without touching my lips, thus avoiding a greasy mouth or nose. I think I may say that I was a very apt pupil.

When, some months later, I met the Seraxa in the Gheddahìa pastures, the chief's mother again invited me to supper. This time I passed the test with flying colours. The formidable old lady regarded me with immense satisfaction and approval, and during coffee, with one of her rare smiles, she said, 'Now, my son, you may eat even with a sultan. May Allah bless and prosper you.'

★ ★ ★

An even harder nut to crack than the Seraxa were the Qouafi – a sprawling, more numerous tribe who wandered deep in the hinterland between the mountains and the coast. Although they had avoided fighting openly against us and it was now eight months since they had taken any part in the rebellion, they were a bellicose and turbulent people. It was said that their chief had quarrelled with the leaders of the revolt and – more wily than they – had called a halt until he saw which way the wind was likely to blow. Little was known about them, and on all the official maps the word 'Qouafi' appearing on the various pasture areas was always followed by a question mark. Some informants had met prominent members of the tribe almost at the gates of Misurata, while others asserted that they had seen their camels as far away as Shemek, well over a hundred miles from the coast.

One day I received an urgent summons to headquarters. A message had been sent by the head of the Qouafi to say that his only daughter was ill, and asking that a doctor be sent immediately with everything necessary to restore her to health.

I went, of course. The rainy season was just over; the scent of jasmine rose from the dry walls and gibbet-like well-heads, and the palm trees stood dark and clear against the cloudless night sky as my little caravan moved out of the oasis of Zawiet el Majoub. At first there was not a glimmer of light in the east, but after some miles the sun rose suddenly and in the distance, among palm trees and bushes flooded with honey-coloured light, we saw the tents of the Qouafi.

The deep dawn silence was suddenly broken by the braying of a donkey and the barking of dogs, and between two sand dunes figures dwarfed by the distance and indistinct in the golden morning mist began to move about the wells.

Inside the Bedouin tent I found a girl lying flat on her back, her glazed, dark-ringed eyes, in which the night's delirium still flickered, staring unseeing into space. Every now and again the word 'water' came from her cracked lips.

The mother was bending over her, watching every breath and movement; she gripped my hands and arms with a force that surprised me in such a thin and seemingly fragile woman.

I had never met the chief of the Qouafi but I knew that he was reputed to be an aggressive and violent character, and a source of considerable concern to the Government. At that moment there stood before me only a man bowed down and stripped of all pride, a man in the grip of fear, who started at every sound, and who watched in anguish where his daughter lay, prostrate between life and death.

The mother had turned back the girl's *ḥāik* and tucked it under her armpits, but in her feverish tossing, unable to bear the heat, the patient had thrown off the covering; her hair was soaked with sweat and as she tossed her head this way and that the braids loosened, scattering coins, trinkets and the amulets worn as protection against the evil eye.

I called her by name: 'Fattûma, Fattûma . . .'

She fixed her eyes on me and murmured: '*Râsi yuja' fîhā* . . . my head hurts,' and with difficulty raised her hand to her forehead.

Her chest was marked with little inflamed patches and she groaned when I sounded it with my fingers, and shuddered at the contact of my cold ear on her breasts. Below the ribs the stomach was concave and there was a gurgling sound as I pressed it. The dark shadow between the legs showed that the hair had not been removed for a week: the girl's brow puckered and in spite of her weakness she put out a thin hand to cover herself.

The mother whispered to me that during the last few days the girl had lost a lot of blood from the nose. How was it, she asked, that the evil spirits had not also departed together with all that blood?

I was only able to establish a very fragmentary case history but it seemed fairly certain that the evil spirit in this instance was the Eberth bacillus. There among the Qouafi camels it was not possible to carry out a laboratory test, but I had little doubt that the girl was suffering from typhoid or paratyphoid fever.

It was seven o'clock in the morning, and the under-arm temperature was ninety-nine point five, from which I deduced that the disease was probably in the second week. Should I attempt the only treatment – a drastic one – that might arrest it? I again examined the girl from head to foot: I did not want any unpleasant surprises. The heart seemed in excellent condition and a summary analysis convinced me that the kidneys were functioning satisfactorily. We would try.

Seated on the edge of the mat, I felt the girl's arms to see which it would be better to use for the operation. I could feel the father's breath on my hair as, tense and watchful, he followed my every movement; the mother's eyes were fixed on me from the other side of the mat, and I tried to avoid them.

Mohamed ed Dernàwi tied an elastic band round the arm I indicated. The vein protruded under pressure and I dabbed the copper-coloured skin with iodine. A syringe full of clear protein solution was ready; I stuck the needle into the vein and the blood flowed into the syringe, turning the contents red; I pressed the pump and the liquid became white again and, while Mohamed untied the elastic, flowed slowly, carefully, into the vein, leaving an opaque patina on the inside of the syringe.

'And now . . . ?' asked the father while I washed my hands outside the tent.

'Now there will be a high, a very high, fever,' I replied, adding in answer to his troubled, bewildered look: 'and the fever, if it is God's will, will cure her.'

The great chief bowed his head: 'God is Compassionate and Merciful.'

The hours passed and the fever mounted with exasperating slowness. By five in the afternoon it was little more than a hundred. After sunset, however, the first sudden rise set in, and at ten o'clock it touched a hundred and four. The girl was so hot that the warmth could be felt at a hand's breadth from her body. The pulse under my fingers galloped at an increasing speed.

As I sat on the floor I could feel the eyes of the mother and father drilling the back of my neck. Behind them were the servants, and the tent was filled with a continual low murmur of prayer.

At midnight the thermometer registered a hundred and five point one. The girl's body jerked convulsively up and down and the skin had become lifeless. It gave no reflection in the light of the lamps and was so taut and hot that it seemed it must split.

Suddenly the crisis was reached.

The pulse became less tumultuous, the arteries less turgid. Beads of sweat broke out on the forehead and the skin of the body began to shine and to become soft and wet. Rivers of sweat poured from the neck, under the arms, down over the breasts, gathered in the hollow of the stomach and ran over the thighs and legs. The heart became stronger, helped by the caffein.

The mother continually wiped away the perspiration which now ran from every pore in the girl's body; the mat had to be changed and placed in another corner of the tent because even the ground underneath was soaked. The chief tried to help, but the women pushed him out of the way into a corner: he was more hindrance than help, staggering about like a blind man, with a stunned expression on his face.

At six in the morning the temperature had dropped to ninety-six point five.

The fever did not recur during the next four days. I remained in the camp for another week, however, in order to supervise the feeding of the convalescent and because a persistent swelling of the spleen made me fear that there might still be a relapse, but my fears proved unfounded.

When I declared the daughter to be out of danger the mother wept silently but the father kept his eyes on the floor and then suddenly raised his head, spread out his hands, palms upward as though they carried the open book, and in a voice suffocating with emotion recited the first *sūra:*

> '*Praise be to God, Lord of the worlds!*
> *The Compassionate, the Merciful . . .*'

Allah had willed that his daughter should live, and five camels waited before my tent to conduct me back to the city.

★ ★ ★

Three years later, when I was again in Misurata, there was a sequel to this story.

We were nearing the end of August, the hottest time of the year, when the wind blowing up from the south seems to come from an open furnace.

My man-servant, Jemberié Igzaou, shook me, and continued to shake me until I was properly awake. The darkened room throbbed with the heat and the pitiless Misurata afternoon sun filtered through the shutters, throwing a streak of light around which the buzzing flies circled incessantly on the dusty air.

'Outside an Arab.'

I was still sleepy and did not grasp what Jemberié was saying.

'An Arab?'

'An Arab.'

'Couldn't you have told him to wait until five o'clock?'

'He say me he cannot wait.'

'Well, why didn't you tell him to come back this evening?'

'He say cannot come back.'

'But what does he want? Is he ill? Is he wounded?'

'He quite very well.'

By this time sleep had fled, and being completely awake and resigned to it, I told Jemberié to show in this Arab in excellent health who appeared to be in such a hurry.

A Bedouin entered, tall and lean, wrapped in a kind of burnous widening over the shoulders and falling like a hood down the back. At a sign from me he sat on the floor in the middle of the room while I remained looking down on him from my vantage point on the edge of the bed.

He seemed young, even very young, with delicate features and large, dark, velvety eyes, but the otherwise adolescent face was transformed into that of a warrior by the hooked nose, lean cheeks and jutting chin.

After the first greetings he fell silent. From time to time he lifted his eyes, caught mine for an instant and immediately lowered his own again, repeating timidly, 'Kef' alēk ... how are you?'

When I replied that I was well, he placed his outspread hand on his breast and muttered, 'El hamdullillāhi ... God be praised.'

Finally he made an effort and started to speak. He spoke hurriedly in a low voice, keeping his eyes half closed, as though reciting something he had learned by heart but of which he feared to forget a word or phrase.

The chief of the Qouafi sent his greetings; he sent many greetings, and prayed that God would have me in his keeping and prosper me.

When I questioned him, the boy raised his eyes and replied in his normal voice: being no longer the mouthpiece of his chief he could resume his ordinary tone.

No, he did not belong to the Qouafi tribe; he was a Sirtic nomad; his name was Ali, son of Hajj Mansûr, son of Abubekri, son of Hajj Idris, son of Said el Mālek. He threw in the four generations in a perfectly natural manner in order to indicate that he was not a nobody, but a 'son of the great tents' and the scion of a long line.

After this brief parenthesis he relapsed again into his recital: the chief of the Qouafi sent me greetings, many greetings, and his blessing; the chief of the Qouafi was my son ...

I interrupted him again to ask where the chief of the Qouafi was, what he was doing, how he was.

The chief of the Qouafi was with his people in the Bu Rêya pasturage; the chief of the Qouafi was well (more praises to God who protected the chief of the Qouafi and kept him in good health).

The voice became less montonous and faltered a little: the chief of the Qouafi had a daughter, and he sent me a letter . . .

I was not listening to him any longer. As I sat staring unseeing at the flies circling round and round in the streak of sunlight my mind had slipped back into the past.

Only a few seasons had come and gone but I realised that until that moment I had completely forgotten those ten days spent among the Qouafi in the pastures of Zawiet el Majoub. And now, two words from this Bedouin had recalled the whole scene – I saw again the thin face and large, fevered eyes of Fattûma as though I had seen them that morning. I remembered too the desperate hunted look of the chief, and heard again the toneless voice of the mother speaking to me in monosyllables. I wondered what had happened to Fattûma. Perhaps she was ill and her father wanted me to see her again – for Ali ben Hajj Mansûr, observing that I was preoccupied with my own thoughts, was now patiently repeating that the chief of the Qouafi had a daughter and that he sent me a letter . . .

And, in fact, the chief of the Qouafi had a daughter and he *had* sent me a letter. It was written in the hand of a teacher of the Koran; the signature of the chief in a corner was almost illegible, but his seal, lower down, made the message authentic. It read as follows:

Greetings to our Lord Pirajno the physician.
May God have him in His keeping. Amen.
With regard to the following, so that your health is good, by the mercy of God and His blessing, we ask a good word from you by your grace.
Who brings you this is our honoured friend Ali of the Ulad Sleiman, son of the pilgrim Mansûr, God protect him.

Now he desires to marry my daughter who is our only issue.

We are satisfied and may God's will be done.

But although Allah gave us a daughter, he also permitted you to give her a second life when death was upon her.

So we ask that you listen to the request and tell us if the prayer for the betrothal may be said.

And we wait for your decision.

And God be with you.

I looked up to find our honoured friend Ali, son of the pilgrim Mansûr, watching me with an anxious expression, endeavouring to read my thoughts. He could not guess just what those thoughts were.

For I was touched to the heart. What caliph, I thought, what sultan of *The Thousand and One Nights* had ever rewarded his physician in a more princely manner?

Ali ben Hajj Mansûr left with my consent to his marriage and a pair of silver *khālkhāl* for Fattûma's ankles. I went with him to the door and with difficulty disengaged my hands which he kissed with vehement gratitude. When all the various formulæ of blessing had been exhausted, he leapt into his saddle and I watched him disappear in a swirl of dust which remained suspended above the road like a cloud of gold.

★ ★ ★

It is time to talk of Jemberié Igzaou.

Jemberié Igzaou had followed me from Buerat el Hsun to Misurata and was my valet, general factotum and confidential servant.

He was an Abyssinian of the Gojjam, enrolled in the mixed battalions composed of Amhara and Eritreans. He was short, as black as coal, and had certain negroid characteristics but, being a good Abyssinian, he was convinced that he was white and maintained that the whites were red, basing his conclusions on the colour of their ears seen against the light.

In Amharic Jemberié means 'My sun', and Igzaou 'may God guide him'.

Alberto Denti di Pirajno

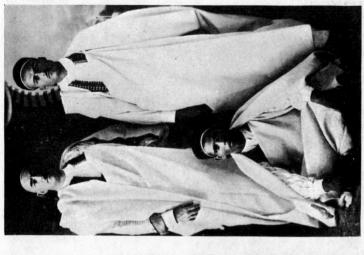

The author with the Duke of Aosta (*left*) and with Mohamed ed Dernàwi and Aissa ben Jahia (*right*)

'My sun – may God guide him' was of indefinable age; he seemed a young boy but could not have been less than twenty-five years old. His account of himself was somewhat confusing. According to him, he ran away from home at the age of six and went to Eritrea, where he was made director of the railway. In reality, as a boy he had worked as a stonebreaker along the railway line and after some time was promoted to foreman. He joined up as soon as recruiting beyond the frontier began, and at the time of our story he considered himself a veteran in the Askaris and was only surprised that he had not yet been promoted *mumtāz* or corporal.

He was a Coptic Christian and very proud of his religion; he paraded among the Arabs adorned with a brass cross so large that an archbishop might have coveted it. He had a great contempt for all Mohammedans, although occasionally he might mention to me with a certain condescending approval some particularly educated Moslem or eminent local personality who happened to follow the Prophet, and he would treat a hardworking and honest Moslem craftsman with benevolence. Jews, however, male and female, of any age or condition, he abhorred without discrimination. All the laundresses of Misurata were Jewesses – and Jemberié insisted on washing all our linen so that it should not be contaminated by such an unclean contact. In the first house of the ghetto down towards the sea there was an exceptionally beautiful laundress who was undoubtedly a direct descendant of the women who did King David's washing at the wells of Bethlehem. When I mentioned this lovely creature to Jemberié and suggested that he might allow her to come and take away my dirty handkerchiefs and wash them, he looked at me severely and said that never could I blow my nose on handkerchiefs touched by the hands that had crucified Jesus. In vain I sought to point out to him that obvious chronological factors made it impossible that the girl had had anything to do with it. He replied that all Jews were responsible for Christ's death, even those then unborn.

His ideas about disease and remedies were more or less those of primitive man. He was convinced that a stroke of lightning

could make a woman pregnant, that a man became impotent if
he touched a chameleon, and that to urinate facing the moon
gave you venereal disease. When he had a headache he opened
the vein across his forehead and, bending over a basin, let the
blood flow until the headache ceased. He first began to respect
medical science when he found that a white powder relieved his
headache without any blood-letting.

He was of peasant stock and – like all peasants the world over
– his reluctance to spend a farthing was positively sordid. But
he was also an Amhara and, therefore, as vain as a peacock: when
it was a question of appearances, of 'making a show', he did not
consider expense and in order to adorn his *tarbūsh* with a huge
and irregular silk tassel he would cheerfully spend three weeks'
pay.

My incapacity to bargain with vendors and the ease with
which they got the better of me inspired him with an angry
compassion, for he was as avaricious with my money as with his
own: nothing upset him so much as to find that I had myself
gone to the market to buy a mat or a leather cushion. And it
must be admitted that he was much more successful than I.
When he had to buy a coffee-pot or a dish or a broom he went
to the market in good time, entered the shop with a polite
greeting for the proprietor, removed his *tarbūsh* and sat down.
With a nonchalant air he would ask the price of the most
dissimilar objects, none of which he had any intention of buying,
and smile sarcastically at every price mentioned, saying that
evidently the shopkeeper had risen in a good humour and liked
his little joke. At a certain moment he would remove his
sandals and ask for a cushion in order to make himself more
comfortable.

In the meantime, among the various objects offered to him,
the dish or mat on which he had had his eye from the beginning
would appear; on hearing the price he ceased to smile and began
muttering something to the effect that the police should know
better than to allow thieves to operate undisturbed in the city.
He checked himself immediately, however, declaring that, in
any case, he would not dream of buying such rubbish: his

master, the *tebīb*, would throw it in his face if he dared to take it into the house.

At this stage the shopkeeper would begin to weaken and to reduce his price, but Jemberié pretended to take no further notice and with a serious face would call attention to the fact that he had been sitting in the shop for more than an hour and so far no one had offered him a cup of coffee. When the coffee arrived, Jemberié would request a double ration of sugar in it, and a glass of orange-flower water, because coffee by itself upset his stomach.

As he sipped his coffee he would sigh and make nostalgic references to the great cities in which he had lived – places where all self-respecting shopkeepers offered to those who deigned to enter a richly assorted *meze* – a tray filled with morsels of salted fish, pickled olives, pieces of roasted liver, small meat pies, roasted almonds, chickpeas, peanuts, and buns running with honey; naturally, such liberality was not to be expected in a miserable little market noted only for its rapacious and extortionate vendors.

By now the shopkeeper would have realised that he was no match for such an adversary and so as to waste no more time he would spread out a mat or polish an object with his sleeve and name an even lower price. But Jemberié was still not listening: with his head thrown back he would sniff the air, wag his forefinger and whisper, smacking his lips: 'Today you are eating eggs with cumin – I can smell them. They are good – eggs with cumin; I have a special weakness for eggs with cumin . . .'

Desperate at these broad hints and at the horrid threat to his dinner, the vendor then threw up the sponge and pressed the dish, the broom, the coffee-pot – anything he liked – into the hands of the Askari, in order to get rid of him.

Jemberié would return in triumph and display his purchases. Cheaper than you buy another week. Much cheaper. You have pay four lire; I pay one lire seventy, and maybe – maybe – he give it for one fifty, but I not want waste time.'

In all my wanderings across Tripolitania, from Buerat el Hsun to Misurata, from Nàlut to Ghadames, Jemberié Igzaou was my faithful shadow. When, after some years, I entered the colonial administration, he resigned from the army in order to stay with me. He went with me to Tripoli, where I ended my first period in Libya, and when I was assigned to Eritrea he followed me and was with me during all the years I spent between Massawa and Agordat.

When, in Asmara, I had an attack of septicæmia and for several days was hardly expected to live (we were still far from the discovery of penicillin), Jemberié never left my side. He refused to eat or sleep and when I was convalescent I hardly recognised him: his face seemed all eyes, and instead of being black had taken on a look of marshy green.

It was in Asmara too that he informed me he was about to be betrothed. I congratulated him and asked him what type of marriage he was contemplating. He gave me a stern and scandalised look and said that, naturally, he admitted none but the canonical, regular and indissoluble form of marriage.

In explanation of my question and of Jemberié's answer it should be mentioned that among the Copts there are three forms of marriage: the religious marriage which is indissoluble, the civil marriage which can be dissolved on payment of a fine, and the temporary marriage for a stipulated period, against payment. Jemberié, however, informed me that God Himself only recognised one of these forms – that which joins the two parties for life. To clinch the matter still further, his future father-in-law was a *cashi*, a very austere priest extremely scrupulous about the observance of the divine laws.

Jemberié's few remaining relatives were far away at Bourieh in the Gojjam and, in any case, his father had been dead for some time. It would therefore be necessary, he said, for me to take the place of his deceased father at the ceremony. He took it as the most natural thing in the world that I should do this; he did not ask it as a favour but merely spoke to me about it so that I should know what I had to do, and make my preparations in time.

Of Jemberié's wedding, celebrated in a stuffy little church at the gates of Asmara in the oppressive heat of the dry spell between two rainy seasons, I have only a very hazy recollection in which the predominating elements are blinding sunlight, torrid heat, clouds of reddish dust which dried the throat, the smell of fermented honey and water, of rancid butter, and dense clouds of incense.

I had learnt my part very carefully. I was surrounded the whole time by a group of young men who, in the nuptial choreography, represented the friends of the bridegroom, including Jemberié's future brothers-in-law – robust peasants from Anseba. Fortunately for me, the half-caste wife of an Italian tradesman who was a friend of mine was also taking part in the proceedings, and in the ceremonial ritual to which the women were admitted, or when the father of the bridegroom had to address his daughter-in-law, it was Eleanora who acted as interpreter and often prompted me in what I had to say.

After having drunk some *tech*, the native beer, with the men of the bride's family – who pretended to be unaware of the reason for my presence and continued to assure me that they did not know the whereabouts of the girl I was looking for – I was led by the women into a hut close by, where I found an enormous bundle of clothes piled on the floor. It was the bride. She was parcelled up in about a dozen *shamma*. The women, singing something composed entirely of trills, lifted her up from the floor and removed her wrappings one after the other until she was dressed only in a long *fūta* which fell from her face to her feet, completely concealing her form. On her head, pulled down to the level of the eyes, which were the only part of her still visible, she had a wide-brimmed straw hat of the kind worn on the beach by ladies of fashion.

Supported by her women friends, the girl knelt down in front of me and I spread my hands in blessing on the crown of her straw hat. We then formed a procession outside: preceded by a chanting priest, I walked at a slow pace with a guiding hand on the shoulder of the bride at my side – the two of us under the shade of a parasol which an enormous and vociferous man held over our heads, his arm stretched straight out in front of him.

I had a vague impression of looking extremely ridiculous and dared not catch the eye of Eleanora who, beside me, was covering her mouth with her handkerchief – either to smother her laughter or to protect her throat from the dust. All round us the bridegroom's friends sang and shouted at the tops of their voices; the occasional joyful crack of a rifle added to the noise, and the wind blew so hard that we were enveloped in clouds of red Eritrean dust.

We passed through a crowded entrance into the semi-darkness of another hut. Suddenly I was amazed to find that there were apparently two brides – absolutely identical, with the same wide straw hat, the same sack from head to foot. In fact, the second turned out to be Jemberié, adorned in exactly the same way as his betrothed. They were of the same height and it was impossible to distinguish between them.

I blessed the couple. Jemberié's father-in-law made me a speech in Tigrinya and passed to me the authority over his daughter which he had exercised until that day; I in return embraced him, kissing him on both cheeks and on the forehead. We emerged in procession once more; I was now between the bride and bridegroom and we all three carried lighted candles. At the door of the church, priests under great, multi-coloured umbrellas offered us crucifixes to kiss and led us into the crowded, malodorous church where the rising clouds of incense made everything nebulous and indistinct.

The ceremony began. All the priests started to shout at once, reading from their bibles and making a terrific din. Huge black acolytes greeted each climax in the ritual by blowing loud fanfares on twelve-foot trumpets. Meanwhile, the bride's girl-friends, by whom I was surrounded, never ceased their singing and screaming for one moment. All this continued without pause for an hour or so, and I remember nothing but the noise. But the couple at last were wedded, and they symbolised the fact by turning round and blowing out the candles which we all held in our hands.

After the ceremony we emerged into the red glare of the afternoon sun and sat ourselves in the great tent which had been erected in the churchyard. In my role as the groom's father I was the guest of honour and I sat on a mat between the bridal couple with the bride's father crouching opposite. The air in the tent had reached a pitch of sweltering suffocation; all kinds of delicacies floating in red pepper sauce were served and we washed them down with tankards of native beer.

At last the serving girls brought in a whole roast lamb and this was set ceremoniously before me. Nobody moved; all waited politely. Then the bride's father stuck a finger into one of the lamb's eyes, skewered it forth, displayed it for all to see and placed it in my mouth. The eye, which appeared to be my perquisite, certainly tasted better than the finger that accompanied it. This little ceremony being completed, the feast could now begin, and everyone set to. We ate solidly for four or five hours.

Gorged, dust-choked and weary from the heat, it was a relief when the time finally arrived at which the bride and bridegroom could decently retire. We, the men – the brothers of the bride, the father of the bride and I, the father of everybody – conducted them to their hut. Everyone kissed hands, and the bridegroom shut the door. It was over; I could now go home and take a bath.

★ ★ ★

On the eve of the war in Abyssinia I went back to Italy, and as I took leave of Jemberié on the quayside at Massawa, in the shadow of the liner which was to take me home, he asked me whether we should ever meet again.

Eight months later, recalled to the Colony, I disembarked at Mogadishu and from there went by plane to my new station in Harar.

Harar had only recently been taken by General Graziani's columns; sniping was still going on in the mountains; the Abyssinians dominated the Chercher, and military ambulances journeyed by night bringing the wounded into the city. There was no regularly constituted government, Governor Nasi had not yet arrived, and my functions were of a universal nature which imposed upon me all kinds of responsibilities and left me without a moment to breathe.

There were no houses and in order not to live in the official government building I took up my abode in a native *tukul* which the military engineers had converted outside the city, on the slopes towards Faïda. I had taken on as personal servant a Galla boy of the name of Digaro' who was as stupid and as lazy as a marmot.

I had been in Harar a month when, returning home one evening, I came upon Digaro' huddled on the footpath, blubbering and holding his behind. He seemed not to hear my questions, and kept repeating that he was not a slave, that he was not a bastard. I could get nothing else out of him and so, losing patience and having called him the few improper names I knew in Galla, I continued towards the house. Digaro', still blubbering and holding one side of his buttocks, followed me at a respectful distance.

There was a light in the window of the *tukul* and when I opened the door I was struck speechless: in the one and only room, Jemberié was remaking my bed and preparing it for the night.

He turned and came towards me and, without the slightest fuss and with his usual inscrutable smile, shook my hand and asked – for all the world as though we had parted yesterday – 'You well, signore?'

I fired a string of questions at him and he answered me with the greatest simplicity that at Addis Ababa he had heard of my arrival at Harar and, naturally, had come to resume his service with me. The shadow of a smile passed over his face: obviously, he told me, the great ape he had found in the *tukul* was not the kind of servant for me.

Through the open door, the great ape in question could be seen spying from behind a tree, and Jemberié made a motion of disgust in his direction. 'I find great ape behind *tukul* and say him: "What you do in master's house?" He say me: "Go away Abyssinian. Now Galla give orders here." I kick his behind and

say him: "Shut your mouth, you ugly bastard negro slave."
Throw him out and shut door.'

We remained for about a year at Harar and when Mangashà
Ubié, the Ethiopian governor of the western territories, left I was
sent to replace him and to organise the politico-administrative
districts in the vast region along the Sudan frontier, extending
from Kaffa to the Blue Nile.

During that thirty-four days' odyssey from Addis Ababa to
Gambela on the Sudanese frontier, Jemberié never left my side.
We journeyed five hundred miles across regions without roads,
with thirty-two motor lorries and six caterpillars, preceded by
hordes of men armed with poles, scimitars, pruning knives and
pickaxes whom the village chiefs, notified in advance, had sent
to improvise a track over which our column moved no faster
than a snail.

Jemberié stayed with me throughout my time in the western
territories and followed me in all my vagabonding through the
country of the Anouak and of the Nouers, in the Anfhillo forest,
across Wallega, into the Beni Shangul in the sultanate of the
legendary Sheik Khôjeli, and on up into the region where the
Blue Nile (which constituted the northern limit of my territory)
crosses the frontier and flows down to Khartoum to mix its
waters with those of the White Nile.

It was a period of intense and ceaseless work. There were
interminable caravan excursions on mules over almost unknown
country, among people of different races, tongues, customs and
degrees of civilisation.

Slowly but surely, the organisation of the territories began
to take shape: Commissariats were established, and to them
the Residencies were attached. As the government gradually
extended its political and administrative control, the country
began to settle down and to adjust itself to the new order.

The various regions were acquiring their own individual
physiognomies and I was just beginning to see the first results
of my work, when the Tall Young Man – with whom I had
spent those previous years in Libya – was appointed Viceroy
of the Empire, and was good enough to express the wish that I

be attached to him not, this time, as his physician, but as his *chef de cabinet*.

It was a great honour, but I was sorry to leave the work I had only just started – and in my heart I had some misgivings: I felt that the tall crusader was taking upon himself responsibilities which, in my possibly antiquated orthodoxy, I considered unsuited to a prince of the blood. Jemberié, however, was not afflicted by any such doubts and lived in a state of complete beatitude.

'After sweating like navvy you now real gentleman,' he told me, with immense satisfaction.

He had always found it extremely mortifying that I had been obliged to pass months at a time in caravans with hordes of Galla and packs of negroes, travelling on the back of a mule in all weathers, sleeping very often under the stars with a pack-saddle for my pillow. Now that, after my nomadic and uncomfortable existence in the western territories, I lived in the villa of the Empress Menen, on the same property as the *ghebi* in which the Viceroy had taken up residence; now that I slept in an enormous four-poster bed with a canopy bearing the lions of the Negus's coat of arms; now that I had engaged the ex-cook of the dissolved American Legation, Jemberié at last considered that my way of living was suitable to my rank.

Moreover – and this completed his satisfaction – he had been promoted *bölük-bashi*. To mark the occasion he had bought himself a *tarbūsh* at least three inches higher than the regulation measurement; on his sleeve he wore the insignia of his new grade, and in honour of my position he had considered it necessary to tie round his middle a regimental scarf of pure silk.

The only fly in his ointment was the increased expenditure in which we were involved. 'Here money run like water,' he grumbled, shaking his head. I had to keep up appearances to a certain extent, and as I received invitations to dinners and receptions I was naturally obliged to return them. Moreover, my new cook was an artist, and the guests did full justice to the dishes he produced. Jemberié however was shocked at such prodigality. On the morning after a particularly successful supper party he brought in my coffee with a funereal air and said in a lugubrious voice, 'Yesterday everyone very pleased, eat everything. Lady with red hair eat two helpings sweet. Very expensive; nothing left. Cook he say, "My cooking very good." Perhaps better he cooking badly so people eat not much and not come again.'

I found that my position as *chef de cabinet* did not altogether exclude the *tebīb*. One afternoon the Viceroy felt ill and complained of pains in the stomach; I at once called in Professor Scollo. The next day, in white overall, mask and rubber gloves, I assisted him in one of the most delicate appendectomy operations I have ever witnessed. When he had opened the peritoneum, Scollo lifted the diseased appendix with the pincers and looked at me: it was perforated and discharging pus.

Twenty-five days later the Viceroy was again at his desk, and as the organisation of the various departments of his office was now complete I felt that I could withdraw. I was offered other assignments in other parts of the empire but, although I was gratified, they did not tempt me and I preferred to go home. I was, however, very ready to accept an invitation from the Governor of Eritrea to spend two weeks with him in Asmara before leaving.

It was three years since I had been in Asmara and I found that the town had spread like a drop of oil. The buildings had changed and thousands of unknown faces thronged the streets, making me feel a stranger, although the friendly hearts and smiles of the men and women I had known remained the same.

Sad hearts they were, and dejected smiles. The romantic nineteenth century used to say: '*Partir, c'est mourir un peu.*' I could not know that when I took leave of the empire I was abandoning a dying patient, but I was sad because I felt that another chapter of my life in Africa was closing for ever.

After many years, I can still see the quayside at Massawa in the merciless June sun, and the arcade of the *Magazzini Generali*. Its columns and pillars provided shade but did nothing to cool the group of friends who had come to see me off and who took shelter beneath them. For even out of the sun the atmosphere was like an oven.

The magnificent arms and shoulders of Donna Ly, my assistant's half-caste wife, seemed to be modelled in bronze, and beside her dark beauty and Eleanora's phosphorescent smile, the bloodless pallor of the European women seemed almost unhealthy. All the men were dressed in white and looked like figures in plaster. Jemberié's *tarbūsh* made a splash of scarlet.

The steamship 'Mazzini' towered above us on the other side of the quay, and when the moment had arrived, Commander Matarazzo leaned over the side and made a sign to me.

'When you come back,' said Jemberié, 'you say me and I come meet you in port.'

From the bridge I watched my friends waving handkerchiefs, berets, caps – and beyond the others, against the background of the store's white façade, I saw the flaming *tarbūsh* of Jemberié Igzaou. As the 'Mazzini' drew away the figures on the quayside became smaller and less distinct, but the splash of red remained there, immovable, and was lost to my sight only when the ship turned towards the Abd el Qader fisheries.

That was the last I ever saw of my faithful friend. I never returned to those parts and so Jemberié never came to meet me at the port.

In later years I returned instead to Tripoli, was taken prisoner and, after a time behind barbed wire, was repatriated to Italy.

For several years after that I continued to write to friends in Africa and to question those whom I met, trying whenever I could to find out what had become of Jemberié Igzaou. I could obtain no news of him from anyone; it seemed as though he had been spirited away. Although various people thought they had caught sight of him at Massawa or at Asmara, no one knew where he was living. I finally came to the conclusion that he had returned to his native place in the Gojjam or had rejoined his wife in the Anseba valley.

Then, in 1952, a letter from Eleanora in Asmara informed me that Jemberié had died fighting in the battle of Keren.

As I held the sheet of paper and stared at the thin, upright handwriting in the style of twenty years ago, I was invaded by a vague remorse: excellent Jemberié – with my suppositions I had belittled him. He had neither taken refuge in his native country nor sought the peace and security of the Anseba pastures where he would have been safe from the storm that broke on his second fatherland. When the empire fell and Eritrea was invaded, when all was already lost, he rallied to the flag under which he had grown to manhood, and gave his life defending it.

★ ★ ★

Although, as I have said, Jemberié had an extremely low opinion of Mohammedans, every now and again he came across an Arab of whom he thoroughly approved, and on these occasions he gave me no peace until he was allowed to present the person in question to me – 'he great man; he heart like milk; he have everything in his head'. Shortly after our arrival in Misurata he met Hajj Ahmed es-Sed and fell a victim to the charm of that Fatimid of ancient race.

Hajj Ahmed es-Sed was a person of importance: not only did he possess houses, land and livestock, but he had also made the pilgrimage to Mecca (as indicated by the title 'Hajj'). Moreover, he was called 'Sed' which means 'Lion'. He was tall, with a long beard reaching to his chest.

But it was not on account of his imposing appearance, riches or titles – and still less on account of his religion – that Jemberié admired Hajj Ahmed. He was left gaping and amazed at the generosity of this Moslem towards the crowd of poor people which gathered every Friday in front of his door, and was touched by the simplicity with which the noble pilgrim placed himself on the same level as the humble people to whom he gave alms. Although his own innate thrift was outraged by so much liberality, Jemberié was nevertheless shaken by such regal munificence bestowed in the name of God.

Above all, however, Jemberié was moved and fascinated by a great misfortune that had fallen this unhappy man. It seemed that for some time Hajj Ahmed had suffered from atrocious stomach pains. Naturally, a person of his rank could not be afflicted with the ordinary vulgar complaints to which common

men are heirs: extraordinary people must have extraordinary
diseases. In fact Hajj Ahmed, having had occasion to go to Sirte,
had spent a night on the Wadi Soffejin and while he was sleeping
a serpent had entered his mouth and curled itself up at the
bottom of his stomach. And there it had remained. From that
night he had been tormented with disturbances which could
obviously be explained only by the presence of this unwelcome
guest. Moreover, if any doubt had remained about the matter,
it had been dispelled once and for all by his deceased father who,
in a dream, told him that not only was there a male serpent in
his stomach, but also that it was a particularly malignant and
dangerous reptile.

Unfortunately, a native healer had also confirmed point by
point this message from beyond the tomb, and had added that
unless Hajj Ahmed could somehow succeed in getting rid of the
serpent, the latter – which was none other than an evil spirit
from the infernal regions – would certainly kill him within a few
months.

In the meantime, Hajj Ahmed suffered the tortures of the
damned at the hands of quack surgeons, blood-letters, composers
of amulets and matrons who knew mysterious remedies. He had
tried one cure after another, visited all the marabouts and experi-
mented with the whole gamut of peculiar medicaments which
compose the Arab pharmacopœia.

From the moment when he first acquainted me with this
startling history, Jemberié never ceased talking about it and
begging me to give to his noble protégé the medicine 'who make
serpents run'. He was convinced that, just as an extract of male
fern frees the intestine from tape worm, so there must be a
medicine capable of ridding the stomach of serpents which have
chosen to take up their abode there. At the same time, he pestered
the pious Mussulman to try my cures, and the unfortunate
man, desperate after so many unsuccessful experiments, finally
acquiesced and decided to consult the Christian doctor.

From that moment my life became an absolute hell.

For three months I was at the beck and call of Hajj Ahmed
es-Sed's serpent. He came to the dispensary in the morning and

in the evening. If I would not see him, he waited for me in the street and followed me home. Sometimes he got there before me, and when I arrived I would find him installed in the salon with a cup of coffee which Jemberié had hastened to offer him.

The truth of the matter was that Hajj Ahmed was in the period of the male menopause: he was suffering from disorders of the circulation, glandular disturbances and nervous illusions which made him feel that his stomach was swollen like a water-skin and that he had a suffocating stoppage in his gullet.

'But I have not told you all,' he confided, 'you should know also that the serpent will not allow me to touch a woman; perhaps he wants them for himself. When I lie with a woman the accursed thing breaks my back, cuts my nerves, and I am as limp as a eunuch ...'

A very painful situation for anyone bearing the name of 'Lion'.

For two whole months I tried by every means to convince him that there was no serpent in his stomach and that he must follow some serious treatment. He let me speak, listened patiently without taking the least notice of what I said, and then resumed his discourse about the serpent, the accursed serpent which was 'devouring his life'.

I found it quite easy to demolish the arguments of the Arab blood-letters, but I was powerless to dispel the impression made by the dream in which his dead father had pointed to the pit of his stomach, whispering the fatal words: 'There, there lies the serpent; there is your assassin.'

After months of this persecution, I came to the conclusion that either Hajj Ahmed must succumb or recover, or I would inevitably be placed in a padded cell. It was then that I decided to cross the narrow line that separates the physician from the charlatan.

One evening, Hajj Ahmed was waiting for me at the corner of the piazza as I left the dispensary – waiting for me with his hand on his stomach and the expression of one condemned to death. As soon as he saw me he cried, 'O *tebīb*, will you not liberate me from this serpent which is killing me? Do you not believe the words of my dead father?'

I took him home, and as we drank our coffee I talked to him.

A father's words, I said, are sacred, but very often words heard in a dream are imperfectly remembered and it is often impossible to discern their exact significance. God, however, knows all and I might have been mistaken in my incredulity. How could we find out the truth? Hajj Ahmed could, of course, go to Tripoli where the radiologists would be able to confirm or deny the presence of the serpent. But if this evil spirit were cunning enough to assume the form of a reptile, it would certainly be easy for him, would it not, to make himself invisible to the rays? Hajj Ahmed gravely approved my reasoning and assured me that this demon, if not Eblis, the Prince of Evil himself, must certainly be one of his ablest lieutenants.

There was only one way to find out whether the serpent was there or not: to open the stomach.

'O Hajj Ahmed, if there is no serpent, I will close the stomach again and will say to you: my brother, I was right. If, on the other hand, I find the serpent, I will drag him out and you shall crush his head so that he shall never again trouble the sons of Adam.'

Hajj Ahmed became so excited that he upset his cup of coffee. 'You can truly free me from the accursed thing, O *tebīb*, and give me back my life?' I left him in transports of expectation.

With a great deal of cautioning I confided my plan to Mohamed ed-Dernàwi, the dispensary nurse who, flattered by my confidence in him and pleased to play a part in the conspiracy, swore to carry the secret to his grave. It could all be done in the evening, he said, when that gossip Aissa and the porter had left; the dispensary would be empty and the city preparing for sleep.

Mohamed ed-Dernàwi had worked for three years in the operating theatre of the Tripoli hospital and had administered chloroform when Testori was operating; the narcosis would only last a few minutes and there was no risk. Mohamed would also provide the absolutely indispensable element for the success of our undertaking: a serpent. He professed to know where serpents were to be found, and in his excitement he promised me serpents of such a size that I was obliged to curb his enthusiasm and to remind him that a human stomach could not contain a python.

Hajj Ahmed arrived punctually, late in the evening, with the negroes who were to carry him home after the operation. His servants remained in the courtyard. With his face towards the *Qibla* he recited the evening prayer and then, naked, mounted the operating table. Putting on my rubber gloves, I covered his chest and stomach with three sterilised cloths, leaving uncovered the epigastrum which I duly disinfected with alcohol and tincture of iodine. Mohamed fixed the chloroform mask on his face. The pious man was praying; his voice became muffled under the mask and very soon the words faded away and he was breathing deeply and regularly.

The moment had arrived.

I took up the lancet and cut the skin along the median line from the sternum to two inches above the navel: this seemed to me sufficient for the extraction of even a young crocodile. I stopped the bleeding and with fifteen stitches sewed up the wound. Mohamed executed a most artistic bandage.

Hajj Ahmed was still sleeping. The negroes carried him away on a stretcher. I watched them go, followed by Mohamed ed-Dernàwi who carried under his arm a cardboard box, carefully closed and tied with string, containing an unfortunate and furiously struggling serpent.

On the following day I went to see Hajj Ahmed at his house. I found him extremely well. He was, of course, resigned to remaining in bed for a fortnight, since it would be unwise to take risks after such a serious operation. But he was radiant and sought with great magnanimity to comfort me.

'We may all make mistakes, *tebīb* – only God is all-wise. You see, there *was* a serpent; my father did not lie and I did not misunderstand his words.'

Deeply moved, he embraced me: he did not wish me to take my mistake to heart; it saddened him, he said, to see me confused and mortified.

'But you have saved me, O wise one!' He embraced me again,

patting me on the back to encourage me. 'It was you who had
the idea of opening my stomach to liberate me from the accursed
thing! I had tried all the remedies, all the exorcisms and spells,
but the healers shrugged their shoulders; only you were able
to cure me. Praise be to God, Who has granted you knowledge
and wisdom.'

It had not been possible to keep Jemberié in the dark and I
had let him into the secret. At first he did not understand. What
need was there, he had asked, to catch another serpent? Wasn't
the one in Hajj Ahmed's stomach enough? And if there was no
serpent in his stomach, why did I want to put one there? When
I had explained to him that the serpent was only an illusion of
the patient and that in order to cure him it was necessary to
remove the illusion, he was first astounded and then advised me
to have nothing to do with it: Hajj Ahmed, he said, was certainly
too intelligent, too highly educated and too clever to be taken
in by such a vulgar trick.

After the miraculous operation, Jemberié visited the convalescent with me and was dumbfounded when he heard the
description of the operation based on the fantastic picture
painted by the incorrigible Mohamed, and saw the great man
weeping on my neck as he eulogised my prodigious performance.
In a moment all Jemberié's admiration for the noble gentleman
of Misurata evaporated and he banished him forthwith to the
amorphous crowd of Mohammedans whom he despised. After
the third visit, as we were leaving the house of the patient who
had now almost completely recovered, Jemberié said, 'He just
like all Arabs: only he plenty more ass.'

★ ★ ★

For a long time I had been contemplating an excursion to Sliten
to visit the sanctuary of Sidi Abdesselām, and I had promised
Aissa ben Jahia, my native assistant, that he should accompany
me. When at last I was able to make the journey, Mohamed
ed-Dernàwi and Mahmud Ferjiani were so anxious to come
with us that in the end I consented to take them as well.
Jemberié, who did not approve of my pilgrimage to the tomb

of a Mohammedan saint, stayed at home very shocked and in a bad temper.

In those days no one had thought of the motor road with which Balbo later linked Tripoli to Cyrenaica. There was only a narrow, dusty track between Misurata and Sliten; Giuseppe Volpi had not yet established his imposing agricultural undertaking along it, and the association for the colonisation of Libya, which was later to build the agricultural village of Garibaldi and the Moslem settlement of en-Namia, was not yet in being.

In our dilapidated truck we crossed the great oasis of Zawiet el Najoub and the smaller oasis of Bu Rêya and staggered down the slope, past the imperial ruins of Ras Ma'agol and the Roman remains at Shifé. The track then became level and wound along the coast. Soon after we had passed Suq et-Tlata, the first houses of Sliten came in sight and we entered the city through the Nisurata Gate. We stopped in the Viale del Re, close to the *zāwiya* of Sidi Abdesselām. This was our goal and we entered.

The building contains two mosques – the tomb of Sidi Abdesselām and the cemetery of the saint's descendants. Aissa ben Jahia and Mahmud Ferjiani, overawed by the air of sanctity which emanates from the old stones, moved about like somnabulists with their hands on their breasts, and even Mohamed ed-Dernàwi, in spite of his pretensions to sophistication, spoke in a whisper and regarded the votive ornaments on the walls of the saint's tomb with a certain awe.

It is here that flower-bedecked sheep are sacrificed during the prescribed feasts in the pilgrimage period of Milud, the birthday of the Prophet. Parents who have asked Sidi Abdesselām for children and whose prayer has been granted come here to offer a slaughtered lamb in payment for the child they have received. In this very courtyard the saint performed the ritual ablutions during the last years of his life. There are those who maintain that the water still spurts from the walls of the tomb; it seems that from the jar used for the ablutions – which was buried with its owner – there runs at times a crystal stream which, Mohamed assured me, cures fevers and many skin disorders. A cousin of his, at the third washing, found himself free of an eczema with which he had been afflicted for years.

But Mohamed's account of the water's powers was nothing at all: legend has it that when a great-grandchild of the holy marabout – an only son – died at the age of twelve, his mother in desperation prayed to her venerated ancestor for another son to replace the one she had lost. The holy man appeared to her in a dream and commanded her to bathe in the miraculous water. The woman did as she was commanded and nine months later gave birth to a son 'as beautiful as the archangel Gabriel'.

On the threshold of the Great Mosque we met the Imām who told us how, before the miracle, before sterile men and barren women began coming here in pilgrimage, snow-white rabbits were seen to enter the sepulchre of the marabout and to emerge with their bellies so swollen that they 'rolled against the ground'. A harlot noticed these prodigious rabbits which by merely crossing the mausoleum became heavy with young, and recognised them as the mischievous jinniyah female spirits who, in order to show human females the way, had taken the form of the animal which symbolises fecundity. The wretched woman, who for a long time had desired a son for her redemption, ran to pray at the tomb and her prayer was answered. Since then, the sanctuary has overflowed with 'virgins who are becoming embittered by their celibacy, barren women, and mothers whose offspring have been cursed with some affliction'.

The most propitious moment, it seems, is Friday after the mid-day prayer, and the pilgrimage must be repeated three Fridays running. The woman visits the tomb and after having craved her particular boon she lights the coloured candle she has brought with her and throws perfumed seeds into a brazier. After praying, she takes a jar and descends into the pool, removes her clothes and, when she is as naked 'as a child washed by the midwife at the ceremony of the seventh day', she performs the ritual of the great ablutions.

It is only very rarely that a woman does not become pregnant after this operation. The disappointed ones comfort themselves with the thought that their failure to conceive may be a blessing in disguise, since Allah often imposes a seeming misfortune on those for whom he has a special predilection.

The Imām was loquacious. Perhaps he was a little flattered by the interest of a Christian doctor in his religion. He explained to me that in ancient times the spring flowed not with water, but with blood – the blood of a jinn of the infernal regions – but the evil had entered into a serpent and disappeared, leaving only the benevolent element behind.

When I asked him what had become of the serpent full of maleficent power he smiled in a gratified manner and told a story which left my companions open-mouthed.

One morning, it seems, the people of the city found at the spring a colossal serpent wound fifty times round upon itself, and asleep. It was as black as night and when it awoke it was seen that fire flashed from its eyes and smoke poured from its nostrils. Every now and again it threw itself a hundred cubits into the air, above the tallest palm trees, and then fell down again into the pool and drank it dry with one draught.

The terrified men and women ran to the saint, invoking his protection.

On the following night, at the head of a procession of un-known persons (who were without doubt saints and inhabitants of the kingdom of the good spirits), Sidi Abdesselām went to the spring. From a distance the listening crowd heard the murmur of the supernatural assembly, at times drowned by the chanting voice of the holy man pronouncing the most terrible exorcisms. In the meantime, the serpent lashed out furiously, tearing up centuries old olive trees with its tail and rending great holes in the ground. From that night the spring became pure and holy, and the serpent was seen no more.

Mahmud Ferjiani paid a very high price for a little of the dust from the wall of the tomb, with the intention of making it into plasters as soon as he returned home, to cure his child of ringworm.

I was beginning to suspect that four-fifths of human ailments responded to Sidi Abdesselām's influence and I felt that it was

rather mean of this four-centuries-dead saint to set himself up
as a rival concern.

'But why – if the holy man can cure all ills,' I asked, 'do so
many sick people come to be treated at the dispensary?'

'Ah, but you see,' Mohamed ed-Dernàwi explained to me, 'at
the dispensary they do not pay.'

★　★　★

Rebecca Buaron, the proprietress of the Misurata brothel, was
a voluminous Jewess. She was only about forty years old but
the premature blooming of the oriental woman, love of good
food, and excesses of all kinds had aged her before her time.
In her youth she was famous for her beauty throughout the
whole of North Africa; she had inspired the wildest of passions
and driven the more frenzied of her admirers to every sort of
folly. In her life and loves she had undoubtedly provided enough
material for a new *Decameron*.

Being a pious and deeply religious woman, she maintained
that all her friends had been sent to her from God. God in his
infinite goodness had certainly been generous, filling this beautiful creature's life with an unending cavalcade of men of every
age, occupation, race, colour and estate. Among the many, some
of the most remarkable included the rebel chief Ramadan es-
Shetàwi, General Ameglio, an Egyptian who could dance the
polka with a pack mule across his shoulders, an Italian minister,
a learned student of the Byzantine liturgy, and the most rascally
Greek tradesman in Libya.

Her vast and varied experience had endowed her with a frank
contempt for the sons of Adam of whatever race or colour, and
she spoke of them with long-suffering compassion as though
they were deficient beings in need of protection and guidance.

When I told her that I had heard wonderful accounts of the
perspicacity of the rebel chief Seff en-Nàsser who still maintained the revolt against us in the South, she shook her head in
protest and said, 'All stories. Seff en-Nàsser is an imbecile because
he has not thrown you back into the sea, and you are fools
because you have not destroyed him. Mark my words, *tebīb*,

the world goes on because God has distributed a measure of stupidity to everyone, for it is certain that Seff en-Nàsser could drown you and he does not do it, and you could wipe him out and there seems no likelihood of that either.'

I passed on these words to our military commander and he – a hard-bitten old colonial – told me that he had for a long time been considering entrusting the direction of his political department to Rebecca, but was afraid the appointment would not meet with approval in Tripoli.

Her pessimistic view of the male sex had not embittered Rebecca or made her unpleasant or malicious. Now that for her the season of love-making was over – a fact not unduly regretted – she was able to take an interest in other people's love affairs and was almost as proud of the successes of her girls (whose sentimental vicissitudes she followed with intelligent understanding) as she would have been of her own. She guarded her protégées with a jealous affection not unlike that of a mother, but she had no illusions about their defects and shortcomings. 'Have you noticed Khadijia's eyes? If she had a brain behind them she would turn the world upside down.'

She was a Jewess, but she was a complete stranger to the avarice which those who have seemingly never known a close-fisted Christian believe to be the prerogative of Jews. She treated her girls with a disinterested generosity which was really remarkable in one of her profession. Unfortunate creatures from brothels all over Libya, who had been exploited by grasping madams, begged to be allowed to come and work in her house in Misurata. Even Jemberié, with his hatred of the Jews, said of Rebecca, 'She very good old strumpet.'

When the girls came to the dispensary for the regular medical check-up, Rebecca accompanied them and kept them close about her, rather as a hen gathers her brood together. The little prostitutes would cross the courtyard with a bored air, dragging their sandals over the uneven cobblestones and crowding outside the room where I awaited them beside the iron bed.

They stretched themselves languidly, their arms up over their heads, twisting their bodies from the waist and yawning silently; for them the hour was early and they vented their resentment at losing their sleep by making faces at Ehlia, the nurse appointed to attend to the ills, great and small, of Venus Pandemia. Ehlia, in order not to be obliged to notice their impertinent grimaces, would bend her fat and sullen face over the steriliser.

I called them in by name. One at a time they entered, undressed and mounted the bed, letting fall their sandals one after the other. Before lying down, the more daring among them would blow a kiss in the direction of the speculum in my hand, as though to propitiate it. With their savage humour, they called it *zebb el hukûma* – the phallus of the Government – of the Government which subjected them to this control. But even the most shameless of them, before undressing, always cast an uneasy glance towards the courtyard where Mohamed ed-Dernàwi waited with his cards and register – for even these women have their modesty. If this glance was intercepted by Ehlia it always brought a sarcastic smile to her face. Ehlia despised the girls on account of their profession and the girls detested her because she was a Jewess. Even in this little world of shipwrecked humanity the brotherly love which should be engendered by religion did not operate very effectively.

Every time I plunged my hands into a bowl of disinfectant after the examination, the victim would raise her head and ask anxiously, 'Am I well?' When the answer was, 'Yes', all the benedictions of Allah were showered upon me, as though I had some part in their escape from the perils with which their path was beset. Sometimes, however, my verdict was less consoling.

'Am I still ill?'

'Yes.'

Then there were tears and lamentations, exclamations and invocations; and the names of God and of the most venerated saints were mingled with my prescriptions.

'*Ya Sidi Abdesselām*,' prayed Khadijia, who was from Sliten and attributed to the marabouts of her native country powers that in fact belong only to the anti-syphilitic drugs.

Sometimes Rebecca, authoritative and massive, was able, in

her wisdom, to comfort them: she had seen too much in her lifetime not to know that time arranges most things in this world, and that if there are ills for which no remedy exists, hope must never be abandoned. So she would clasp the patient to her ample bosom, help her dress to the accompaniment of jingling bracelets and ornaments, and whisper to her the absurd words which mothers address to their children. As she twisted the *ḥāik* round the girl's hips she would turn a pleading face to me and say, 'Isn't it true, *tebīb*, that Mabruka will get well? Such a lovely creature, *wallàhi!* A little patience, some medicine and Allah's help. Allah is merciful. In a little while this princess will smile again. The blessing of Allah upon her.'

In the meantime the other girls would be gossiping and chattering under Ehlia's baleful eye. While I bent over the washbasin one of them, on the pretext of speaking to me, might come near enough to see herself in the glass on the wall – and turn away, confused, if she met my glance in the mirror.

The most famous of all these girls was Mné. She was lithe and slim, with small features, huge liquid eyes that slanted like an antelope's and beautiful hands and feet. She was a desert girl from the *qibla*, and had been sold into her profession by caravaneers. Her beauty had already brought her a host of admirers; she had even had a novel written about her; and the girls were flattered to have her in their house.

When the girls left the dispensary, accompanied by Rebecca, Mné usually brought up the rear, and as she passed Ehlia she would put out her tongue at her. Ehlia would lose her temper at last and hiss '*sharmouta*' through her teeth. The insult would bring a fresh and delighted smile to Mné's face, and bending towards the Jewess she would mutter something like (and here the translator feels it necessary, owing to the misuse into which the magic of language has fallen, to leave the passage in the original) '*Che tua madre non si stanchi di scondinzolare sulle pisciate dei maschi e possa il Consolatore toglierle il vizio di mordere.*'

Rebecca Buaron had taken a liking to me – because I was a doctor, because my hair was prematurely white, and because I treated her for nothing. '*Wallàhi*, I am not sure yet whether you are my father or my son – but I am very fond of you. Fond from the heart, you understand?' I was not much taken with the imaginary relationship, but the remark was well meant.

When she summoned me to treat her for one of the liver attacks to which she was subject, or when I called on an official visit without notice, she always kept me to tea and told me some story from her highly coloured life. She would tell of how they had played darts for her when she was a child; of how the rebels had seized and kept her in their camp, and how in the midst of a battle she had remained for hours flat on the ground, pressed as close as possible to the earth, while bullets riddled the tent in which she had taken refuge; of her stay in a harem in Tunis, covered with gold and jewels, and of her desperate flight after having abandoned all her possessions, walking for days and days towards the frontier of Tripolitania with her clothes in rags and with bleeding feet. She had been so happy to find herself in her own country again that she had given herself, on a sand dune, to the first spahi she met after crossing the frontier.

Sometimes she invited me to mid-day dinner in her house in the deserted street, which stood dazzling white in the sun except where a corner or a verandah cast a sharp-edged violet shadow across a wall or down on the cobbled lane. In the long white wall, punctuated at regular intervals by shuttered, half-moon windows, there was no apparent entrance to welcome the visitor out of the glaring light into the shady, peaceful courtyard beyond. But as I turned the corner into the alley, where the sun-baked mud preserved the imprint of bare feet and sandals, a door was thrown open and the *bakkūsh*, a deaf-mute porter, was there on the threshold to receive me with a festive whimper. The unfortunate creature, unable to speak, clapped his hands and emitted guttural noises to announce my arrival.

Graceful phantoms gowned in rustling silks greeted me timidly in the cool shade of the darkened corridor and escorted me with care so that I should not stumble up or down the invisible steps.

In the luminous courtyard the girls crowded round me: for

these occasions they put on their most gorgeous attire; from the *sanduq* they unearthed their finest ornaments of brass, silver and gold. Khadijia was peacocking in a *ḥāik* made of cloth of silver, which shone like moonlight; Salma, the monkey, paraded a triple necklace of Turkish coins and gold filigree medallions which gave the impression of a medieval gorget; Yasmina wore a silver belt a hand's breadth wide with a clasp as big as a fist; Fatma's ear-rings of old silver, encrusted with coral and other semi-precious stones, reached to her shoulders, and Mahadia displayed a pair of gold chain cuffs which covered her arm from the wrist to the elbow.

I pretended to be overcome: the more they were expected, the more were compliments an obligation.

Could it be possible that all this finery was in honour of the *tebīb?* Were these Rebecca's girls, or had I fallen among princesses escaped from the seraglio of Istambul? They must all tell me their names because I could not be expected to recognise the girls I knew among these dazzling creatures. I covered my eyes to protect them from so much splendour, and the little multi-coloured crowd, perfumed with sandalwood and carnation, chirped and fluttered round me like flustered, exotic birds in an aviary.

Through the open window of a ground-floor room, Mné could be seen sitting back on her heels intent upon putting a final touch of *kohl* on her half-closed eyelids; at the noise, she turned and looked at us, surprised, with the mirror in one hand and the antimony-stained fingers of the other spread out fanwise, in an attitude that made us roar with laughter.

The girls' laughter prevented me from hearing Rebecca Buaron who, in a peach-coloured *holy* stretched tightly over her exuberant bosom and heavy hips, sailed like a battleship across the courtyard and took us in the rear with raucous exclamations like fire-crackers; her extended arms were ajingle with gold ornaments, and a broad smile masked the shrewdness of a face in which obesity had not altogether cancelled the traces of her earlier beauty.

It would almost seem that she had forgotten her invitation.

With feigned and festive surprise she would ask: can it really
be that the *tebīb* has come especially to eat with her and with
her girls? But what would he eat, seeing that there was nothing
in the market that morning and the new cook had not the
slightest idea of what a meal should be? In the meantime I must
certainly be dying of hunger while these brainless hussies had
kept me so long listening to their senseless chatter. She turned
a severe look upon the girls and began giving orders as though
she were directing a military manœuvre: she shouted awful
threats in the direction of the kitchen, and made frantic signs
to the deaf-mute who was busy arranging cushions in the room
prepared for the banquet.

When we were seated, two of the girls would enter carrying
an enormous dish – holding it high so as not to mark their dresses
– from which emerged a steaming hot mountain of *cuscus*. The
cook, apprehensive about her masterpiece, followed them with
her eyes from the door of the kitchen where she stood with a
frying-pan in one hand and a cloth in the other.

In the long, low room, seated on cushions arranged upon the
carpet, we stretched out our hands for the food in that religious
silence which, in all countries, accompanies the beginning of a
meal.

At my side, Rebecca eyed the best pieces of mutton surrounding the pyramid of *cuscus* and with her fat fingers smothered in
rings she handed them to me with a brief and dignified inclina-
tion of the head.

The small, henna-tinted hands of the girls carried the food
to their mouths with movements full of grace; faces which were
as open books in the light of day bent towards the steaming,
greasy mouthfuls of food; busy, flashing tongues gathered up
the grains of semolina and fragments of meat that remained on
their fingers.

The mountain of semolina became a vast crater; from the fat
sheep's tail I selected titbits that dissolved in the mouth with a
delicious flavour of spices.

The moment for congratulations had come. The cook was
a negress with a face like a monkey and a body like a statue;

she leant indolently against the doorpost and accepted our compliments with obvious pleasure and without any false modesty.

But Rebecca was not satisfied: the *filfil* was not ground fine enough; in that season sheep were thin; the right quality of semolina could not be found; I had eaten nothing; there must surely be something or other with which I could satisfy my hunger?

With a great effort, levering herself up with one hand on my shoulder and another on that of Mahadia, she rose, breathing heavily, and disappeared into the kitchen.

When she returned she was followed by the negress and the *bakkūsh* bearing a long covered dish. Rebecca had wished to introduce into an Arab meal one dish of her own people. 'We Jews,' she said, with an air of gastronomic pride as she lifted the cover to show me the *kharâymi* – a colossal fish swimming in a fiery red pepper sauce. Rebecca had prepared it, she told me, with her own hands, and she cast her eyes to heaven, calling upon God to witness the truth of what I was evidently supposed to consider an impossibility.

The earthenware jug which kept the water cool passed from hand to hand as we attempted to put out the fire which the potent *filfil* had started in our gullets.

Sweets now followed sweets. Our already overburdened insides found difficulty in giving the welcome they deserved to the delicious concoctions of sugar, honey, cinnamon, pistachio. After *baglāwa* in the shape of lozenges, Khadijia offered me half-moons dusted with vanilla: the Tunisian *brīk*. During her long stay in the hospitable houses of Tunis, Khadijia had acquired a heavy necklace of 'Napoleons' and the secret of making little puff pastries which imprison a fragile egg yolk. She was proud of her ability and between one mouthful and the next she would tell us stories of her imaginary adventures in Tunisia: the Arab notabilities who had ruined themselves for her; French officers who had wanted to abandon their careers in order to marry her; the Greek shipbuilder who had offered her a villa at the Goletta. Gesticulating in the excitement of her fantastications, she broke a *brīk* in her hand and the egg yolk spattered her nose, to the infinite delight of her companions.

Finally, the cook advanced with a jingling of silver anklets. In one hand she bore a copper bowl containing a water jar and soap; on the other arm she carried a pile of hand towels. A thin stream of water was poured over our soaped hands and ran into the bowl; we dried ourselves as the aroma of rose-perfumed coffee rose from the cups which the *bakkūsh* had placed in a circle in front of us.

It was the hour of the siesta, but the presence of an unaccustomed guest kept these slaves of the Court of Love from their sleep and invited confidences which they whispered into the doctor's ear, punctuating their recitals with sighs and pensive silences.

Yasmina told me of her troubles, which I already knew: the story of the disease with which she was afflicted in the past; with a face as grave as a child's she talked to me of ulcers that corrode the flesh, of gnawing pains, of unsuccessful treatments, of ineffectual doctors. She showed me the marks left on her arms by clumsy injections: in the curve of the elbow I noted that, under the pressure of my fingers, a swelling appeared beneath the velvety skin. This caused all of them to inspect their arms with concern, and the name of the 'great sickness', spoken with awe, passed from painted mouth to painted mouth.

Mné dragged herself across the mat to rest her head against my knee. I looked down upon her sharp profile; the heavy meal had brought a flush to her face; her cheeks were rosy and the light and shade reflected from the courtyard outlined the bone structure. I could feel against my knee the grace of a body which interrupted pregnancies, disease and the profession she followed had not yet succeeded in deforming. She told me in a voice veiled in tragedy the details of her last abortion – the pain, the hæmorrhage which emptied her veins, the child extracted in pieces. As she spoke of these things a certain reticence caused her to lose herself in roundabout phrases when she could not find a discreet expression with which to replace the vulgar one that sprang spontaneously to her lips.

Mabrouka, lying by the window, sang in a languid *mezza voce* the song of Shiara Misrani, a popular ballad which perpetuates a *crime passionel* committed many years ago; she drew out the notes in a long cadenza, rocking her head from side to side. Blonde curls, at variance with her dark face, escaped from one side of the scarf round her head. They were the result of an application of peroxide of hydrogen which I had given her some time ago when she fell from her bicycle and her scalp was torn by one of the pedals.

Salma, who had accompanied her to the dispensary and had been present during the treatment, imitated Mabrouka's shrieks as I had sewed up the wound: 'Ah—oo—ah—oo!' Mabrouka took offence; she could see nothing funny in the incident: according to her, she had fractured her skull. 'Is it not true, *tebīb*, that I had a big hole in my skull?' Salma made a face and clapped her hands in protest. But Mabrouka was not to be denied and, kneeling in the middle of the room, she parted her blonde curls so that everyone should see the terrible scar – a fine red line about three quarters of an inch long. She remained thus, her hands raised to her head, her small breasts firm under her *surīya*, miserable because they were making fun of her, because nobody took pity on poor Mabrouka.

The summer afternoon's languor, after the Pantagruelian meal, slackened the limbs and made the eyelids heavy. No one took any notice of Gmera who – always rowdy – was shaking her savage locks to a dance rhythm.

Rebecca snored in a corner, sunk deep among the cushions, her chin on her chest, her head lolling. Two flies buzzed round the drops of sauce which had fallen on to the mat.

Mné was sleeping, her head still against my knees; I slipped a cushion under her, gently, so as not to wake her: her face as she slept was disconsolate and wet with tears.

At last, on the tips of my toes, stepping over the bodies of the sleeping girls, I made my way out of the room; in front of the door the cook was lying flat in a strip of shade, fast asleep and grunting.

But my precautions were in vain: as soon as I put my foot

into the street, Rebecca's flock wakened and overtook me. The
stifling air hit us like the heat from a furnace; the girls were
blinded by the strong light, but with their fingers to their lips
they made me the formal farewell speeches:

'God be with you in the evening.'

'May your night be happy.'

'May God prosper you.'

'God keep you in health.'

'Fare you well.'

'Farewell.'

Mizda

An Abyssinian slave girl

Mné

Chapter Three

BERBER COUNTRY

In 1927 I was transferred from Misurata to the Berber territory in the mountains near the Tunisian frontier, and for the first time I was to add political activities to my medical functions.

My field extended over a very wide area. It included the whole territory from the mountains in western Tripolitania down to Ghadames and the Sahara, a region which we had not yet occupied but where we were already in touch with local leaders. Contact was also maintained with the distant oasis of Ghat, far to the south, where lived Bubaker ag Legoui, king of the Azdjer Tuaregs.

The population was entirely Berber. These people are said to be the descendants of the ancient Libye who once inhabited the North African coast, but there are many highly coloured stories concerning their origin. An Arab historian of the thirteenth century even affirms that the Berbers came from Palestine, where their king Goliath was killed by David. One fact is certain: the Arab invasions of the seventh and eighth centuries broke the dominion of the Berbers, who were driven southwards, into the Sahara and the fortified mountain villages.

Although for twelve centuries they have lived in close contact with other peoples, the Berbers have never been absorbed by their conquerors, and even today, although they may speak Arabic outside their homes, in their family circles they still preserve their own tongue.

The two peoples live side by side without any serious trouble, but they cordially detest each other. The Berbers consider the Arabs obtuse, thieving and treacherous, while the Arabs maintain that the Berbers are 'as hateful as Jews, as poisonous as asps and as immoral as prostitutes'. Possibly they each tend to exaggerate the defects of the other.

93

My new headquarters were at Nàlut, the chief town of the Jebel Nefusah, on the brow of the mountain which dominates the desert.

The dwellings – with the exception of the Turkish fort and a few government buildings – are some of the most curious in the world. They are cut in the rock and to reach them it is necessary to climb down steep steps also cut in the rock. There is an open space in the middle which serves as a kind of common courtyard for all – like a collection of molehills.

But the grottoes of Nàlut were typical of this mountain country; everything here was rock: there was not a plant or a tree to be seen.

On the highest point of the promontory rose the castle, almost part of the rock itself. Within it, along corridors the width of a man's shoulders, hundreds of minute cells had been carved out of the limestone, one upon another. Each family rented one of these for the storing of its provisions which were deposited in the keeping of a guardian.

Under the Italian administration there was a native body composed of wide-awake local notabilities through whom it was possible to exercise efficient control over the whole region.

The head of these native officials was Messaud ben Aissa, a man who had preserved the Turkish title of *Kāymakām*. He was a massively built Berber, with a child-like face camouflaged by a fierce-looking beard that gave him the appearance of a brigand. In reality he was a mild, good-natured man for ever indulging the whims of a capricious wife and somewhat under the thumb of an authoritative sister.

During the rebellion, the rebel chief Chalifa ben Asker, who did not trust this fat, comfortable, keen-brained, but goblin-faced man, kept him for several weeks tied hand and foot to an old Turkish cannon. The mere mention of those days reduced Messaud to a jibbering condition; he was quite unable to express his feelings on the subject and lost all control over words and gestures. Now his days passed evenly and placidly between the not very onerous work in his office, interminable discussions with the *Cādī*, and verbose descriptions of the varied but always harassing symptoms of his arthritis. He lived in an attractive subterranean house the inner walls of which had been hewn with a pick-axe; shelves and cupboards had also been cut into the rock and then fitted with wooden doors.

His sister was a sturdy mountain type with a pleasant face and a perennial smile which disguised the indomitable energy lacked by her brother. One day, when I was taking tea with Messaud's wife, this sister – while busy about the house – opened the door of one of the chests in the wall and out sprang a horned viper which bit her on the chin. At her cry we ran to see what was the matter. I immediately injected permanganate of potassium all round the bite – knowing that owing to the slackness of the Italian Government the Pasteur Institute's phials of anti-serpent serum always arrived at the dispensary at least three months after the potency time-limit had expired.

Zilukha bent Aissa did not die, but for many months she was not the same person. The active, strong-willed woman who had ruled both her own family and that of her brother with a rod of iron and, surrounded by daughter-in-law and grandchildren, had always been the autocrat of the clan, now passed her days in a torpid dream, seated by the brazier with her hands in her lap, staring into space, while those who had depended on her pottered uselessly round, unable to take the initiative or decide anything for themselves.

Rahima, the wife of the *Kāymakām*, tried to take the place of her sister-in-law, but the remedy was worse than the disease and her impulsive interventions only added to the confusion. Messaud ben Aissa, who was nearly as dazed as his sister, moved about the house like an automaton and came constantly to see me at the dispensary or at my office to ask with exasperating regularity when Zilukha would recover. He asked with some diffidence if I was quite sure that the viper which had bitten his sister had been really a viper, because it was a well-known fact that female evil spirits could with the greatest of ease assume the form of any animal. With some hesitation and embarrassment, like a child caught out in a misdemeanour, he confessed that he had tied round his sister's neck a little bag of miraculous powder that

a witch doctor had sold him for a gold piece, but that the effect
of even this powerful remedy seemed to be slow in showing
itself.

In reality, although Zilukha's harassed relatives who saw her
every day failed to observe it, her condition was slowly but
steadily improving; after a time I noticed at each visit that her
brain was clearing and that very slowly she was beginning to
take an interest again in what was going on around her.

The first time she reproved a grandchild, her complaint was
greeted with joy and they began to hope. Slowly her bad temper
reasserted itself, and when she was again nagging at her brother
and making her daughters-in-law, sons, sons-in-law and grandchildren tremble before her, Messaud announced, delighted,
that his sister had recovered.

★ ★ ★

During my early acquaintance with the *Kāymakām*, I did not
know what to call him. 'Messaud' seemed to me too familiar and
'*Kāymakām*' too formal. For some reason or other I decided that
his rank entitled him to be called 'Bey'. When I first addressed
him by this honorary title, however, Messaud began to laugh
and exclaimed, '*Ala limîna yā Bey:* to the right, O Bey.' Seeing
that I was puzzled, he told me the story of the unfortunate Bey
of Fassato.

Under the Turkish rule, an ambitious and purposeful man of
Fassato made up his mind to obtain the title of 'Bey'. Prepared
to make any sacrifice for the satisfaction of his vanity, he went
to Tripoli and began to look up old connections, to make the
acquaintance of other and more influential people, to noise
abroad his own good deeds and to invent them when there were
none to talk about. However, he soon became aware that all this
talk was getting him nowhere, and that if he was to obtain what
he desired, a great deal of grease would have to be applied to the
wheels of the complicated Ottoman administrative machinery.
The commissionaire at the door, the secretary, the chief administrator, and even the governor himself were all ready to hold
out their hands for tips and presents, the *bakshish* that opens

doors, obtains favours, speeds up the signing of important documents.

Thus, in order to propitiate this crowd of vampires great and small, the stocks of barley at Fassato were exhausted, the fields, olive-groves and orchards were sold, and the goats, sheep and camels left the Jefara pastures and made their way to market.

At last the unfortunate man obtained the imperial signature, complete with the imposing stamp of the Sublime Porte and the august seal of the Padishah, which conferred upon him the title of 'Bey'. Then he returned to his mountains where his relatives, friends and neighbours came to meet and congratulate him. They addressed him by his new title and the vain simpleton's heart swelled with pride: his life's dream had been realised.

The first rains had fallen and the ground needed ploughing. The authorities in Tripoli, in their benevolence, had left him with a small parcel of land; but he no longer had any servants and there were no horses – he had not so much as a scabby old camel for the heavier work. He appealed to his brother, who agreed to guide the plough. But the 'Bey' himself had to wear the yoke and drag the plough over the ground.

The rope cut into his shoulder; his feet slipped in the soft earth; the sweat poured from him as he pulled desperately with all his strength, heaving, panting, and stumbling at every step.

But he had one comfort: when, bent double in his efforts to drag the plough along, he lost his sense of direction and swerved from the straight course, he heard the voice of his brother respectfully calling, 'To the right, O Bey. To the right.'

★ ★ ★

Though the Berbers were often rewarding patients, physically tough, quick to react to drugs, and loud in their praises when cures were effected, there was one whose cure turned out to be less than a blessing – in fact it almost broke up a marriage. The case was that of Meriem bent Yusuf, the woman with the coral gloves.

Some months before, I had treated her brother, Issa ben Yusuf, for a particularly nasty wound. At that time I employed a certain number of spies who kept up a shuttle service across the frontier from Tunisia to Tripoli. They included Seân camel breeders, Mohajerin livestock thieves, itinerant vendors, army brothel girls, and caravaneers who carried on contraband activities under the pretext of transporting goods and grain and who, for safety's sake, acted as informers on both sides of the frontier.

Issa ben Yusuf belonged to this last category. He was a tall, spare youth without an ounce of fat on his bones: the muscles of his torso, shoulders and hips were as clearly drawn as on an anatomical chart and gave an animal vitality to his body.

He did, in fact, possess the vitality of a wild beast. They had brought him in to me with a great gash running from his collar-bone to his ribs, made by the spear of an Imanghassaten Tuareg. He had travelled for two days in this condition, first on the back of a camel and then for fourteen hours on a bed of empty petrol tins in the back of a lorry. When he arrived at the dispensary he was the colour of ashes from loss of blood, but he was alive.

Five weeks later he had recovered and his friends came from Dehibat, the first French military post on the route to Medenin, to fetch him. They opened their eyes when they saw the scar, laughed, embraced Issa and thumped him on the back with a force that must have put the finishing touch to his recovery.

One morning, several months later, a young Berber woman entered my dispensary and, gracefully removing her headscarf, announced, 'I am Meriem bent Yusuf' – as she might have said, 'I am Greta Garbo.'

When I asked her where she was from, she looked at me in astonishment and said that of course she had come from Tunisia and that her brother sent me greetings and Allah's blessing; she was the sister of Issa ben Yusuf, the young man with his chest torn open by a spear which I had sewn up so well that the scar was hardly visible and his chest did not hurt, not even if he thumped it with a closed fist, and she was called Meriem and her husband was a well-digger: I must certainly have heard of him because he was the best well-digger in the whole region and I could not possibly not have heard of Ramadan et-Tugar, who was the son of Hammuda ben Hamed who was the cousin of the husband of Zilukha, the sister of my friend the *Kāymakām*, and she was to stay with Zilukha who would keep her until the treatment was finished; oh yes, she had come to Nàlut to be treated, because she was ill, very ill, and even the baths at Ain Numin had not cured her.

I finally managed to stem the flood of words and to ask her what ailed her. Silent at last, she unwound her outer garment until she was dressed only in her chemise, and extended her arms towards the window so that I could see them in the full light.

They were beautiful arms, round and smoothly joined at the shoulders without any looseness at the arm-pits, whence the firm, pure line of the breast began. But she seemed to be wearing gloves. A most amazing erythema covered the forearms with variegated nodules ranging in colour from violet to scarlet, and in places the skin seemed to have changed to coral.

During the next two to three months I saw Meriem bent Yusuf five times; under the eye of the *Kāymakām's* sister she followed the treatment very scrupulously and kept meticulously to my prescriptions. Her previous experience of medical treatment had been confined to burning with hot irons and verses from the Koran, so that there was no resistance to drugs and the response to the treatment was incredibly rapid; the injections, the salicylates and liniments acted so effectively and in such a short time that at a very much earlier date than I had expected I was able to tell her that she was cured.

Meriem looked at her arms and her joy took away her power of speech – a phenomenon all the more remarkable in such a talkative woman. She passed and repassed her hands over the smooth skin, smiled at her cousin Zilukha and then turned to me. She would have liked to thank me but became confused and stopped in embarrassment.

I asked her to convey my greetings to her brother, to the police sergeant of Dehibat, to the Mudir and the Cadi, to Sidi Drahib the oil merchant, and to my various friends beyond the frontier. Meriem, blinking her eyes and nodding rapidly in assent, promised that she would remember me to everyone, stammered out the farewell formula and ritual benediction and was gone.

The months passed, the seasons changed. With the spring, gusts of hot wind from the desert blew around the rocky promontory from the top of which the castle of Nàlut gazed out from its empty sockets. Spring brought no grass or flowers to this bare mountain, but the air became heavy with a scent as of new-baked bread and the sky was full of swooping swallows preparing for departure.

Issa ben Yusuf, the smuggler, was taking a cup of green, aromatic tea with me in the dispensary. He had come to pay his respects during one of his periodic visits to Nàlut, before joining the caravan for Tunisia. He had talked a great deal about men and events beyond the frontier and now he spoke to me of his own people. His sister was well, her arms quite cured. As he said this, he lowered his eyes to the cup in his hand, shook his head and laughed. He was evasive when I asked him why he laughed and at first became embarrassed and silent. Finally he decided to explain.

His brother-in-law, the digger of wells, was a good fellow but ignorant and I must excuse him; everyone knew that he could find water, that he dug excellent wells and that the wells dug by him never collapsed; but everyone knew also that he was an ignorant fellow, so that when he talked nonsense no one took any notice.

The fact was that this excellent digger of wells was feeling none too pleased, indeed he was furious. Daily he bewailed his wife's cure and cursed the power of medicine. Slowly, evasively, stumbling for words, Issa ben Yusuf explained the reasons for his brother-in-law's displeasure. It appeared that when his wife embraced him the nodules caused by her complaint had given him the most delicious sensations on the nape of his neck. Now he felt them no longer, for her skin was healthy and smooth. He was furious with the *tebīb* for having robbed him of this subtle satisfaction. It had been the main joy of his life.

★   ★   ★

The Berbers were reluctant to come to the dispensary, and in particular they believed that to bring children there was to expose the small patients to the evil eye.

Therefore, when Harshah the weaver sent to tell me that her child was ill, I made my way as soon as the dispensary was closed down the steep steps into the courtyard, and knocked at the door of her troglodytic dwelling.

The cradle was a hammock slung from wall to wall. As I laid the child down again after having examined it, Harshah, who was holding the lamp, searched my face in silence and then quickly bent over the child which had begun to cry. Turning her head slightly in my direction she whispered in a terror-stricken voice, 'This is the third which has died like this . . .' Leaning against the rough wall of the grotto, I tried, in simple words and giving examples to illustrate them, to impart the elements of child nursing to this young Berber woman who habitually drowned her offspring in her milk which was too rich for organs already inflamed by summer enteritis.

Huddled under the niche in which the smoky lamp was burning, my pupil endeavoured, wrinkling her forehead, to follow the sense of what I was saying but her mind was occupied more with her thoughts than with my words. Suddenly she asked me anxiously whether burning the belly of the child with a hot iron could cure it.

I had to begin all over again, without any show of impatience, for that would have frightened her and made it impossible for her to take in what I was saying.

No fires on the belly, no. Little 'Abd el Qadar was like an overburdened camel: when a camel was exhausted after carrying too heavy a load, the camel-herd let it rest and lightened its load when it took the road again. In the same way, 'Abd el Qadar's stomach must be allowed to rest and the load must be lightened. The mother nodded her head to signify that she had grasped the allusion, and smiled when I explained that she must prepare a 'dummy' of gauze dipped in sweetened water so as to relieve the hunger of the child without irritating its disordered intestine. After three days of sweetened water he could take milk again, but the feeds must be very short and repeated every three hours. Harshah opened her eyes and joined her hands in a gesture of supplication as though I were asking her to kill the child. But by this time I had her under my influence and could dictate.

'You must do as I say because I know more than you know. The feed must be very short: if too much water is put into a water-skin does it not burst? The same happens to the stomachs of children who are put to the breast too often and for too long a time.'

'You are not going to give me any medicine?'

That I had to promise – it was unnecessary for the little patient but indispensable to the prestige of the physician.

In the twilight of the evil-smelling lamp the woman gave a great sigh of relief. She had spent so much on amulets which were to have worked miracles and which had done nothing whatever for the child. She had spent so much, and she was so poor. She put out a hand to rock the cradle – her arm was devoid of bracelets, without even a miserable *mugyas* of horn.

'You know, my husband is a government spahi; he earns eight liras a day and must feed his horse. The government is crafty; it has forbidden the issue of barley and only gives oats, so that we cannot even make *bazina* with the horse's ration. It was the only advantage we had.'

Not only was she poor, but she was also virtuous – and therefore no one made her presents of bracelets. Oh yes – if she were like Manubia, the wife of Said el Maraghni, she too could go to the well loaded with silver . . .

'And what does Maraghni say?'

'Everyone knows that he is blind when it suits him to be so.'

At the thought of all that silver displayed with such impudence, Harshah's tongue began to run away with her: the rancour of the girl who is poor but young and with beauty to offer against the middle-aged woman, overblown but rich in experience and able to play her cards skilfully, got the better of Harshah's discretion.

Yes – Manubia had a lover. A lover without land or livestock.

And the lover was Shoushan. Of course I must know Shoushan. He was called Shoushan because his mother was from the Fezzan – a dirty negress from the Fezzan. But his real name was Daud, and when he was not out in the pastures or with the caravan he always came to the dispensary to have his eyes treated. I knew him well. Could that ragged scarecrow of a Shoushan really be making presents of silver bracelets? Harshah laughed at my wide-eyed surprise. Why, yes, indeed, he could.

Harshah came close to me and whispered a story which, if there was any truth in it, had serious implications. It was a muddled story of places far and near, on both sides of the frontier; a story of mysterious and unexpected meetings with Shoushan when he was supposed to be with a caravan elsewhere; of a camel he guided which, with nothing on its back, was nevertheless extraordinarily heavy.

'Harshah, are you sure of this?'

The woman insisted vehemently, somewhat impatient at my reluctance to believe what everyone knew. On the head of little 'Abd el Qadar, of course it was true. Shoushan, who only pretended to be a fool, was really the boss of the whole traffic. When everyone believed him to be on the Sinawen route or in the Saniet er-Rejel pastures, Shoushan and his associates were at the frontier selling arms and ammunition to the rebels who had taken refuge in Tunisia. From there, by a roundabout route through the 'western territory', the arms and ammunition crossed the frontier again and reached the Zintan, Rojeban and Imanghassàten rebels.

'If you do not believe me, in the name of God stop Shoushan when he leaves for Tgutta and see what he has inside his pack-saddle.'

The lamp in the niche flickered. 'Abd el Qadar was asleep in his cradle. Outside the grotto, in the quiet of the summer night, the entrance to the subterranean dwellings seemed like spent craters of the moon. The dogs barked huskily on the ramparts above.

A month later, Daud ben Messaud, alias Shoushan, was stopped by the *zaptivé* and packets of ammunition poured from his pack-saddle as they tore it open. He certainly had no idea that his misfortune bore any relation to the lack of bracelets on a woman's arm, or to the fact that a child had found it impossible to digest its mother's milk.

★ ★ ★

I was obliged to keep in touch with a great number of people who had no plausible reason for coming to Nàlut and whose presence there would have been immediately remarked – people who wandered along the frontier and often crossed it to reappear in the most unlikely places.

To gather information from these wanderers I often made long journeys to meet 'patients' who generally awaited me at some well along the frontier or under a group of palm trees on an unfrequented route. On one of these trips I stopped at the Aulad Sellam wells where the Mohâjerin, a small tribe of Arabs, had pitched five tents.

Formerly, the whole tribe had taken refuge in Tripolitania to escape French justice, for a price had been put on the heads of the most troublesome among them. They were rebels by instinct and brigands by vocation, and they wandered from one territory to another carrying their curse in their name: 'Mohâjerin', the outlaws.

They were in perennial revolt against all constituted authority, but they also quarrelled among themselves, so that their tents never formed a single camp but were scattered right along the frontier from the mountains to the sea. In me they saw only a physician – albeit a physician with somewhat peculiar ways – but since the time when I had cured the mother of the Sheik Abd en-Nebi I had been treated with a respect they did not accord to everyone.

The chief's mother was a decrepit old lady who had by some miracle managed to keep very young eyes in a face as creased and wrinkled as a baked apple. She was a valuable ally because she knew all the people and territories between Sfax and Nàlut, and the men of her tribe obeyed her without a murmur. In addition, she had begun to take an interest in the game I was playing because the missions I entrusted to her served to break the unbearable monotony of her life in a territory where the police nipped every illicit enterprise in the bud.

There had been a time, she told me, when life in Tunisia was very different: something happened every day. With a rapt expression she described the nocturnal excursions of the men, when the women of the camp spent the night in a fever of waiting; the precipitous flights amid the crying of children and the groans of pregnant women as they bumped about on the backs of camels; the exhausting marches from one pasturage to another; the fights with other goatherds and camelherds, jealous for their own animals; the innumerable halts at the wells belonging to sedentary tribes, and the struggle to obtain water; the days of stark poverty alternating with periods of plenty when raided livestock poured into the camp. Ah, those were the days worth living!

She spoke in a quiet voice, without gestures, but her eyes lit up and a reminiscent smile played over her mouth as she recalled the stormy and violent days of her youth.

So I was welcomed at the Aulad Sellam wells and given dinner there by the Mohâjerin. I ate with three tribesmen who informed me that they were to all intents and purposes corpses, having been condemned to death in the neighbouring Regency for armed revolt. They roared with laughter and teased the youngest of them, who was about to be married. What was a young woman to do with a corpse in her bed? they asked him. She could hardly be blamed if she turned her attention elsewhere, to something more virile.

But my stay with the Mohâjerin had to be short because any prolonged absence from Nàlut on my part without a clearly defined reason might give rise to suspicion. Moreover, I had to see Madhun the next day.

Madhun was a young Berber without any fixed abode who travelled by night, slept on the ground, and washed when he happened to think of it. Nevertheless, he was quite a dandy, and his name meant 'the pomaded one'. He was also my best informer from over the border.

I had arranged to meet him at sundown by the crossroads at Bir el Mitt, and next day I set out to keep the appointment. He was there punctually, accompanied by Aissa ben Ramadan, a jack of all trades, and by Ibrahim, a lad with a stupid, freckled face whom I had never seen before.

The rain poured down and made us shiver under our coats as we huddled around a smoky fire of twigs. The light of the sun had disappeared from the sky; the horizon had vanished behind a veil of rain, and a heavy, leaden bank of cloud stretched from west to east. Close by stood the horses, heads down, their manes sparkling with raindrops, their eyes following the movements of a bird as it drank from a puddle; in the distance a tethered camel was just visible through the rain, raising and lowering its neck behind the misty bushes.

The reluctant flames flared up occasionally among the damp brushwood, illuminating the Saracen features of Madhun wrapped in his dark *uàsra*. Aissa had put the tea kettle on the fire and, with a row of glasses turned upside down in front of him, waited patiently till the water began to boil.

Madhun screened the glasses from the rain as the tea was poured into them. The tinkle of the preparations wakened a greyhound which had been sleeping under Madhun's cloak, and the sharp nose of the bitch protruded from beneath his arm. The light of the fire was reflected in the golden irises of its eyes and shone in pupils that were no more than black, scintillating pinpoints.

The tea was deplorable: the well water was brackish and the sugar failed to disguise its unpleasant flavour. Aissa told us that the well had a bad reputation and that a long time ago a man was drowned in it: last year a camelherd, on drawing up his leather bucket, had found a human arm tangled in the cord.

The serious talk was finished and the boy Ibrahim, who had stood apart, now came and squeezed his small person between the two men, huddled up in his *bāik* with only his face, hands, and the points of his sandals visible. Madhun asked him a question about himself, and without waiting for further encouragement the boy began to tell his story. He spoke softly, and every so often paused in order to throw a twig on the fire or blow on the ashes.

Ibrahim, it seemed, was an orphan without any brothers. Madhun had nicknamed him 'Sheik ed-diâb', the chief of the jackals. Every evening when he was not with a caravan he set traps under the sand in the river beds and along ways which only he knew, working carefully and employing the techniques which long experience had taught him. These traps closed with a snap as soon as a paw or foot touched them. In the morning he inspected his traps and collected the foxes and jackals which had been caught. He sold the animals' pelts in the market, and his wife cooked the carcasses, which formed his staple diet.

This child had a wife?

The boy laughed, exposing an uneven set of teeth. He was not a child, he said, being probably over twenty, and his uncle, the Mudir of Jossh Kebir, had given him a wife two years ago.

And he ate jackals?

Ibrahim was surprised at my surprise: jackals, he said, were very toothsome, and foxes even more so. They must be cooked twice – once to remove the overstrong flavour of wild game from the flesh, the second time in order to impregnate it with the herbs and spices.

He explained to me that foxes and jackals are possessed by evil spirits, so that he had no compunction about killing them, whereas not for anything in the world would he have raised his hand against a gazelle or a dove, which were sacred, *mràbet*. He spoke very seriously, convinced of these things, and there was an awestruck expression on the small face framed in the *hāik*. His knees were drawn up under his chin and as he talked his hands moved in brief and fluent gestures.

In a low voice, as though confiding a secret, he told us the extraordinary tale of a jackal that lived between Tiji and Zigzau and which three times had escaped from his traps; on the last occasion it had got away only by leaving a paw behind. Fifteen days after this miraculous escape Ibrahim met the jackal as he was returning alone from Sinawen after delivering barley there

by caravan. It was a moonlight night and the jackal had recognised him, he said; it had followed him, running along the crest
of the dunes; sometimes it went ahead and waited for him and
then, as he passed, it had raised its mutilated paw and cried out
in its language of howls and shrieks. No one understood this
language, of course, but the jackal was certainly calling down
curses upon him. Ibrahim, terrified, perched on his camel, had
called upon the sacred marabouts for help and had beaten his
animal to make it run. But there had been no need to beat the
camel: it had clearly understood the jackal's threats and curses
and, no less terrified than its master, had careered along at a
tremendous pace until the cries of the jackal died away in the
distance.

Madhun and Aissa, who had smiled at the beginning of
Ibrahim's story, became uneasy now; their mocking words died
on their lips; their eyes flickered stealthily as they looked about
them.

Could it be that the soul of a man, perhaps some long-dead
outlaw, inhabited the body of this jackal? It could be; it was
possible; such things were known.

The rain continued. Within the radius of the light from the
fire the drops scintillated and hung like pearls on our clothes
which steamed in the warmth of the flames.

But it was time to go. The men began to move about among
the horses; the gnome-like Ibrahim mounted his camel and disappeared silently into the darkness. Madhun brought me my
horse and in a moment we were all in our saddles. As we moved
off, Aissa trotted before me, his silhouette from his hood to his
saddle-bags forming a dark triangle against the starless night sky.

Behind us, the dying fire succumbed to the rain.

★　★　★

I think very few people in Nàlut ever knew the real name of the
Cādī. When they addressed him they used his title, and when
speaking of him they called him 'Sleeping Belly'. I never knew
the exact origin of this nickname, but I took it to indicate that
type of vacillating man who is always unsure of himself, unable

to take a decision, and for whom the Sicilians have a name: *panza 'i canigghia*, ('bran belly').

It was said that during the rebellion, when Chalifa ben Asker was ruler of Nàlut, he kept the *Cādī* beside him in order to enjoy his abject terror, and that for some time after the arrival of the Italians the unfortunate man refused to emerge from the well in which he had taken refuge, unwilling to believe those who told him that the rebels had fled.

Although he was not greatly loved, he was esteemed for his knowledge and honesty. He was, in fact, an authority on Mohammedan canonical law and was able to argue the most subtle legal points, embellishing his disquisitions with excerpts from the most famous commentators and authorities with which his tenacious memory was stored.

He often came to see me and was always accompanied by his faithful scrivener, Sassi. Sassi was a little man, with a hooked nose which curved over a fierce Corsair moustache, and he had a great respect for his master's knowledge in his own particular field. So long as the *Cādī* talked on those matters Sassi stood behind him, immobile, with his eyes downcast and an air of humility. But as soon as the other launched into long, illogical discourses on all kinds of other subjects his attitude immediately changed: he smiled into his moustache, winked at me and sometimes even tapped his forehead with his finger to indicate that his master was not quite all there.

The fact was that the *Cādī* was one of those men who are cultured without being intelligent; who are extremely erudite in the field in which they have specialised but who, as soon as they are confronted with subjects they have not studied thoroughly and methodically, collapse under their own innate stupidity.

I realised then why the *Kāymakām* – who was ignorant, but intelligent – lost patience when he was discussing any matter with the *Cādī*.

One evening, after having given me in detail the case history of a family of the Ulad Mahmud and explained why all the people concerned were guilty (the woman and the lover because they were adulterers, the husband because he connived, the mother-in-law because she had accepted money from the daughter-in-law's lover, the husband's uncle because, being in love with his niece, he had attempted to eliminate the lover – only by a fluke was the mule, on which the lover had made his escape, exonerated), the *Cādī* turned to Sassi and told him to leave the room.

As soon as we were alone, he drew his chair close to mine and asked me if I knew that in France they sold women at fixed prices?

I was not sure what he was getting at and suspected that someone had been pulling his leg, so I asked him to explain. With great seriousness he assured me that in Paris there were shops in which attractive young women could be bought, and that people living outside France could send the money and the shop undertook to despatch to them the goods selected.

As the *Cādī's* Italian was somewhat halting he interspersed Arabic phrases and words when he found himself at a loss for the exact expression. He now insisted that the women were chosen from *teswîra*, that is, photographs. I asked him where he had seen the photographs and he replied that there were dozens of them of magnificent creatures; that each had a name and that these lovely girls were to be had for the price of a loaf. Purple with excitement, he fixed his piggish, shining eyes on my face.

I asked him who had given him this information. He replied that he had the advertisement and the photographs, but that Gabriele would give me details.

Gabriele was a young clerk, intelligent, who spoke perfect Arabic and French. He had a quiet, reserved appearance and those who did not know him did not suspect that under this harmless exterior he hid an excessive vivacity.

In the meantime, the *Cādī* had brought out the advertisement and photographs from under his *ḥāik*. It was a three-years-old dress catalogue from the Galeries Lafayette which had somehow arrived in Nàlut. The dresses were worn by models and under each was a name – Simone, Arlette, Yvonne – and the price.

This had obviously been Gabriele's little joke; and patiently I began to explain to the *Cādī* the facts about western commerce. But the old satyr was bitterly disappointed. He had expected more of Paris . . .

★ ★ ★

Sassi, the *Cādī's* scrivener, did not always act in that capacity: he fulfilled also the humbler functions of beadle and doorkeeper, and sometimes I borrowed him to keep order for me when there was a crowd at the dispensary.

He had a large family which he supported partly with his earnings and partly with the produce from a small field of palm trees which he let out every year for the extraction of the *legbi*, the palm wine. He was always serene and smiling, so that I hardly recognised him on the evening when he asked me to go to his grotto to see his son who was sick. In answer to my questions he merely shook his head and sighed as though he would like to say more but could not; his face was ashen and drawn, and casting up his eyes to heaven he gesticulated as though unable to express the anguish that was bursting his heart. His son was ill, very ill. He was the only son God had given him – because the others whom I knew were not his sons.

When Chalifa ben Asker, the rebel, took Nàlut, Sassi was one of the tyrant's first victims. Even now Sassi seemed unable to give any explanation as to why he had been singled out for such persistent persecution. Perhaps it was an instinctive dislike, perhaps, he said, he had failed to offer dates, perhaps he had been slandered by someone seeking to ingratiate himself with the new chief. But perhaps also there was a reason which Sassi did not wish to discuss.

In any case, Chalifa wasted no time: first of all he killed Sassi's sheep and goats, then he sequestered his camel, and finally he threw him into prison.

In prison Sassi had an opportunity of trying out the diet which Dr Guelpa recommended for diabetes – consisting of fasting and Janus water – with the difference that Sassi had to substitute basins of brackish ooze for the beverage so widely prescribed

by the French clinician. Every two days he was given a piece
of bread, but every three days, to even things up, he was given
fifty strokes of the whip.

As Sassi was not diabetic and as beating is not, in any case,
included in any pharmacopœia, after two weeks of this regime
he was in a pitiable condition.

One day when he had been beaten with more than usual
enthusiasm, Sassi, on the floor of his cell, prayed that God would
take his life and thus put an end to his sufferings. All at once
the hand of a woman appeared between the iron bars, and
immediately disappeared again. An instant only, but time to
throw him a handful of dates. Then the hand reappeared and
threw him three fritters still hot and dripping with oil.

Every day this woman brought him some fruit, bread or a
sweet, and Sassi in his cell waited for the hand as one waits for
the moon of Ramadān.

The woman was Chalifa's wife.

Had Sassi known her before? Sassi lifted his eyes to heaven and
swore that he had not known her before. Sassi was a gentleman.

When the Italians arrived, Chalifa was hanged. Sassi married
the widow of his persecutor and became the father of his sons.

But he had desired from his wife sons who should call him
father 'not only with their lips but with their blood'. Sons came,
but God had taken them all back except one, and now this one
was very ill.

Sassi shook his head and silent tears coursed down through
the wrinkles of his drawn and withered face. He lowered his
voice and told me that the other night near his grotto the cry
of the nightbird that kills children had been heard. Seeing my
incredulity he became eloquent and assured me that there was
indeed a bird that killed children; that everyone knew of its
existence and that the mothers of Jebel Nefusah went in terror
of it.

The story is one of a married man who tired of his wife. She
had lost her beauty and, after giving him a son, her health too;
nor had she passed her health on to the son, who was wasting
away beside his faded mother.

Being tired of his wife with the pale and sunken cheeks, the man took a second wife who entered the sad, silent house and filled it with boisterous gaiety. She laughed at the prematurely aged woman who had seen the sun set on her husband's love, and who now trembled for the life of her son which flickered like a flame in a lamp without oil. When, after a painless pregnancy, the second wife gave birth to a son, she announced with a triumphant laugh that the master had been born, and extending her right hand with the five fingers outspread, she cursed the first wife's son.

The child died the following night.

Then the mother too prayed for death. But she could not die as believers die: she knew that she did not merit hell but she knew also that no paradise could purge her hatred, so she called to her aid the demons, the sprites, the jinns and the spirits of evil; by the use of their spells she was transformed into a bird and her desire for revenge taught her to fly.

She flew away – and she still flies, even today, over houses where mothers fear for the lives of their children or exult over the beauty of their sons as they rock their cradles. Since even Allah cannot restore to her her lost son, this unhappy mother, to whom sorrow has given wings, desires that all mothers shall know her anguish and become crazed with the same pain that tore her heart.

Her cry in the night is an omen of disaster, and when the irreparable has happened she laughs at the tears that are shed.

Sassi had heard the cry of the nightbird, flying above his home. Now he sat silent, waiting for the inevitable and wondering why Allah, who is gracious and merciful, permits such things to happen.

★ ★ ★

Every two or three months I passed a few days in the Ghadames oasis, the important junction south of Nàlut on which converge all the caravans from the coast, from the Fezzan, from Tunisia and Algeria. I have covered the two hundred miles between Nàlut and Ghadames by 'plane, car, motor-lorry and caravan –

and although it may not be the most comfortable, there is
certainly no finer way of travelling over the sunbaked tracks
than on the back of a slowly moving camel. No one who, after
many days in caravan, has at last emerged on to the brow of the
el Bab plateau and gazed from the back of a camel over the oasis
of Ghadames spread out in the light of the setting sun, can ever
forget that moment.

Ghadames is a strange country.

There is a saying that it was once a prostitute, and in the local
dialect it is, in fact, called *Bembaka*, which means just that. Like
all prostitutes, in order to live it needed protectors. The Tuaregs
– 'the veiled family' (the veil covering the men's faces while
those of the women go shamelessly naked) – set themselves up
in this role.

They escort caravans going to Ghat, to the Fezzan and to the
Sudan, and accompany those coming from the country of the
blacks across the Sahara. It is they who control the 'traffic routes'
and guarantee the safety of the trade on which Ghadames lives.
In fact, Ghadames is so grateful for this protection that if a
Tuareg assaults a Ghadamese, or steals a camel, or rapes a woman
of the oasis, it makes no protest but smiles at its protectors – who
may be light-fingered but who are always indispensable.

Yes, Ghadames is a strange country, and I learnt many things
in the shade of its palm trees.

The Ghadamese speak Arabic with the Arabs, Tamahàk with
the Tuaregs and Haussa with their servants, but among themselves they use a Berber dialect which no one speaks outside the
walls of the city. The population is housed on three levels: the
servants on the street level, the free men on the upper floors and
the women on the terraces above, from which they descend only
on very rare occasions after sunset in order to go to the mosque.

Enclosed within their oasis and isolated in the vast desert, the
Ghadamese nevertheless maintain contacts all over the world;
they combine the flabbiness of sedentary people with the broad
vision of the nomads. The Ghadamese tradesman, huddled in
his little hovel stuffed full of goods, will talk with the greatest
simplicity of his stays in Paris and London, or of the letter he

has just received from his representative in Marseilles or New York.

Ghadames is indeed a strange country.

Hajj et-Talatin was the most important and authoritative merchant of Ghadames. He was a man no longer young, but robust and extraordinarily active, although he gave quite the contrary impression. He seemed lazy because he never hurried, and he watched the world through great, slow, bovine eyes: when he was listening, he lowered his tinted lids so that his glance filtered through a mere slit. In Ghadames it was said that Hajj et-Talatin could see even when he was asleep – and that the man was not yet born who could get the better of the old fox.

I had treated him, and continued to treat him, for a number of ailments great and small, due to his age, his sedentary life, excessive coffee-drinking and smoking, and previous infections. When I arrived in Ghadames it was always difficult to refuse his hospitality and maintain my freedom of movement.

On one occasion (after we had known each other for about a year) he told me that one of his wives was ill and asked me to visit her.

He accompanied me up to the terrace of his house. His short, square figure preceded me along dark corridors punctuated by streaks of white light from the narrow high-walled courtyards, across ramparts outlined against the fiery glow of the sunset, and up narrow stairways cut into the walls or passing externally from one floor to the next. Finally, passing through a large, whitewashed room, we came out on the highest terrace of all.

I was invited to sit down on a pile of carpets the top one of which was a rough Bedouin hammâl. Lifting a corner, I observed underneath it the bright colours of a Kayruan rug; underneath that I found the long, soft hair of a Moroccan carpet, and underneath again my hand encountered the silk texture of a Shiraz. Last of all, I discovered a wonderful peach-coloured Bokhara decorated with roses worthy to be strewn before the feet of a sultana.

The delicate sensibility of these people delights to place beautiful things before guests and then to leave them the joy of discovering them for themselves. From the terrace there was a view of houses, terraces and covered ways, of the surrounding oasis and beyond the sea of palm trees the desert glowed in a golden haze that veiled the horizon. From the distance the murmur of prayer floated up to us, the lament of a beggar, the voices of the servants round the Jumenta fountain.

A cushion was placed for me. On my right was a dried-up old woman whose face I could not see because, in order to hide her embarrassment, she remained bent over the teacups or busied herself with the tea kettle and stove. In front of me sat two young women with their heads and faces covered.

Hajj et-Talatin threw away the stump of his cigar and took leave of me without deigning even to glance in the direction of the women. Perhaps he wished to devote himself to evening prayer or perhaps, leaving me alone with his women in this way, he wished to make me understand that he considered me as a brother.

The departure of the master of the house, however, made the silence even more embarrassing and when I pronounced the words of greeting I received only an indistinct murmur in reply. For a split second, over their veils, the women scrutinised this phenomenon they would never have believed possible: a Christian on their terrace!

Which of the two women was the patient?

When I put the question to the old woman she replied without raising her head that the patient was not there but that she would come. The younger women seemed to exchange a significant look. Finally, one made an effort and informed me that, God be thanked, she was well and she wished me prosperity. As she spoke she uncovered the upper part of her face and I saw with astonishment that her eyes were green.

These two women were Hajj et-Talatin's first two wives; the sick one was the third. They were pale-complexioned women, whiter than many Europeans. The wife with the green eyes had beautiful hands, plump in comparison with the hands of Arab women. When I called her 'Signora foreigner' she exclaimed and clapped her hands with surprise. How had I guessed? She was indeed a foreigner, she said; she was born in Morocco on the Rif mountains. Removing her head covering she showed me that she had red hair.

The other was a Ghadamese and dressed like one. She was laden with bracelets, armlets, necklaces and ear-rings that jingled as she moved; her hair hung in two coiled plaits at each side of her head, and on her forehead she wore a *mrabba*, a large tassel of red wool. She stretched herself from the waist with a feline movement, and looked at me out of the corners of her eyes; in execrable Arabic she informed me that she was ill, so ill that no medicine could cure her. She turned her head over her shoulder and in the local dialect said something to her companion which made the Berber woman blush. It was evidently something extremely improper, for the old woman swiftly reproved her in the same dialect and the young wife covered her mouth with her fingers pretending to be confused. But she smiled at me with her eyes.

In order to relieve her embarrassment I asked her how many children she had. This simple question had a most disconcerting effect: the two whispered together and giggled, digging each other in the ribs. The old woman threw me a glance which was meant as an apology and in a vibrating voice let loose on the two women a torrent of words of which I was unable to understand a syllable. There was, however, no doubt about her authority, for the other two subsided at once and cast sulky looks in her direction.

The old woman offered me a glass of tea and sought to distract my attention by asking me how long I had been in Ghadames; if the air suited me; if the water made me ill; if the climate was as I liked it. She served me with one glass of tea after another, varying the ingredients and aroma.

Presently, at a sign from the duenna, the two young women withdrew. There was still no sign of the third wife and it seemed she had made it clear she would not come.

When we were alone the old woman became more natural and talkative. The sick wife, she told me, was Sitta Mamuna, the youngest of Hajj et-Talatin's three wives; he had married her eight months ago; she was a Tuareg woman, of the Ifoghas tribe. She was very ill because some months ago she had fallen a victim to the 'spirit that sits on the shoulder'. The matron lowered her voice and spoke in a serious and worried tone. Did I know *elli 'ala ktefha*, the spirit that sits on the shoulder?

Yes, I knew him – the turbid spirit of the women's quarters, the unhappy symbol of all the aberrations of cloistered women. This perverse demon rides women in their first blooming – in fact, the Berbers say that he 'takes only beautiful young girls', and if an older woman complains of his torments, the young women turn their heads away and laugh.

The manifestations of the spirit's malice are infinite: the woman who has him on her shoulder may fall into convulsions, suffer from the most peculiar sensory hallucinations, laugh or cry without cause, endure periods of madness during which she will remove her clothes and soil herself, or else imagine she is an omnipotent empress. She may even speak languages she does not know, or be taken with prophetic delirium.

The duenna (who was a poor relation of Hajj et-Talatin, a distant aunt) informed me that Sitta Mamuna had had every kind of cure, but all had failed: even a composer of amulets had obtained no result from his magical formulæ; neither had any of her own remedies availed her. Perhaps in order to distract me from the subject which was worrying her, she went on to inform me that she knew how to cure many maladies and that she was famous throughout the country for her remedies.

I made a show of being impressed by so much wisdom, and with a fleeting smile (did she believe it, I wondered, or was she laughing up her sleeve?) she told me the story of how the older women had learned witchcraft and acquired the power of curing diseases.

In ancient times the matrons had decided to catch the devil and get rid of him.

'How can we get him here among us?' they asked.

The devil always appears in the midst of fights, so the women began to shout insults at each other and to take one another by the hair. The devil appeared and immediately the imprecations turned to groans and lamentations.

'Why do you weep?' asked the devil.

'We weep,' they replied, 'because the devil is dead.'

'Rubbish! I am the devil.'

'But we tell you he is dead. What do we know about you?'

'But I say I am the devil. I ought to know. How shall I prove it to you?'

'We don't believe you. If you are the devil, prove it by getting inside this oil cask.'

The devil entered the cask and the women popped in the wooden bung and sealed it with palm tow and wax.

'Let me out,' shouted the devil, struggling inside the cask.

'Ha, ha! – we shall never let you out again,' replied the women.

'Bitches!... Camels!... Harlots!'

'You blasted oak!... You one-haired monster!'

'My daughters, let me out and I will do you good.'

'How can you do us good, father of Evil?'

'I will teach you witchcraft; I will give you the secret which will make the spirits that cause disease obey you.'

The women agreed and the devil kept his promise.

However – in the case of Sitta Mamuna the devil's tricks had had no effect. The unfortunate girl had inhaled all kinds of aromatic herbs, swallowed all manner of nauseating concoctions, covered herself with every conceivable magic pomade, slept under a mountain of amulets. The one who 'sits on the shoulder' had remained firmly in the saddle.

Sitta Mamuna never came up to the terrace; she lived shut up in herself, often falling into convulsions which left her prostrate and exhausted. For days at a time she might seem to be normal, but even then she remained in her room, laughed immoderately, wept without cause, and was full of feverish vivacity.

Should we go and see her?

The room was dark. Amid hisses and explosions there was the sound of someone pumping a pressure lamp, which with a sudden bang produced a blinding light. The only piece of furniture in the room was a coffer heavily ornamented in brass.

At my feet a completely naked girl was stretched out on a mat. On seeing me she sat up, crossed her legs and made me a sign to sit down opposite her, for all the world as though she were closely covered and veiled, as every God-fearing Mohammedan woman should be.

Behind me were the old aunt and a servant. The lamp had been placed on the floor between me and Sitta Mamuna so that grotesque shadows danced on the walls and ceiling. The girl was very young, but not beautiful. She had high cheekbones and a wide forehead; her thick, pouting lips were those of a spoilt child; her breasts were high and firm and her skin of a whiteness that seemed artificial in the phosphorescent light of the petrol lamp. She took my hand and laid it against her cheek, and as she dragged herself along on the mat towards me I was assailed with the scent they call *dongria*, a kind of incense to which is attributed therapeutic powers. The aunt made an effort to pull her away from me, angry at such shamelessness, but the girl turned on her and bit her arm. The room was filled with the cries of the old woman and the shrieks of the servant, and Sitta Mamuna took refuge in a corner where she immediately had a fit of classical hysterical convulsions. Rolling and twisting herself jerkily, she suddenly fastened head and heels to the ground and arched her body into a bridge. She remained in this acrobatic position for a few moments, her eyes closed, the abdomen rising and falling to her heavy, hurried breathing. Then she relaxed and her breathing became more regular. She opened her eyes and gave me a tired smile.

When I had completed my examination she bent towards me and, as though continuing an interrupted conversation, asked me if I knew that Aishah was a bitch. I explained that I did not know Aishah and that, therefore, I could not say to which zoological family she belonged. The girl replied that Aishah was a prostitute, a *bembaka*, like all Ghadamese women. She was speaking, it seemed, of Hajj et-Talatin's first wife. It appeared that the Ghadamese woman hated Sitta Mamuna, who was a Tuareg of noble race and could therefore have nothing in common with a vulgar *bembaka* like Aishah.

In order to change the conversation, I asked news of Hajj et-Talatin, as though I had not seen him for some time. At the mention of his name she became suddenly uncontrollably hilarious. With her hands she described his pot-bellied outline and laughed uproariously. Did I know the great fat thing? Was he a friend of mine?

The aunt endeavoured to restrain this outburst, so unbecoming in a young wife. But the bite was very recent and when Sitta Mamuna jumped to her feet she backed away, shielding herself with the body of the servant.

The girl now began to parade up and down the room, swaying her hips, striking suggestive attitudes and gesticulating in an affected manner. She was obviously imitating someone, and the pantomime was evidently meant to be offensive for the old woman covered her face with her hands and the servant turned to the wall in order not to see.

We again sat down on the mat. The girl took my arm under hers and leaned her head on my shoulder. She was in confidential mood. Did I know that she was a Tuareg princess? I replied that she was not alone, since the Moroccan wife of Hajj et-Talatin was a Berber princess.

She looked into my face and gripped my arm. Did I know Zayida the Berber too? But I must not say she was a princess because she was not, even though her skin was softer than silk. She caressed her lip with the tips of her fingers, closed her eyes and bent her head back in ecstasy.

I stood up, but the patient threw her arms round my knees. Would I not stay with her?

I promised to return later in the night when her husband would be sleeping, and the wives too.

'They do not sleep,' she said as she bade me farewell, 'they are bitches.'

With a sigh of relief the aunt opened the door of the room and piloted me back across the labyrinth of corridors, ramparts, antechambers, stairs and steps, down again into the courtyard which was now in darkness.

The darkness, in fact, permitted a frankness which would have been impossible if we had been able to see each other.

'You will give me a cure, *tebīb?*'

Certainly. I had very effective remedies for women tormented by the 'spirit that sits on the shoulder' – but I must know all the facts.

The old woman was not without imagination. Yes, perhaps Mamuna had wept when they brought her to the house of her husband, or perhaps she had lost a sandal during the marriage ceremony; or perhaps the evil spirit had jumped on her shoulder at the moment when her husband removed her veil.

I agreed that, of course, all kinds of incidents of that nature might cause no end of trouble – but that the physician must know all. How many times a week did Hajj et-Talatin visit Sitta Mamuna?

The breathing of the lady aunt became more audible in the darkness. I must know that Hajj et-Talatin was the most important merchant in Ghadames and his trade with all the countries of the world kept him busy night and day.

I admitted that Hajj et-Talatin was certainly a man of many activities.

The old woman grasped at my words and talked rapidly and at length of Hajj et-Talatin's many occupations, insisting on the respect he enjoyed.

But this highly respected merchant was also a virile and full-blooded man – and yet he did not approach his women? Was that not strange, *signora?*

Her breath was now coming rapidly and she mumbled confused phrases. I caught a garbled citation from the Koran about it being a sin to suspect one's fellows, and to the effect that every man was free to do as he thought best so long as he did not offend against the law, and even the law admitted that every caravan might have its 'wife'.

This hint was sufficient for me. The *signora* was quite right, I said: Ghadames was full of caravan 'wives'. When Sitta

Mamuna was parading up and down the room was she not perhaps imitating a caravan 'wife', a *zâmel?* These young men did, in fact, sway their hips and gesticulate in the same affected manner. Hajj et-Talatin then, having three pretty, fresh young wives, preferred the company of a *zâmel?* And yet with these strange tastes he had married three wives? O Allah, Lord of the universe, what playthings you make of the sons of Adam!

And the wives? Why did Aishah detest Mamuna? Were they jealous? Jealous of whom?

The old aunt hinted that I wished to know too much: only God was all-wise, she said.

Was it not true that after her marriage Sitta Mamuna waited on the terrace with the other wives for the attentions of an evasive husband? While they waited had there not sprung up between Sitta Mamuna and Zayida, the Berber with the skin softer than silk, one of those morbid attachments which are engendered among women deprived of men? But Zayida was already Aishah's property, was she not? And so the spirit that sits on the shoulder had leapt upon the young wife. Was this not the cause, *signora?*

I lit a match in order to look into her face. The old lady shook her head in protest: she had no desire to stir up such muddy pools. In any case, what purpose did it serve? God knew all. She became almost angry. If I was a physician I should be able to prescribe the right medicine. Had I the medicine, or had I not? The other matters were beside the point.

It was only a brief moment of irritation, however, and when at the door of the house I whispered in her ear the name of the medicine which would cure Sitta Mamuna, she turned and placed her head on her arm against the doorpost so that I should not see her smile.

Chapter Four

THE VEILED PEOPLE

ALTHOUGH the Tuareg people are the traditional protectors of Ghadames their proper territory is the vast desert region lying to the south. Here, in south-west Tripolitania, live the tribes belonging to the great Azdjer family, whose sovereign in those days was Bubaker ag Legoui. He had his residence in the Ghat oasis and in 1929 I took the opportunity while I was at Ghadames of paying him a visit.

The Tuaregs suffer from a complex which the psycho-analysts call hypertrophy of the ego: they are sincerely convinced that they are superior to all other races. They are 'the veiled family' and, according to them, the noblest line on earth, their warriors the bravest under heaven, and their women alone able to 'illuminate the night with a smile'.

Throughout North Africa, from the Sahara to the Niger, there are less than 200,000 of them and of these I have treated not more than thirty, but my limited experience has convinced me that when the veiled family disappears from the earth, decimated by disease or absorbed by other populations, it will be the end of a fascinating people whose singular characteristics place them in a unique category of mankind.

They are divided into noble and vassal tribes – the *ihaggaren* and the *imghad*. The vassals are richer than their masters because they own livestock, work the land, supply the caravans with camels and run the economy of the territory. The feudal lords, on the other hand, live a life of ease. When the opportunity occurs they carry out a raid, but mainly they live on their subjects and spend their time composing songs in honour of the beautiful women of their clan. From their appearance, these nobles might be beggars: they are dressed in cotton rags, their feet thrust into worn-out sandals. In spite of this, however, they

124

A Berber family at the Nàlut food cells

Massawa

are as ceremonious and pompous as a sultan on his throne and as proud as a Spanish *hidalgo*. When a dirty, louse-infested *ihaggaren*, with his face veiled and his hand on his sword-hilt, asks a passing stranger for an object to which he has taken a fancy, and insists like an importunate beggar, disregarding refusal or rebuff, he manages to maintain such a superb air of superiority that one begins to understand why the *imghad* are almost grateful to their noble lords for allowing them the honour of supporting them.

These aristocrats are wonderful fighters, and the history of the Tuareg people abounds with episodes of heroism, of chivalry and of generous folly worthy of Charlemagne's court or of King Arthur's Knights of the Round Table.

The warrior of the Azdjer Tuaregs who, on a hill and surrounded by enemies, ordered his servants to retreat to safety and remained fighting alone until he was riddled with bullets because, as servants, they might be permitted to flee, whereas he, as a patrician, could not turn his back on an adversary, was blood brother to that Roland who, at Roncesvalles, overpowered by the Moors and with the icy hand of death already gripping his heart, refused to retreat by so much as a step.

The infiltration of the European powers into Africa and the consolidation of their rule brought these heroic deeds to an end and the decadence of the patricians then set in. Up to relatively recent times, however, it was still their function to defend the tribe's pasturage, to raid other people's livestock, to sack the camps of their enemies, to extort tribute, to impose tolls, and to protect their vassal tribes from oppression by the nobles of other Tuareg tribes. With the passing of the system whereby armed barons defended the rights of their vassals, the patricians' *raison d'être* also disappeared, leaving only pretensions for which there was no longer any justification. The result has been that the feudal lord, incapable of any other activity, is today a mendicant living on charity.

The patricians, belonging to a class which produces only warriors, are completely ignorant of anything but warfare. Very few of them speak Arabic and hardly any are able to write *tifinar*,

E

the strange Tuareg characters which may be written from right to left or from left to right, from the top down or from the bottom up. Only very rarely does a patrician hold any public office, except that of king of the confederation, or tribal chief.

These deficiencies and limitations are both the cause and the effect of the supremacy of the women in Tuareg society. The Tuareg woman can read and write *tifinar;* she generally speaks Arabic, and quite frequently writes it. She has a passionate love of poetry; she preserves and hands on the family traditions; she plays the *rebaza,* a four-stringed mandolin, and the lute, called the *umzad.*

The matriarchal system of the ancient Berber communities from which the Tuaregs are descended still continues among the 'veiled people'. They say that 'the womb gives its colour to the new-born child' and that, therefore, the child belongs to the caste of the mother and not to that of the father.

As a result of their social predominance the women control not only the tribe's economy but also its property. And, although there may be other countries in which women have the upper hand (either openly or by guile) there certainly is none where they enjoy a greater sexual freedom.

Among these people, the sexual function is woman's chief attribute. The family, the tribe, are built around the woman's femininity, which is understood as being exclusively an instrument for the exercise of love – but not a passive instrument, for the Tuareg woman is not a chattel or an object of conquest: on the contrary, she has the uncontested right to choose her men. It may be extremely mortifying for the male sex, but I am obliged to admit that, in so far as their women are concerned, the function of these proud Tuareg warriors is more or less that of the male bee in the hive.

In a Tuareg community, a woman becomes independent when, on reaching puberty, she is excluded from religious practices. In fact, this period is called *ba-n'amuk,* the suspension of prayer. With the first menstrual blood she is considered impure, and is therefore not permitted to pray, but the occasion is celebrated by the family and clan as her coming-of-age. For the first time she sits as a woman outside her tent. She is dressed in a fine new blouse dyed with a shiny, greasy indigo preparation, and covered with ornaments of metal, silver and ivory, much too heavy for her childish form; her face is plastered with yellow ochre and her eyes disfigured with make-up, and she sits like a freshly varnished doll between her father and mother, surrounded by relatives and friends of the family. It is the ceremony which consecrates her as a woman: from that day she can paint her face, play the lute in public, frequent the 'courts of love' and proclaim herself in a state of *asri*. While she is in the state of *asri*, the Tuareg woman takes as many lovers as she likes. She receives them in her tent, or invites them to the 'court of love' where the girls play the *umzad*, surrounded by warriors who kiss their hands, improvise poems in honour of their beauty and beg forgiveness for a too audacious compliment by lightly brushing the foot of the offended goddess with their lips. When the madrigals have ceased, when the moon is veiled, the couples disappear behind the patches of lentiscus, behind the rocks, into the stony river beds, into the tents.

These dissolute and cavalier customs may be the legacy of a cynical, amoral and decadent civilisation, but other Tuareg traditions and habits form a striking contrast to such subtle refinements.

The Tuareg – man or woman – goes through life without washing. For the ritual ablutions, sand is used. To invite a Tuareg to wash is to invite a curse upon him since he is touched by water only when the washer of the dead takes over his corpse. Their magnificent bodies, therefore, acquire a patina which is a combination of decades of filth and indigo dye from their cotton garments. The dye runs into their skin so that a naked Tuareg looks as if he had been daubed with blue varnish.

The women grease their hair abundantly with rancid butter, and as the hair is never washed the superimposed strata of fetid grease are a happy hunting ground for lice. In addition, they wash their garments with a root which produces a generous lather but gives off an absolutely pestilential odour. Finally, the noble Tuareg woman chews tobacco and is extremely skilful in launching mouthfuls of yellowish saliva over immense distances.

Perhaps it was on account of these strident contrasts, this extraordinary mixture of magnificence and poverty, of pride and grovelling, of beauty and filth, that the Tuaregs were also referred to by the Arabs as 'the mad people'.

★   ★   ★

I had for some time been in correspondence with the great chief of this strange and contradictory people, Rubaker ag Legoui of Ghat, and every so often he sent a message to me by one of his sons – either his legitimate son for whom he seemed to have little fondness, or his bastard son who was the apple of his eye.

In order to reach Ghadames, the small band which accompanied the chief's son, whichever it might be, had to cross country dominated by the rebels, and to avoid trouble they were often obliged to make long detours off the beaten tracks. On one occasion they had to fight their way through for a whole night. They arrived in the morning, exhausted with thirst, with one of their number hunched up on a camel, his belly slit open and his intestines held in by a scarf. After I had sewn him up he recovered quickly and returned some days later to his tribe in the highest of spirits.

But almost any evening one of the sons of Bubaker, tall, lean, and wrapped around like all Tuaregs with three or four long garments, might appear on the terrace of the fort. He would murmur his name and, to prove his identity, come close to me, place his face a hand's breadth from mine, and for an instant raise his veil so that I might recognise him.

He would present me with a letter from his father, and after I had read it he would begin to talk. He would talk for hours, until the stars faded and the sky in the east lightened, becoming tinged successively with pink, gold and blood red. He would tell me all that the letter had omitted, because Bubaker, like a good Tuareg of ancient lineage, entrusted the important news to his son's mouth and made use of writing only to ask for money, watches, yards and yards of cotton material, gramophone records, and once even (a request which somewhat surprised us) a bicycle.

In that year the drought had dried up the pasturage and whole populations had moved northwards with their animals in search of grass. One of the rebel tribes, the Imanghassàten, had also moved, and this worried Bubaker ag Legoui, because they were armed and always ready for a fight.

It was essential that pacts of good neighbourliness be established if the Shaamba and the Ifoghas, local sedentary tribes, jealous of their pasturage areas, were to be prevented from starting trouble with the new arrivals.

Our military authorities had sent into the desert a man whom the official reports described as, 'the well-known Bosu', an informer of mixed breed who succeeded in reconciling and satisfying all who paid him – and they were many. I did not altogether trust the 'well-known Bosu', and so, armed with my medicine chest and instrument bag, I had followed him, accompanied by Califa ben Yunea, a Berber who spoke four languages, in search of patients to treat, wounds to dress – and men and women who would talk.

The Tuareg people I met on that occasion may not be as fascinating as those of Antinea – but mine are real.

Shaoui ag Ibejji, nephew of the chief of the Teghehé n'abbar clan of the Imanghassàten Tuareg, had been bitten on the hip by a camel. I had been treating the wound for twenty days and it had now healed. He was the Beau Brummell of his clan, tall and lean, and he appeared before my tent like the ghost of an ancient warrior.

His head and neck were wrapped in a red and white striped headcloth. His face was covered from the forehead down and from the chin up, the merest slit remaining across the bridge of his nose. Over his breeches *à la Zouave* and his sleeveless undershirt he wore three long blue-black, bell-sleeved garments tightly gathered at the waist into a leather belt from which hung his takuba, a long-hilted sword. A brick-red mantle fell from his shoulders to his feet; from the upturned points of his large, boat-shaped sandals long straps were attached to his belt.

He was magnificent. When he appeared in the opening of the tent which I used as a dispensary he assumed immediately a statuesque attitude: head up, chest out, one foot advanced and all his weight thrown back on the other, one hand on his sword hilt and the other extended in a dignified salute. He was so superb that at first sight one did not notice that his headcloth was in shreds, that the dye in his tunics had run and that they were mended with different coloured cottons, that his mantle was a mosaic of patches and that his sandals were held together with string.

Inside the tent, into which he brought a stench of goats that could be cut with a knife, he took half an hour to undress. Finally, he stood naked except for his headcloth and the black veil over his face – for the Tuareg tradition demands that a man shall at all times and in all circumstances keep his face covered. Even when he eats in the presence of strangers or of women, a Tuareg does not uncover his face; he passes the mouthfuls of food under the lower veil which is raised a little from the bottom: it would be extremely improper to expose the 'hole through which food passes'. Only later did Shaoui raise the frontal veil just far enough to uncover his eyes as a sign of confidence in my powers as a physician and in order to show that he was pleased with the gift he had finally wheedled out of me.

The bandage was crawling with lice again, but the wound was now firmly closed and the mark of the stitches was already fading. When I told him, through Califa the interpreter, that he was cured and that there was no need for him to return to the dispensary, he began to question Califa who became annoyed and, instead of interpreting, took up the argument himself in an indignant tone. The dialogue became heated, and in order to prevent it degenerating into a fight I interrupted and ordered Califa to explain what was happening.

After having used the most injurious epithets he could call to mind regarding the women of the Tuareg's family, Califa informed me that Shaoui was asking for a handsome present as a reward for having recovered so quickly and so well.

From the day the camel bit him this noble lord, by prayers and insistent begging, had succeeded in taking off me a pair of rubber heels (which he immediately stuck on to his down-trodden sandals), an enteroclysis tube with a hole in it (which he tied round his arm), and a broken paper knife (which he stuck proudly in his belt). He had now, it seemed, taken a fancy to an old and battered cigar lighter of mine. He began by asking if it was an amulet, if it contained magic; and when I explained that it must be filled with petrol before it would light up, the idea of a metal object which 'drank water and spat fire' filled him with enthusiasm. In vain did Califa explain that a cigar lighter in the hands of someone who did not smoke and had no petrol was as useful as a lamp in the hands of a blind man.

'And who told you I should keep it in my hands?' asked this noble mendicant in a supercilious tone. 'I will tie it round my neck for good luck and every time I touch it I will think of your master.'

It amused me to keep him on tenterhooks, and while he was dressing, Califa repeated to me some of the ingenious arguments and entreaties which Shaoui used, interspersed with his own views on the behaviour of this barefaced beggar.

'Make him a present of a cord to hang himself with,' he advised me in deep disgust.

Finally, as Shaoui bent himself double to leave the tent, I put into his hand the object of his desires. His eyes danced with joy like those of a child, but the gesture with which he accepted the cigar lighter was restrained and full of dignity. He paused, laid the metal that spits fire to his heart, kissed it and whispered the ritual benediction.

As soon as he was in the open, he drew himself up to his full height, placed his hand on his sword hilt, pressed it down so that the point raised a corner of his mantle and, in a tone of great condescension as though conferring a favour on a servant, said to Califa: 'Tell your master that I shall compose a poem in his honour.'

He turned and walked slowly away with the characteristic undulating gait of the Tuareg patrician – which is achieved by flexing the knees while scarcely raising the feet from the ground.

★   ★   ★

The head of the clan, Shaoui's uncle, was a big man, so dark that he looked more like a Sudanese than a Tuareg. His mother, however, was niece to the famous Sheik Ofenàit, chief of all the Imanghassàten, and her stock had ennobled him and entitled him to become chief of his clan in spite of the fact that his father was a slave.

He told me of the fortunes and misfortunes of his people, speaking nostalgically of the glorious days of the great raids, of furious pursuits and desperate battles, when the camps rang with the roars and cries of plundered beasts, when the women had so much silver they did not know where to put it, when at the 'courts of love' the beautiful musicians sang the exploits of the fallen heroes.

The chief, however, was such a liar that the facts of a story, as given by him, were never twice the same.

When he spoke of the women of his youth he became excited and positively lyrical. He conjured up girls with wasp waists and bodies as slender and flexible as serpents, with voices so soft and sweet that they 'cut the nerves' of those who listened. In those days, he said, Tuareg women were women indeed and dispensed their favours without bothering to look upon the face of the male, obeying to the letter the popular precept: 'Whoever loves you, love him in return – even if it is only a dog.' Those were the days of certain women who had since become legendary, of famous lovers who staked their claim to renown not only in the arms of free men but also in the furious embraces of the *iklan*, the negro slaves.

To whom did he allude? Califa, frankly disgusted as he interpreted these effusions, kept interrupting to tell me what he thought of this 'son of a prostitute with more horns than a hedgehog has prickles'. He now explained that the chief was referring to his own wife who, when she was young and in a state of *asri*, did much honour to her name, 'Tara', which means love. Since I had been living among the Tuaregs I had, in fact, often heard of Tara ult Isakàn, the boast of the clan and glory of the tribe.

It was said that when she was young she had taken every man in her clan as a lover, without exception – from young boys who were wearing the veil for the first time to old men obliged to lean upon their swords for support as upon a stick. Immediately after she reached puberty she conceived a mad passion for the septuagenarian Si Baska ag Urzig, the celebrated Inennan-kàten brigand. After the death of the old man, who expired in her embrace, she promised herself to every one of a band of warriors who were setting out to sack the tents of the Kel Uhat. She kept her word, and received under her tent the eleven members of the expedition who returned alive from the bloody encounter.

Shaoui, proud of such an aunt, confided to me that 'two camels were not enough to carry all the gifts she received from her admirers; in her arms boys became men, and old men renewed their youth'. When Tara played the *umzad* in the 'courts of love', warriors flocked from the Shati, from the Tassili, from the Wadi Tarat, covering hundreds of miles on the backs of racing camels, spurred on by the hope of spending a single night in her arms. 'The poems written in her honour cannot be counted,' declared Shaoui, always lyrical when he talked of this shining light of his family: 'Her body was a mandolin and whoever played upon it remembered the melody for the rest of his life.'

Alas, the mandolin was now mute and had lost its strings. Tara had passed middle-age. She was tall even for a Tuareg, with a square face and prominent cheekbones – a large face in which the nose and mouth were lost in heavy cheeks which were all one with the double chin and neck. Her body was shapeless, her arms were huge and flabby and her pendulous breasts swung low upon her belly. Of her beauty nothing was left but the smile which the years and endless tobacco-chewing had not dimmed. Nevertheless, even as a ruin Tara continued to have a legendary quality about her, for when the old men looked upon her they remembered unforgettable nights of long ago, and the young men saw in her the exemplary Tuareg woman who, after having dispensed her favours to innumerable men, had then chosen her husband and remained tenaciously faithful to him.

And when Tara talked to me in her halting Arabic, when I listened to her shrewd remarks about her people and noted her authoritative judgements, her knowledge of what lay behind the scenes of the limited but complicated politics of the Azdjer confederation (to which the Imanghassàten belong), I came to the conclusion that she was the real chief here, that it was her big, strong hands, unsoiled by work but so long skilled in love, that guided the fortunes of this turbulent Teghehé n'abbar tribe.

★ ★ ★

One of my patients, Kemmeda ag Ermès, considered himself a highly evolved Tuareg. He was serving in the South Algerian Oases Command when the French President visited Tunis, and he took part in the grand military review and remained in the town for a week. He had, therefore, seen the sea, a train, and trams; he had discovered that glass in windows was invisible metal, that an electric bulb was a bottle in which light was kept and, above all, he had learned that in the country of the *frangi* everything had to be paid for. I removed a cyst from his scalp and he was much troubled at the thought of what I might demand for my services. When finally he made enquiries of Califa and was told that he would not have to pay a cent, he took on a new lease of life and even went so far as to express a desire to do me a *tanfust* – a service – but without being out of pocket.

While I was sitting outside my tent trying to clean myself as effectively as possible and wondering why fleas do not exist in the desert whereas lice abound, Kemmeda approached me with his slow, undulating step, accompanied by the 'well-known Bosu' who, true bastard that he was, fussed around him, delighted to show me that he was the friend of a pure-blood Tuareg noble-man. They sat down and followed my patient efforts in silence. Kemmeda showed great interest in the insecticide powder and

Bosu took upon himself to give him a complicated explanation, in Tamahàk, so that I was unable to understand what kind of story he was telling.

When I had finished and was about to put on my shirt, Bosu informed me that Kemmeda was worried about the health of his cousin's daughter. (In a country where a cousin is called 'brother' and a man's wife 'the daughter of his uncle' it was not always easy to discover the exact relationship between people.) It seemed that this relative of Kemmeda was sick and Kemmeda wished me to visit her, convinced that as soon as I laid eyes on her the sickness would disappear because, he said, I was a great physician. Bosu multiplied the compliments, and made a long speech in the Tuareg language. He must have excelled himself in his account of my prowess, for Kemmeda struck his thighs in wonderment and emitted admiring exclamations from under his veil.

They seemed unable to tell me what was wrong with the woman in question, however; I could not discover whether her bones ached, or her head; whether she vomited or was feverish.

My suspicions began to be aroused by the insistence with which the Tuareg, through the half-breed, advised me not to forget to offer gifts to the sick girl because 'girls are very susceptible to gifts from foreigners'.

It was evident that the girl was young, but when I asked Bosu her age he pretended to consult Kemmeda and, after a long confabulation, informed me that the girl had 'suspended prayer' only six months ago; that she was educated and could read, write and speak fluent Arabic as well as Tamahàk. Then, fearing that I still did not understand, he whispered in my ear that she was as beautiful as the sun, that she was in a state of *asri* – and as lively as a colt, which was the meaning of her name – *Tahûk*.

Kemmeda obviously knew exactly what the half-breed was telling me, and confirmed the interpreter's words with rapid nods. I had met a number of Imanghassàten patricians, but this was my first procurer among them. The collection was now complete.

★   ★   ★

In the low tent, which I had to enter almost on my hands and knees, Tahûk was sitting on the ground, wrapped in an outsize garment from which only her head emerged. She smiled at me, displaying a wonderful set of teeth. Their sparkling whiteness contrasted sharply with her dark, full lips which were thickly plastered with a wine-coloured cosmetic.

The smile accentuated her prominent cheekbones and lit up a sea-blue reflection in her enormous, liquid eyes, edged with their darkened lids; the antimony extended the outline of the eyes towards the temples and faded into green where it blended with the ochre colour with which the whole face was covered. What really made this Tuareg woman astonishingly beautiful, however, was her auburn hair which was dressed in curled masses on each side of her head.

The disconcerting colour of the make-up on her Mongoloid features, combined with the mass of gold-copper hair, made her look like a bewitched oriental idol. The girl's face so fascinated me that I almost failed to notice the odour of her unwashed body.

My visit was not unexpected and Tahûk received me in a natural manner, using the traditional greetings in Arabic and addressing me as 'my lord' as she invited me to sit down beside her. She gravely accepted the first present I offered her, which was a mirror. Her hands were beautiful and all her movements full of grace as she held the mirror here and there to catch her reflection. When I produced a bottle of hair lotion, however, she snatched it up with an exclamation of pure joy and held the bottle to her nose, breathing the perfume with eyes half-closed and biting her lip as though she were about to swoon with ecstasy. With a sudden movement she seized and kissed my hand, leaving a wine-coloured stain upon it. She turned back her sleeves to the shoulders and spread the perfumed lotion on her arms, holding them to her nose and murmuring ecstatic words. She passed them under my nose also so that I too might enjoy the scent.

All at once she remembered that this was a doctor's visit and that I had come to discover her sickness and – possibly – to cure her. She hurriedly put aside the mirror and the bottle and began to tell me how ill she was: she had pain here and pains there and a troublesome cough that split her ribs. She carefully recited what she had obviously been told to say, but when I questioned her she stumbled over her replies and, becoming impatient, insisted that she had pains everywhere.

Under her outer garment she wore a kind of Sudanese '*gandurra*', a sleeveless garment slit up the sides as far as the hips. She removed this with the rest because, she said, she wished me to hear how bad her lungs were.

Her adolescent body – soft and supple as a cat's and stained all over with indigo – did not seem to belong to the chrome-yellow face. Her arms were slender but not thin; her breasts, stained with blue, were like variegated marble, rose-tipped. Her waist was so small that she could enclose it within her two hands, but her hips curved like an amphora and her legs were long, slim and straight, right down to the short feet with their rows of neat toes diminishing evenly in size like tiny organ pipes.

After I had examined Tahûk from head to foot I came to the conclusion that I had rarely found a human organism in such perfect condition. When I told her so she was not at all pleased. For a moment she began to sulk, but immediately her eyes lit up with a mischievous smile. She lay on her back, completely naked, with her head resting on my knee. She threw me an upward glance of interrogation – but I was watching her wonderful hair, fearing that at any moment a procession of lice might emerge from that gold and copper jungle and begin to swarm all over me.

There was a long silence, in which I was quite at a loss for words. Then the young Tuareg noblewoman spat skilfully against the side of the tent, and asked me in a low voice if I knew how to ride a colt . . .

★   ★   ★

Very often Tara, the chief's wife, would call me to her tent so that I could examine and treat a selection of her women friends, all of whom seemed full of the fancies of sickness. So one stiflingly hot afternoon I found myself on my knees in front of an elderly woman who sat cross-legged on the floor, holding her head back so that I could put drops in her eyes, the lids of which were swollen with conjunctivitis.

Tara ult Isakàn sat beside us and followed the operation with great attention. So far, she had translated the patient's Tamahàk into Arabic, but when I had finished and finally sat down the patient spoke directly to me and I could hardly believe my ears, for the Tuareg woman spoke French. Putting a hand on my knee, she said, '*Merci, mon vieux: t'es un frère*'.

Tara did not understand the words, but seeing my astonishment she broke into a Homeric laugh which made her breasts and stomach dance. The patient laughed also, but silently, her shoulders heaving, her hand over her mouth as though she knew it was no longer beautiful.

When their hilarity had subsided a little, Tara informed me that this woman not only knew the language of the *frangi* but had also crossed the sea and lived a long time in their country. 'Ask her how many Christian *frangi* she held in her arms when she was in a state of *asri*.'

There was no need to question her in order to hear her story. She was so amused at my surprise, so pleased with the joke she had played on me, and so delighted to be able to speak the language of her youth that no insistence on my part was necessary.

Damesa ult Adu did not belong to the Azdjer people; she was of the Taitôk clan and had been born far away in the Kudia, in the Algerian Sahara.

She was born in troubled times when the whole desert was ablaze with civil war and when the caravan routes were infested with brigands. The French authorities had only just begun the excellent work of penetration which was to lead a few years later to the pacification of the whole territory.

Surprised by the incursion of a squad of Sahara police which descended upon them from Ain Salah, the Taitôk put up a desperate fight but, armed only with swords and spears, they could not stand against the rifle fire. Damesa saw her parents, her brothers, her friends fall around her, and she herself was picked up by a French sergeant who carried her off to Algeria as the spoils of war.

He was, she said, a good enough fellow, except when he had been drinking (which was practically always) or when he was jealous, and then he became very violent. Damesa was therefore not sorry when a lieutenant took advantage of his seniority to commandeer her and take her with him to Rabat in Morocco.

He had evidently been the '*grande passion*' of Damesa's life. Women whose lives have been filled with men often hold tenaciously to the memory of an early lover whose image the subsequent crowd of anonymous and vaguely remembered faces is powerless to erase. Perhaps because it is an image which symbolises their youth.

Damesa could not remember how long her idyll with the lieutenant lasted. He was a blond young man with eyes of '*bleu horizon*' and whiskers soft '*comme la soie*'. Neither did she remember anything of Rabat – it was all too long ago. She could recall only the little house outside Bab al Alu from which she could smell the sea; it was above the Christian cemetery, which at that time boasted very few crosses.

Damesa accompanied the lieutenant when he was transferred to Oran, but some months later he was sent home. He provided for her with a generosity that freed her from economic pre-occupations. He also suggested that she should return to her country, to her own clan, but Damesa was too young to appreciate the wisdom of such advice.

The semi-conjugal life she had led had left her with too much unsatisfied curiosity; her passionate temperament was not yet satisfied, and her feminine instinct and the innate rapacity of her race made it difficult for her to forego opportunities to which she felt her beauty would open the door. She therefore left Oran and went to Algiers.

She was a little vague about her reasons for this decision. Undoubtedly the blandishments of a mature and seemingly respectable lady from Spain who had brought a collection of model dresses to Oran had a great deal to do with it. She was a woman of vast experience, full of advice, 'who passed for my aunt but who was not really an aunt at all – *tu me comprends, n'est-ce pas?'*

In the house of the Spanish woman in Algiers Damesa made the acquaintance of soldiers, civilians, Arabs, Jews, Frenchmen and other foreigners. It was a prosperous period; money circulated freely, and Damesa, thrifty and parsimonious, put by the golden Napoleons, the blue French banknotes, the European jewels, and the Arab ornaments of gold wrought by Jewish goldsmiths. When she became aware that the Spanish dowager kept the lion's share of all that her admirers offered her, she set up on her own account. '*Après un an j'étais dans mes meubles et la maison et le jardin étaient à moi*,' Damesa informed me.

Stockbrokers who became rich after a morning of shouting and gesticulating on the exchange, shipbuilders who made large sums by cheating over their contracts, Government contractors who knew how to get in by the back door – all contended for her favours. She could have lived at peace, made the most of her good fortune, put her money in the bank where it would have earned more money, shut her jewels away in the safe (after getting them valued, of course): but no – when one is young one is foolish, said Damesa.

Unfortunately for her, however, she began to see her men as they really were. In the country of the *frangi* if a woman wishes to make the most of her chances she must learn to look at men without seeing them. She, Damesa, had not had the wisdom to do that. She observed that her rich Greek merchant was bald; that the Moslem notability was ridiculously pot-bellied; that the Armenian banker stuttered when he was excited. And she suddenly found that she could no longer put up with baldness, obesity or stuttering.

She was in this state of mind, dissatisfied with herself and with everyone else, when an impresario offered her a part in a colonial exhibition which was about to open in Marseilles. He promised her sea and mountains and appealed to her vanity by assuring her that an authentic Tuareg – 'a desert princess' – would create a furore and be the principal attraction in the North African pavilion.

She signed two pieces of paper, and the next thing she knew was that she was on a ship which skimmed over the water puffing smoke and gurgling like a lovesick camel.

It seemed she was a born sailor. She ate ravenously, was delighted when the prow rose on the crest of a wave, laughed at the flying fishes and tantalised the middle-aged captain by telling him the secrets of Tuareg love-making – compared with which, of course, love as Europeans understand it is, she said, '*de l'eau pure*'.

Her work at the exhibition was not onerous, but she had never imagined it could be so boring. She passed whole afternoons and evenings in a vast room filled with cheap carpets, stools and tables inlaid with mother-of-pearl, and trashy Moorish lamps. In the midst of this medley of oddments, dressed according to the popular conception of a sultana, covered with heavy ornaments and false jewels, Damesa was required to sit, stand, take tea, recline in languid attitudes on piles of cushions, and play the lute – while the public, from which she was separated by an enormous glass window, gazed at her as they would have gazed at a monster at their local fairs, and drank in the inventions of the showman who presented her as the 'Sultana of the Blue Mountains'.

There were moments, she said, when she would have liked to scream, tear off her multi-coloured garments, pull faces at the spectators, break the glass window and spit in the faces of the louts who stood staring at her open-mouthed, as though she were a two-headed calf.

When, in the next room, from which only a thin partition separated her, they installed some Moroccan girls who from morning to night performed their indecent native dances to the accompaniment of strident piping and the enthusiastic hand-clapping by the lecherous onlookers, she could bear it no longer. She broke her contract, paid the penalty, and found herself alone in the great unknown city.

But she was not alone for long.

While she was in the 'Desert Pavilion' Damesa had noticed a dark young man, very shiny and spruce, who smiled at her through the glass, winked and made signs which she did not understand. A few hours after she had left the exhibition she came face to face with him, more highly polished than ever.

He was very young, with the soft, velvety eyes of a woman, and with a sinuous walk which made the Tuareg woman – hypersensitive after three months of seclusion – ready to swoon. When he proposed an excursion to the Riviera she was delighted and consented at once.

They were glorious days. She was not in love, she assured me, but the little man from Marseilles was very polite and knew how to treat a woman. *'Il me clouait au lit toute pantelante,'* Damesa informed me – and she was an expert in subtle technical distinctions.

When they returned to Marseilles, the spell continued but the money was finished. In order that the dazzling smile of her friend should not be dimmed, she began to draw on what she had saved in Algiers. Even when that was finished the young man continued to smile, because although the money was gone, he said, there was still Damesa – and Damesa in his expert hands would be a goldmine.

In a short time the Tuareg woman (made to look half European and half African) became the queen of all the haunts of doubtful reputation, the night clubs, dance halls, gambling houses and brothels which, during the first war, sprang up at every street corner. It must have been in this period that Damesa enriched her vocabulary with those terms which are the ordinary jargon of the French underworld but which I found so disconcerting in the Wadi Buhan. I was, for example, thunderstruck when I heard her call five franc pieces *'thunes'*, women of the street *'pierreuses'*, their occupation *'turbi'* and their clients *'mecs'*.

They called her the 'Queen of Silk' but she was really only a poor cotton queen, for it was her friend from Marseilles who pulled all the wires, decided which were the most profitable of her admirers, supervised the work and pocketed the proceeds. The ideal lover of the nuptial trip among the palm trees of the Riviera had vanished and in his place was a slave-driver of the type for whom each country has its own name and which, in Marseilles, is called a 'nervi'. He was all smiles and sweetness when affairs went well and when the Queen of Silk was docile, but when there was a thin period, or if the unfortunate woman showed any reluctance, he immediately became brutal. More than once Damesa had gone to bed covered with the bruises inflicted by the young gentleman. One evening he did not return home. He had been caught in an unauthorised gaming house and the police had put him in the cooler. When Damesa went to the police headquarters in the neighbourhood to ask for news, she too was arrested. She never saw the smart young gentleman again, for a few days later she was ordered to be deported.

Her return journey in the middle of the war, at the prow of an unlit cargo boat, was depressing in the extreme, and she found the sight of Algiers, in the pouring rain, equally so.

She was without a penny; but she still had the house, furniture and garden, and of her past magnificence there remained a few silver ornaments, a necklace, a pair of ear-rings, a bracelet or two. These she was obliged to pawn immediately. Her former friends had disappeared: some had gone to another country, some had married, a few were dead, and quite a number had gone bankrupt.

She was too tired to begin all over again to compete with a younger generation which was moving forward to the assault with short skirts and shingled hair. Even though her mirror assured her that she was still pleasant to look upon, she had sufficient common sense to know that youth – real youth, that indispensable thing – had gone.

Moreover, she felt tethered, like a camel to its grazing ground. Her compulsory repatriation papers described her state of *asri* in a way which deprived it of all romance and placed her in a category of women who were continually under the eye of the police. This was new to her, and she found insupportable both the incursions of the police into her home and the sanitary check-ups. It was at this point that the advice given her long ago by the blue-eyed lieutenant with the silky whiskers returned to her mind. It now no longer seemed a crazy thing to do, and she turned the idea over and over in her mind, considering ways and means.

The increasing difficulties with which she was faced due to the continually rising cost of living eventually decided her to take action. She sold everything she had and departed.

It was a journey full of incident, with sudden halts, unforeseen delays and hurried flights. Southern Algeria was in revolt, the great majority of the Tuaregs were on a war footing again, and communications with the Sahara regional centres were constantly interrupted for long periods.

After an enforced and prolonged stay at Ain Salah, on the edge of the desert, during which she was the joy of the officers' mess, the chance to buy some contraband camels presented itself. It went against the grain to pay the price they asked for three scabby beasts, but she bought them, and on a night when there was neither moon nor stars she managed to slip past the military guards and reach the route which led, through Arak and Inniker, to her homeland, the Kudia mountains.

She broke off her story to tell me of the strange sensation she had experienced on feeling the camel rise on its four feet beneath her, on placing her bare foot on the beast's neck and feeling the crisp, warm hair between her toes. In that instant the years fell away from her – her conjugal life at Rabat and then Oran, her state of *asri* in Algiers, the fantastic and unhappy life in Marseilles – everything melted away as a dream disappears on waking.

For a month she wandered about from mountain to mountain, but her people, the Taitôk – what remained of them – had gone. They had migrated towards the south and were lost among the Shaamba, the people of the Tuat, the Senussite Arabs and all the rabble that had poured into the Sahara to increase the anarchy that had turned the country upside down.

Homeless, tribeless, Damesa made her way cautiously east, dropping down out of the mountains through the Abalesse Pass, and mounting again up the Wadi Minhero as far as Tarat, where she discovered a group of the Imanghassàten who received her kindly. They were the Teghehé n'abbar, the clan of Tara ult

Isakàn, who befriended her. Among these people she became again the Tuareg woman she had been before, the woman she had never ceased to be at heart: *'Une femme taitôque avec le visage barbouillé d'ocre et la bouche rouge de safran; oui, oui, une femme taitôque, rien que cela . . .'*

★ ★ ★

Meanwhile, a new governor had arrived in Tripoli.

It seems to be in the nature of all new Governors to deplore their predecessors' mistakes and to hasten to justify their own existences by introducing some would-be epoch-making innovation in the hope of thus achieving immortality.

Immortality is a harmless desire so long as its manifestations are confined to the scratching of tourists' names on the columns of Greek temples; but the bee becomes really dangerous when it gets into the bonnet of an ambitious governor.

Of course, the erratic behaviour of new administrators could also be due to the fact that the various governments of Italy seemed to go out of their way to appoint as governors of overseas territories distinguished men with no very precise ideas concerning Africa. Their knowledge of the coloured races was usually confined to what they had gathered by watching swarthy acrobats in circuses or the dark-skinned doorkeepers of cinemas.

On this occasion, the new Governor of Libya's opening gambit was to decide that a report should be drawn up on industrial and agricultural activities during the twenty-five years of the colony's life. And I, having passed during that period into the ranks of the colonial administration, was called to Tripoli to compile this report.

I was reluctant to leave the Berbers of the mountains and the desert – for the simple reason that I have an incorrigible habit of getting interested in my work, however modest it may be. Moreover, the provincial town atmosphere of Tripoli irritated me, and I was not at all pleased at the idea of a longish stay there.

Jemberié, on the other hand, was delighted with the change and happily installed himself in the new house, although he deplored my choice of an Arab *fonduq* near the oasis, in the area where later the garden city was to spring up. Mortified at his master's strange and vulgar tastes, Jemberié was much astonished when, on opening the door one evening, he found himself face to face with the Bishop of Tripoli, who had come to visit me. The idea that such a high dignitary was ready to enter a newly whitewashed *fonduq* quite upset him, since he could not decide which was the greater – the honour of such a visit or the shame of being obliged to receive such an eminent person in a hut until recently used only by camelherds. The Apostolic Vicar, however, was not bothered by such considerations.

He was a man of over fifty, thickset, obese and shortnecked. He looked at people through half-closed eyes behind thick glasses, his nose raised like a hound on the scent and his fingers, on one of which he wore the episcopalian ring, combing his bushy beard. After he had listened to an argument and made up his mind about it, he would join his hands as if in prayer and in a deep, ponderous voice, would define the situation or give his view in a few precise and unadorned phrases which admitted of no further argument.

He had an excellent knowledge of Hebrew, Arabic, Persian, Turkish and Albanian. No one in the whole city, with the exception of the head of the Muntasser family, was able to converse with him in classical Arabic, which was a delight to hear. When the chief's nephews were present, they listened open-mouthed without understanding a word, and the Bishop would turn to the chief and, speaking in the local dialect, say that he was astounded to find young Moslems unable to understand their own tongue; feigning indignation, he would call attention to the fact that he, a Christian and foreigner, knew Arabic better than they, who were Arabs and Mohammedans. The old Muntasser was greatly diverted and rubbed his hands with glee at their discomfiture.

Mohammedan canonical law held no mysteries for the Bishop; his knowledge of it was such that the High Court often submitted to him the most complicated questions, asking for his opinion.

The first time he invited me to his house he refused to let me examine him, talked to me of his diabetes as though it had no connection with him, and finished by telling the history of Mòhy ed-Din ben Aràbi, a famous Arab mystic of about the year 1200, of whom I had never heard, but of whose life he knew every detail.

I had already lost the thread of this story when the *Cādī* entered with a packet of papers under his arm. They put their heads together and began to talk rapidly in lowered voices. The papers were passed from one to the other, turned over and back, while with their forefingers they ran along the lines of text, stressing phrases and words. Every now and again the Bishop struck the papers with the back of his hand, exclaiming that there was no doubt at all: the case was exactly that. The *Cādī* assented and then whispered some suggestion which started the examination of the case all over again.

Suddenly the Bishop turned to me and announced that it was absolutely indispensable to know the exact formula used by the husband to repudiate the wife: although there were formulæ which left no doubt, there were others which were only valid in certain clearly defined situations; there were expressions which signified repudiation in the opinion of some commentators while for others they were merely a reproof without any juridical significance. It was, however, inadmissible, he said, that a man could repudiate his wife by the use of the words reported by these witnesses.

He puffed into his beard, raised his shoulders, spread out his hands and wagged his head. Furthermore, he went on, this was a case of conditional repudiation and – what made the whole thing extremely ticklish – the condition was difficult to prove: the question lay in the terms used and it was useless to cavil.

By this time my head was swimming and I was grateful when the *Cādī* interrupted him to point out that in the case under examination the husband wished above all to prove that he was the offended party.

The Bishop replaced the papers on the table, and in an even tone declared that on that point the husband was indubitably in the right, since the one thing about which there could be absolutely no argument was that the husband belonged to the category of cuckolds. He repeated the word, savouring it between tongue and palate.

★   ★   ★

To disease, the Bishop put up a passive resistance. He followed the prescribed diet as scrupulously as though it were one of the many limitations laid upon him by the monastic rule – for with a certain pride he maintained that his position as Bishop did not exempt him from any of his duties as a monk.

For some reason or other he took a liking to me. The incorrigible vulgarity of my speech in Arabic amused him. In a fruity voice, with his hands on his hips, he would ask me in what low haunts I had picked up such unorthodox expressions.

One day as I copied the title of a collection of elementary Arabic prose which lay on his desk, he snatched the note from my hand and asked if I was not ashamed to write Arabic so badly. I replied that I was not, seeing that I had had no teacher and had taught myself by copying out of a dilapidated Koran school spelling book, with the help of an old sergeant of a Libyan regiment. The Bishop remained silent and thoughtful for a moment and then, with a brief, authoritative gesture, invited me to sit down at his writing-table. He put a piece of squared paper before me, placed my fingers round the pen to show me how it should be held, and began to dictate to me the letters of the Arabic alphabet. When the letter was well formed and contained exactly within the square, I heard a grunt of approval at my shoulder – but more often I heard a threatening rumble that warned me I had better begin again. Sometimes he took the pen from my hand, wrote a letter which seemed printed, and then I did my best to copy it.

These lessons became a habit which I would have enjoyed even more but for the pedagogic methods employed by my unusual teacher. I was evidently his first adult pupil and he applied to me the methods he had used in the Franciscan schools in Palestine and Syria where, many years ago, he had taught children the first elements of writing, rapping their knuckles with a ruler when they made a mistake or allowed their attention to wander. I was amused – but only up to a point. When I did not succeed in joining the *lām* to the *alif* in the proper way, or in giving the right curve to the tail of the *sīn*, a ruler would descend like lightning on my knuckles. He did it with such Olympian unconcern that although I swore under my breath I was never able to bring myself to the point of asking him to desist.

As time went on, I realised that this unusual patient did not consider his illness as real: to him it was simply a tiresome idea which would go away if he refused to notice it. This, no doubt, was why he spent hours debating with the *Cādī* or giving me lessons in Arabic caligraphy, or reading abstruse books, giving full rein to his extraordinary versatility.

Whenever I asked him questions which, as his doctor, I had to ask, his brow clouded with annoyance.

'There – I was feeling so well. I was just re-examining these photographs of twelfth-century Selyuk coins. Do you notice the reproduction of the traditional Greek and Byzantine designs? Look at this wonderful piece of Kaykosroway II: he was so much in love with his wife that he had her features stamped on his silver coins. It is magnificent. And then you come in with that professional air which I detest and spoil everything with your questions. You force me to think about my complaint and make me feel ill all at once.'

Numismatology was one of his specialities.

For him every coin represented a piece of history with which he was familiar. Tossing a Septimus Severus *sesterce* or a Persian *dinar* in the palm of his hand he would discourse of dynasties, of peoples, of wars and invasions, of vanished civilisations and of those which had replaced them to disappear in their turn, of artistic traditions passed down from one minter to another. In the fringe of a cord, in a device or in the details of a figure, he would discover an echo from a buried epoch, the influence of powers that have ceased to be.

He had presented a valuable collection of Alexandrian coins to the Jerusalem museum. When I asked him why he had parted with it he replied, with a smile, 'You forget that I am a Franciscan' – adding more seriously and with great simplicity, 'In any case, those coins had nothing further to tell me.'

He had an exceptional capacity for seeing the grotesque and humorous aspect of people and of situations, and this contrasted strangely with his grave appearance, his dignified bearing and the solemn episcopal vestments with their amethyst-coloured buttons.

The Jewish community had at its head a Rabbi who was universally respected for his integrity and for the soundness of his doctrine. This worthy Talmudist was afflicted with a nose of such melancholy proportions that it overhung his mouth. Added to an unfortunate arrangement of the wrinkles on his face and to a chronic inflammation of the eyelids, it gave him such a permanently desolate expression that he always seemed to have just left the Wailing Wall. I asked the Bishop why the Rabbi had such an unhappy air and what could be done to console him.

'Nothing,' he replied, with a grave shake of his head, 'absolutely nothing. This man, who knows the Talmud as very few know it, has every reason to look like that. I wonder how many times you have pulled a long face waiting for a train which was half an hour late? Well – you can hardly expect light-heartedness and jollity from someone who has been waiting thousands of years for the Messiah.'

★ ★ ★

It was the same Bishop who introduced me to his best friend in the town – the Arab mayor of Tripoli.

The friendship between the Bishop and the pasha was one of the most extraordinary I have ever seen. I have never met two men who were, on the surface, more directly opposed in temperament, and rarely have I come across a deeper and closer friendship. The Italian was of modest origin, the Arab the head of a princely family which had once ruled the country; the Bishop held to the simple and pure faith of St Francis of Assisi, the prince was a fervent and practising Mohammedan; the humble Christian had an encyclopædic erudition, the Moslem nobleman was illiterate.

For a long time I pondered this friendship, trying to discover the mysterious affinity which undoubtedly bound two such utterly different beings together. I did not know either of them well and for a long time I saw only the superficial differences which divided them without discerning the deep similarity which bound them together.

The pasha did not know how old he was. He knew that he was old, very old – but he did not trouble to fix the exact number of years: perhaps eighty-five, perhaps ninety. He counted on his fingers, and in order to get somewhere near the truth he would mention incidents of many years ago, trying to guess what age he was when this or that happened. He must certainly have been about ninety, but he was as straight as a rod and had a constitution of iron. What on earth was the use, he asked, of cudgelling his brains to find out his age when he was in splendid health, could still ride a horse and, he added, with a prodigious wink and digging me in the ribs, when he still knew what to do with a woman?

This man who, somewhere about his ninetieth year, still talked of his relations with women, had been a virgin until he was forty. I was never able to discover the reason for his abstinence, or why at a mature age he had changed his regime. When I asked him, he replied jokingly that he had wanted to conserve his forces in order to be able to feel young when he was old. On other occasions, he would say that God caused men to act in different ways and that it was useless to try to find out why he led his creatures along one path rather than another.

At that time many of his sons were still small, and I often met him walking along the seafront holding one or two of them by the hand. Sometimes I joined him and we would sit down at the foot of the castle where, until the last century, his people had lived as sovereigns. Here I would listen to his talk, while the boys amused themselves throwing stones into the sea.

I treated him for a mild attack of influenza which for a few days had given him aching joints and a fever. When the attack had passed I advised him to stay at home and rest until he had regained his usual strength, but it was impossible to keep him quiet during the period of convalescence, and he seemed to make a special point of going to his office, of visiting relatives in the country, or walking about the town. He was surprised when I reproved him, and seemed to think I should be grateful to him for being so active, because – he assured me – if he had remained shut up in the house people would have said that the physician had been unable to cure him, whereas, seeing him about they thought: a great physician has cured him, a wise man has strangled the disease and prevented it from growing.

Sometimes when he boasted of his age and strength, he would take my hand in a grip of iron and defy me to free it. With the pleasure that old men find in recalling the past, he would talk of remote events, of the pomp and splendour of the courts of the Constantinople sultans; of the days when there was a slave market in Tripoli; of the Corsair pirates who infested the Mediterranean long ago.

He never refused alms to a beggar, but he became irritated if the beggar recognised him and called him *sīdī*, 'my lord'. Then, with a gesture of impatience he would wave the mendicant away, muttering with annoyance, 'Your lord, my lord, is Allah.'

He was not rich, and his trousers were often a little threadbare at the knees – but every day food for about forty poor people was prepared in his kitchen.

On one occasion I met him as I was on my way to a suburb to visit an old patient, a camelherd, who had just gone down with an attack of malaria. The old man wished to accompany me, and protested loudly when I suggested calling a *carrozzella* so that he should not tire himself. He walked with me along the dusty road which borders the oasis, and at a point where I began to be uncertain of the way it was he who piloted me under the palm trees, through the maze of alleys, to the *fonduq* where, behind a courtyard crowded with men, camels, saddles, sacks, waterskins, my patient, his teeth chattering, was laid out on a mat.

After I had attended to him, the caravaneers wished us to take tea. They knew the pasha by name but they had never seen him, and they sat round us, keeping their distance and not daring to address him.

The prince knew their countries: the mountains in the heart of the desert, the oases, the wells, the routes that converge upon the city at the coast. He had talked with the fathers and the grandfathers of their chiefs; he had met face to face the legendary bandits of former times. As they listened to his perfectly natural references to people who to them were mythical figures and legendary heroes, the youngest among his audience stared with the same amazement I myself experienced when, as a boy, I heard the centenarian Count Greppi describe how, on entering the diplomatic service, he had had an audience with Prince Metternich.

The old man talked of the rough, wearing and solitary life of the nomads as though he himself had wandered 'in search of rain' along the routes between the mountains and the sea. Almost a century of experience, together with an imaginative understanding of human nature, enabled him to enter naturally into other men's lives, however poor and wretched they might be, and to grasp all their implications.

He talked with the caravaneers – who now flocked around him devouring him with their eyes – with a natural simplicity as though he had known them all his life. In fact, he had always known them: his religious sense of the oneness of all creation, the human sympathy which enabled him to recognise a reflection of himself in every son of Adam, made it natural for him to treat these ragged, bare-foot, lice-ridden caravaneers as his equals – and that without detracting an iota from the respect due to him.

On that occasion I was able to appreciate to the full the infinite variety in Arabic of the familiar form of address in the second person singular, which may be used to a sultan or to a beggar. The word he used when chatting to the head of the caravan was not the same as the form he employed when addressing the boy who offered him a glass of tea; the one he employed when he spoke to me was yet another – but the form by which the caravaneers themselves addressed him had all the solemnity of an invocation.

Before leaving the *fonduq* the pasha expressed a wish to say a word to the sick man, and as he left him he put into his hand all the silver and copper coins he had in his pocket.

★ ★ ★

I had often asked the Bishop about his friendship with the pasha, endeavouring in my curiosity to discover on what it was based. He was always evasive in his reply; sometimes he did not reply at all, and confined himself to raising his shoulders and blowing into his beard.

The more I came to know the Arab nobleman, however, the more I discovered what they had in common – for example, their indifference to illness, their complete disregard of material considerations, their deep understanding of human suffering and misery, and their charity, which was unsmirched by egotism and knew no limits. Both of them submitted to a higher will with the blind faith of children.

At a certain point I realised that, just as the various elements in a mosaic form a single design when pieced together, so the mental attitudes of the two friends were parts of a single spiritual conception which I was at last able to recognise.

One day, as I was helping the Bishop to put his books in order on his library shelves, I announced that I had finally understood why he and the pasha were such close friends; I said that their friendship was a friendship between Franciscans. He continued to turn the pages of a volume he held in his hand, as though seeking a reply there. After a few moments of silence he closed the book and said in a gruff tone, almost annoyed, 'You express yourself badly not only in Arabic but in Italian as well. You ought to know that a Moslem can't be a Capuchin friar, and I myself am too unworthy of the robe I wear to call myself a Franciscan. Suppose we leave St Francis out of it: he is too far above our miserable concerns. The pasha is a man of great heart and exemplary humility who practises the three canonical virtues in a most admirable manner, even though he follows the law of a chieftain who was never a prophet. If I, on the other hand, have been privileged to know the Truth it is by the grace of God and through no virtue of mine. I have learnt much from this man; that is why we are friends. I think you might have arrived at that simple conclusion without any help from me.'

The younger of the two friends died first.

Suddenly the uncertain equilibrium of his metabolism was shaken and the Bishop who had remained a simple friar collapsed.

I was far away from Tripoli when it happened, and only later did I learn how the Apostolic Vicar had died serenely, surrounded by *confrères* and nuns, gripping the hand of his old friend the pasha who in his sorrow seemed turned to stone; while in the cathedral, in the mosque, and in the synagogue men of differing creeds prayed that God would postpone the appointed hour.

★　★　★

By 1930 my work in Tripoli was finished and I was next ordered to Eritrea, which to us in Libya was another world.

Just before I left I received a message from Massauda, one of Tripoli's high-class *sharmoutas*, the biggest in both fame and frame. She had heard of my impending departure and wished to see me in order to read my fate in the coffee grounds. It would be unpardonably impudent, she said, to go into a strange country without knowing what Destiny had in store for me.

I never knew more than Massauda's first name, but it was enough. I had known her for some time – ever since I had treated her for an attack of hay fever. She had remained grateful, and always sent me an invitation whenever she heard that I was passing through Tripoli. She had no secrets from the *tebīb*, and spoke with a disconcerting frankness of her love affairs, recent and remote. She showed me photographs and gave me letters to read which demolished the few illusions concerning my brothers in Adam to which I still clung.

As a girl her figure was superb, but she gradually put on weight and when, during the last war, I returned to Tripoli and found her again, her body had gone to pieces, her legs bulged and her face was like a loaf; her soft, luminous eyes were the only remaining element of her vanished beauty.

At the time of our story, however, Massauda was still beautiful even though she was getting on for thirty, which is the end of summer in the life of a Libyan Jewess.

Her mind was mediocre and vulgar, but she was intuitive and vivacious and these qualities, combined with a certain shrewdness, sometimes deceived people into believing that she was intelligent. It was perhaps because she was not intelligent that she had never succeeded in accumulating anything in the way of a nest-egg. In order to get along at all, she was now obliged to keep four or five girls in her house, although, whether from indolence or from innate kind-heartedness, she did not make much profit even from them. Or perhaps it was because, although she was reputed to be miserly, she was in fact nothing of the kind and let the pounds slip through her fingers while fussing about the pennies. Her love affairs were a standing proof of her impractical attitude: she had given herself for various reasons – out of vanity, or because she had been attracted, or out of compassion, but only sometimes out of necessity.

She seemed incapable of appreciating the idiocy, the incoherence, the aberrations of the men she had known, as revealed by the stories she told me in order to prove how much she had been loved, what delicate sentiments she had inspired, with what youthful gusto she had been enjoyed. To her, their behaviour seemed always a natural manifestation of love, and she was moved by it. In the nickname 'Your rascal' by which an old Minister of State signed himself (the cretin thought he was being dashing), Massauda saw only a likeable pleasantry. A business man, after fifteen days in Tripoli, wrote her a New Year letter in which he described the family Christmas dinner; after mentioning the various members of the family who were present, he concluded, 'I am sure you would like my mother.' This moved her to tears.

When she insisted on my reading the pitiful, pathologically infantile effusions which a general (whom I had always admired

Cunama fantasia: getting ready and the dance

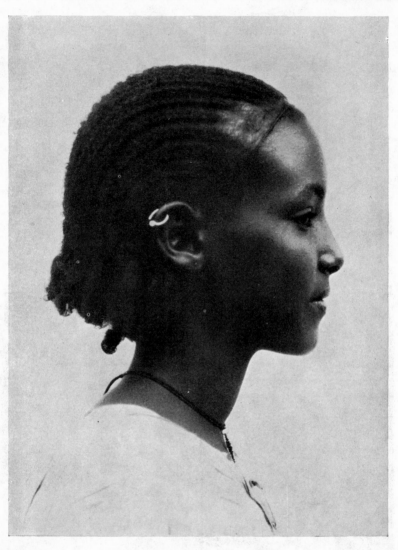

A peasant girl of Tigrinya descent

for his culture, character and sense of responsibility) had written her from Italy – on official notepaper – she was surprised that I was not delighted at the revelation of such an affectionate nature in a valorous soldier.

The subject does not come within the competence of a physician who once ran an African dispensary, and perhaps it would not interest European readers, but nevertheless I have often asked myself whether perhaps such folly is to be explained by the novelty of first contact with a coloured woman. I should like to hope at least that ministers, industrial magnates and high-ranking military commanders do not behave in the same way with white-skinned Massaudas at home.

But I was off now to discover my fate, to learn just what lay in store for me in Eritrea – as revealed by the coffee grounds of the beautiful *sharmouta*.

When I arrived in the cul-de-sac 'Good Fortune' the sound of women's voices filled the street – shouts and laughter accompanied by chords from some stringed instrument.

A young negress hanging over the balcony stared at me with her mouth open and a stolid expression on her face, until I addressed her in the manner to which negro servants are accustomed. She then fled precipitately with a clacketing of her sandals on the wooden floor.

Massauda was waiting on a mat in the ground-floor sitting-room. She was wrapped in a brilliant-coloured *ḥāik* and covered with gold like a sacred image; and she was ready to tell me my destiny.

With her chin on her chest, she kept her eyes fixed on the bowl which she balanced on her crossed legs. The air was filled with the aroma of coffee, with the scent of sandalwood and of women.

She did not speak; she did not even look at me, but raised her hand with its henna-tinted palm motioning me to keep silent. In silence, therefore, I sat down beside her and awaited the verdict.

In a contralto voice and in her comic Italian, Massauda pronounced the fatal words. At the end of every sentence she

F

swiftly raised her beautiful eyes to my face as though seeking confirmation of her predictions.

'You go by Italy in Eritrea. Perhaps going Naples, perhaps going Rome.' She raised her voice and shot me a look from her luminous eyes. 'Not to see this woman, you have understand? Not see this woman. This woman no good, no good. This woman no good for you . . .'

Every now and then she interrupted her predictions to shake a threatening fist in the direction of the floor above, where at times there was such an uproar that the notes of the '*ud* could no longer be heard. Missa, the old hag of a servant, endeavoured to calm her mistress by stroking her shoulder, but when the noise became unbearable she lifted her skirts with two fingers and disappeared on tiptoe up a staircase in the wall. The bacchanalia subsided a little and Missa descended again. This time she huddled herself close to me on the floor and began to tell the most outlandish stories, regardless of Massauda's efforts to restrain her.

Missa was Massauda's wizened, hawk-nosed, money-squeezing go-between; a sergeant with the girls, a pander with the clients. She had a wagging chin, a heavy leer, and a deep loyalty to Massauda. She was the practical side of the establishment, and also a great liar.

'Do you know,' she confided in an affected voice, and with a girlish tilt of her withered face, 'when I go to Italy the prefect comes to meet me on the boat? He does, you know.'

Massauda smiled in spite of herself and then, with a gesture of impatience, silenced the servant and returned to her prophecies.

'Ooooo . . . careful on ship, because on ship if you careful you find your destination. On ship many women, but you staying with men . . . and careful, you understand?'

At this moment, in the room above, pandemonium broke loose. Ear-splitting screams pierced the air, furniture was over-turned, bangs and thuds covered us with plaster, and it seemed as though the ceiling was about to fall in.

Massauda sprang to her feet, leaving her *hāik* behind as though she had discarded her shell; jingling with gold ornaments and unsteady on her high heels, she rushed towards the staircase bellowing at the top of her voice. Missa had preceded her and I followed.

In the semi-darkness the negress and another girl were rolling on the floor, biting, scratching, punching and kicking, dragging out each other's hair by the handful, spitting at each other, panting and vomiting obscenities. In the fury of the battle they had overturned a large sideboard which had held a liqueur service, glasses, knives and forks, plates, a large porcelain clock, and a whole collection of imitation Dresden figures.

The negress broke free like a writhing snake, but her adversary, a muscular Jewess whose face was covered with blood, leapt upon her again and they rolled across the carpet, among the broken china and overturned furniture.

Three other girls who had flattened themselves against the walls were clutching their skirts round them and screaming like magpies. A blind had fallen on to the balcony and the bamboo pole was still stuck through the brass rings.

Like lightning, Massauda took up the curtain rod and began to lay about her in all directions, striking combatants and non-combatants alike. The non-combatants piled on top of one another in the corner and yelled as though they were being flayed alive. With their faces protected by their arms they jumped and bent and twisted themselves in an effort to avoid the blows. It was at this moment that we became aware of the presence of the *'ud* player.

He was a little yellow hunchback, almost annihilated under a fez much too big for his head and a *stambulina* too wide for his dwarf's body. He was standing on a divan against the wall with his head drawn into his shoulders and was holding an enormous lute above his head in an effort to preserve it from the cyclone which was devastating the room. Massauda's fury had terrified him and he was emitting cries so shrill that they rose high above the shrieks of the girls.

Massauda turned and looked at him. She was panting and little bubbles of froth were forming at the corners of her mouth. She let the pole fall from her hands and for some reason a new wave

of fury swept over her and increased the congestion in her
face.

'You ... you ... you dog, you son of a bitch! ...'

She rushed at him, seized him by the front of his clothes, shook
him like a bundle of rags and, reaching up on tip-toe, tried to
strike his face with blows that cut through the air like a sword.
'Ah, dog! ...'

Between my hands I held the bony ones of Missa who, in order
not to be left out, and thinking it a gesture appropriate to the
occasion, was trying to tear her face with her nails. Fortunately
at that moment I was able to push Massauda out of the room. I
persuaded Missa to go with her and put her to bed, so that I
could attend to the casualties.

For this purpose we repaired to another room. I began with
the Fezzanese negress, who was bruised from head to foot and
covered with blood. Every now and again a sob broke from her
as with the back of her hand she wiped the blood from her
nose. One of Messauda's blows had caught her shoulder, and
her back and buttocks were covered with glass splinters which
glittered brightly on the dark bruised skin.

She still had her wits about her, however, and while I was
treating her back, remembering how I had addressed her from
the street, she bent towards the other girls and sounded the
alarm: '*ikàsser ellôza*' – 'Be careful – he cracks the almonds.'

This phrase, in the jargon of most of the North African underworld means: 'this man knows Arabic'; but no one has ever
been able to tell me why. Pretending not to understand, I next
turned my attention to Julia, the Jewess. Her mouth was swollen;
her arms showed the marks of the negress's teeth; one eyebrow
was split open and the weals raised by the bamboo pole made
her back look like a zebra's. She was chiefly annoyed, however,
to see so many people in her room.

'Are you aware that this is my room?' she asked.

The atmosphere was stifling. Through the window opening
on to the alley the night air bore an ammoniacal stench of urine
mingled with the scent of the jasmin which covered the wall of
the house; in the distance, the loud voice of a drunk could be

heard. From a silver frame on the bed table a sergeant of artillery gazed at me with a severe and martial air.

I asked Julia if she would do me the honour to allow me to remain in her room in order to treat her own and her companions' injuries. With a shrug of her shoulders, indifferent to my irony, she replied, 'Make yourself at home,' and balanced a cigarette between her swollen lips.

One of the other girls, in order to give herself courage during the medication, began to sing out of tune in a loud and raucous voice, and when I gave her a resounding smack to make her stop she burst into hysterical laughter.

When we eventually returned to the ruins of the sitting-room, a divan slid out from the wall, and from behind the headboard appeared the fez of the 'ud player, followed by his terrified face.

His appearance caused another outburst of hilarity. The hunchback did not laugh. He ignored the girls and turned to me : I was the physician. With one hand he held the precious lute behind his back; the other he gravely proffered me, pushing it under my nose so that I could observe a few superficial scratches across the knuckles.

'You are the doctor,' he said, 'I am injured.'

I was obliged to close the doors in a hurry so that the ribald shouts and laughter of the girls should not bring Massauda into our midst again. The music-maker, furious because no one would take him seriously, cursed the women and backed away in order to protect his precious instrument from them. Naked, they pressed round him and showered him with a stream of filthy epithets to each of which the dwarf had a ready answer; in fact, to my surprise, he was more than a match for them.

Ghazàla asked him in a pitying tone how it was that he was pregnant: how had he got himself into that trouble? In the local dialect a pregnant woman is said to be 'with belly'. Making a mocking reference to the unfortunate creature's hump, she asked him how it was that he had got himself 'with back'.

'Maybe I *am* pregnant, my beauty,' replied the hunchback with a sneer. 'It can never happen to you because the grass does not grow where the crowds walk.'

He winked at me, satisfied at having thus reduced the impudent Ghazàla to silence, but immediately turned a stream of invective on to the Jewess who, in spite of her bruises and injuries, continued to dance round him endeavouring to bang his fez down over his eyes.

Finally I managed to bundle him out of the room, and soon afterwards I took my departure. The storm was now over and the girls, peaceable as doves, came to the street door to wish me farewell. They were covered with towels, blankets, bruises and sticking plaster, but were quite unselfconscious, and smilingly bade me Godspeed.

I had got as far as Shiara Mizrani, the city centre, when I heard someone calling me, and there at the end of the deserted street the hunchback came running, waving his 'ud like a club.

He had followed me to ask my pardon for his part in the evening's proceedings. He ran along beside me, trying to adjust his step to mine, and threw his head back so that he could look into my face.

Julia was always tormenting him, he said. She mocked him, sneered at him and humiliated him in the presence of strangers. He did not mean me, he hastened to add: I was not a stranger because I was a physician and the father of all unfortunate creatures. She introduced him to people as her eunuch, as her own private procurer, and each time invented some fresh insult – such as, that she had bought him in a Turkish brothel; that she had found him on a dung heap; that she had received him as a legacy from the Sultan of Mahbulistan together with a clyster and a spittoon. The dwarf ground his teeth and rolled his head at the remembrance of her insults.

Dawn was breaking and there were few people in the Piazza dell 'Orologio at that hour: a porter went towards the harbour, a beggar made for his usual stand, a solitary and indolent street-sweeper appeared. The little Arab tavern at the end of the street was, however, already open; from the doorway the large stomach of the proprietor was visible warming itself in front of the fire.

We were the first callers, and the host, surprised at his unusual guests, put us in a little back room which was lit only by a pale gleam from a high window covered with a piece of rusty wire-netting. We sat down opposite one another, with a rectangular table about ten inches high between us.

'Are we really going to eat together?' asked the hunchback, who had not taken me seriously when I invited him to have breakfast with me.

His quick and hungry eyes passed first to the bowls of soup in which eggs, seasoned with cumin seeds, floated on pieces of fried bread, next to the *bazina*, a kind of *polenta* made of fermented barley seasoned with red pepper, and then to the bottle of palm wine.

He chewed every mouthful thoroughly and swallowed it with gusto, making the most of the present in compensation for past hunger and in anticipation of that to come. Every now and again he smiled at me and with his mouth full informed me that the food was excellent – and to prove his satisfaction he belched in the most astounding fashion.

His approval was, in fact, misplaced. The *polenta* was lumpy, the oil rancid and the eggs over-cooked. The palm wine alone was passable, being just at the right point of maturity.

The wine loosened his tongue and he told me he was not from Tripoli; that he was a Yemenite and had always lived at Istanbul. Had I not noticed that he was dressed in Turkish fashion? He looked with some pride at his *stambulina* which should have been black but had become decidedly green; it reached to his knees, and was worn at the elbows and shoulders and threadbare at the seams.

But he had left Istanbul owing to some misunderstanding with the police; and when they told him that there was a shortage of good *'ud* players in Tripoli he had come with his instrument (which was the finest in North Africa) and settled down here. Would I like him to play something? I said that I would – knowing that he offered it by way of thanks for his meal.

He carefully unwrapped his *'ud* and dusting it delicately with his sleeve he tuned the strings.

He began to play, bent over the instrument, plucking at the

strings with the plectrum, now here, now there, now drawing it lightly over them all at once. His left hand seemed quite independent of his right as the flexible fingers twisted over the instrument like the tentacles of an octopus.

Suddenly, he raised his head and began to sing. He sang quietly, in a voice which was surprisingly unlike the squeaky falsetto of his speaking voice.

He sang the song of the *trig el bill*, the camel track, the caravan route:

The wind passes like a caress over the waves of the desert sand
And the caravan leaves no more trace than a bird's wing in the air or a fish in the water.
Let us flee the crowd, for in the multitude there is no salvation,
Let us beware of taking root like a tree.

The sun rises in the heavens and the feet of the camels wearily seek the shadows;
Our throats are parched so that we cannot speak;
The camels' voices sob.

Now the evil spirits that send men mad conjure up before our eyes visions of happiness that are only illusion,
The sound of running water falls on our ears,
The green of palm trees is reflected in a fountain where brightly plumed birds flutter and sing;

The mirage fades and shows only the bones of our comrades, whitening in the sun.
We too shall perish:
There is no escape from death,

But Allah is merciful.
In the Great Void where only God exists, the dying who believe that the Resurrection is certain will find their way to the true oasis.

On the strings of the *'ud* the water gushed forth, gurgled, splashed and spluttered. Three sounds there are that are dear to the ear of man: the sound of money, of a woman's laughter, and of running water.

The caravan was saved.

We shall all be saved.

That is what we have learned on the caravan route.

In our vain search for freedom we shall all lose ourselves in 'the void'; we must renounce what is dearest to us; we must forego what we thought essential to life; we must suffer the anguish of delusion.

The song ended on the solemn note:

'*Ua la shauk fel-Qiyàma:* and the resurrection is certain.'

It was more than Massauda could have told me.

Chapter Five

THE SOLITARY ONE

AFTER the French revolution it was said that those who had not lived before the September massacres could not know the joy of living. It is certain that no one who did not know the Eritrea of twenty years ago can possibly understand how fascinating some colonial territories could be.

In those days Eritrea was governed by a man who was undoubtedly endowed with excellent qualities, but who also had his shortcomings. To begin with, he was honest, and this at once put him in a bad light and made him unpopular. In addition, he was not a politician and had passed his life in the colonial service, starting at the bottom and rising at last to the position of Governor. Because of this he knew all the tricks in the game, and neither regional commissioners nor district officers could pull the wool over his eyes. It was useless to resort to those innocent stratagems which they used to ease their lot when forced to submit to the authority of eminent persons from Rome – men who knew nothing of Africa and for whom the *simoom* might be a cannibal tribe or a monkey, for all they knew.

However, to offset his unpopular knowledge of his job, the Governor had an excellent appetite and liked women.

The presence of a dyspeptic and misogynist Governor can be a disaster. I have myself witnessed occasions on which a mere dish of ice-cream, or a highly seasoned sauce, or even an innocent tartlet of caviar has upset the whole life of a colony for a week. As for the catastrophic consequences of a Governor whose sex instinct is suppressed by that sense of inferiority which leads some austere and disciplined men to abstain from women . . . I remember an occasion on which the effect of an over-audacious *décolletage* on an abstemious and highly-strung Catholic

166

Governor was such that a third of his officers asked to be repatriated.

The Italian Government allocated twenty million lire a year to Eritrea. Salaries were absurdly low, but a goat – if you gave the skin back to the goatherd – cost one lira.

The number of military personnel was restricted and the civilian officials were fewer still. But team-work between civilians and Army was perfect. They mixed readily at the Merlo Café; civilians were welcomed with open arms in any officers' mess, and any officer on mission in a remote area knew that he would find a place at table and a bed in any Commissariat or Residency. At the Asmara Club, officers and civilians danced quadrilles together, under the direction of an archivist who had been in Eritrea for thirty years and who spoke in a mixture of French and Benevento dialect which only the initiated could understand.

There still remained a few of those officers – unknown to Italy – who had built the Colony. They were old, and it was easy to make fun of their peculiarities. In general they were not highly cultured and they all belonged to the 'desert fever' class. But they had worked in the Colony when colonial life was a real adventure; they had organised the people without any police force; they had set up the territories without anyone's help, and without any State allocation they had succeeded in creating an administration which still, decades later, constituted the backbone of the Colony. The younger officials, stuffed with doctrine, were nonplussed and ceased to ridicule these old hands when they found, for example, that the plan for the development of Keren would have to follow exactly the lines traced thirty years before by Colonel Fioccardi; when they heard Colonel Talamonti talk of the people in the upland regions; when they realised that if they wanted to know something about the Baria and Cunama peoples they would have to consult Alberto Pollera's volume on the subject, of which in twenty years there had been no reason to alter a line.

Asmara was a small centre, as yet untouched by imperialistic dreams. The natives went barefoot, attended school and got themselves employed in Government offices without expecting to be appointed Ministers of State.

The thousand or so Italian residents were content to pass their time as pleasantly as possible, working, hunting and making love. The extraordinary thing (extraordinary in these days) was that, in spite of the inevitable scandalmongering in a small community, where everyone knew everyone else's business, these few Italians got along very well together. They agreed, naturally, in maligning the Governor, but he was too intelligent and had too much colonial experience to be upset by that; he accepted the sarcasms and criticisms philosophically and with a smile.

In addition to the Italian men, there were also – though they were less numerous – some Italian women.

The British say that east of Suez anything is permissible to a woman. Let me say at once that the Italian women took advantage of this concession with great moderation. Nevertheless, since a complete change of surroundings will in time alter even the shell of a crustacean, it is inevitable that frail white women suddenly transplanted from their native country to Africa will also undergo some change. A colleague of mine, Professor Tedeschi, surgeon of the Mogadishu Hospital, in a monograph called *The Psychology of the Inter-Monsoon Period* (*Psicologia del Tangabili*) which the instinct of self-preservation prevented him from publishing, made a study of these changes from the viewpoint of the scientist and the experienced colonial.

The pretty wife of a diligent archivist or a worthy accountant (the latter for some unknown reason always enjoyed the reputation of being congenital idiots – so that they had applied to them the Neapolitan saying that 'He who is born a fool dies an accountant or a post office official') or of a junior officer, born and brought up in a simple, middle-class home, began, as soon as she set foot on the ship which was to take her to Africa, to glimpse a world which both overawed and fascinated her.

On board, all the men introduced to her kissed her hand – homage to which she had not been previously accustomed but which was *de rigueur* in our colonies. At tea-time ('But, my dear, what a curious and disgusting drink!') an enterprising young lieutenant or a romantic district officer whispered to her that she had the eyes of a *femme fatale;* at sea on a moonlight night a daring young man kissed her under cover of a ventilator in a way that left her stunned and swooning. She inevitably began to believe that romance had come her way and to make insidious comparisons which placed her husband's obesity in a ridiculous light and made repulsive the tufts of hair which stuck out of his nostrils.

In those days there was a mania for nobility in the colonies. When Suez had been passed, the women who had been to her friends *sciura Rosetta, sora Rosa* or *'a gna' Rusidda,* found she was now being called 'Donna Rosa'; by the time she arrived at Assab she was 'Donna Rosanna' to the ship's officer who read d'Annunzio, and when she disembarked at Mogadishu there was every probability that she would have become 'Contessa'.

In the African Residency she was liable to be the only woman among about ten officials: there were never more than half a dozen Italian women in the small centres, and even in the capital the women accompanying their husbands were always so far outnumbered by the men that a young and pretty new arrival inevitably drew down upon herself the acid disapproval of the plainer and older women, and inspired feverish desire on the part of any male compatriot from the age of twenty to sixty.

Can we in all conscience blame the *sora Rosa* or *'a gna' Rusidda* if sometimes in the Barentù Residency or at Hafun she became a little dizzy among so many famished males, who kissed her hand ten times a day, and if she ceased to be wholly responsible for what she did? I myself am infinitely indulgent, but I do not think that even the most severe judges will deny that in such a case there might have been extenuating circumstances.

In the older African colonies there were women who had been born in Africa, daughters of the first colonisers, of officers of the first expeditionary forces: wives, daughters and nieces of pioneers who for decades had devoted themselves to their difficult task.

Kipling, in a justly famous poem, sings his compatriots who, like him, were born in distant possessions of the British crown. Their fathers, says the poet, acquired the territory by legitimate conquest, but the sons possessed it by right of birth and learned by their 'own good pride' to 'praise their comrades' pride'.

We are poor devils without much ambition, and a very short belt will go round our empty stomachs. Nevertheless, although I am no Kipling, I would like on a humbler note to sing the praises of the unknown Italian women born and bred in our colonies.

White or half-caste, they added savour to success when it smiled upon their men, and rallied their spirits when they were felled by adversity. They remained at their husbands' sides – even though those husbands were not 'men of a million acres' but worked their little plots with a faith to which the presence of these women added an aim and purpose. Even today, when everything appears to be destroyed and profaned, it is still these women, staying on in the lost territories, who sustain the courage of those who fight a daily battle for existence, who keep alive the flame which in the motherland has blackened into soot, who pray on the graves of the assassinated.

No one, alas, will write a convivial ode in honour of these women.

★   ★   ★

As soon as I arrived in Eritrea, in 1930, I was appointed Regional Commissioner for the western lowlands, a vast territory populated by seven different races, bounded on the west by the Anglo-Egyptian Sudan and on the south by Ethiopia from which it was separated by the River Setit.

In Agordat, where I had my residence, I occasionally deputised for the regional medical officer, who was a crack motor-driver and sometimes took part in races either in the Colony or in the Sudan. On the whole, however, I was too busy to give as much time as I should have liked to dispensary work.

Nevertheless, it was at that time that I was obliged to run a long way after one patient – a patient I had never seen and who did his best to escape me. When, after a month's search, I finally caught up with him, guided by the traces of his torment and agony, he was dead. But even had I arrived in time I could have done nothing for him.

It was the period immediately preceding the war against Ethiopia which so scandalised the outraged virtue of the European colonial powers. The atmosphere in Africa was already tense and the Abyssinians, as though conscious of the gathering storm, were busy on the frontier, relieving their anxiety by making constant raids into our territory.

On one such raid two of the bandits – slaves who had escaped from their master to seek refuge in Eritrea – had killed a baby elephant in order to take his milk teeth, and had emasculated four children of a Cunama village because the people refused to help them.

With the aid of the armed bands of the Barentù and Tessenei the raiders were chased back over the River Setit and their chief, a half-caste named Zaccharias, was killed. As, however, some of the *shifta* still seemed to be in the frontier zone, I set out to comb the territory from the Setit to Mount Talasuba with the help of about fifteen armed men of the Cunama and Baria territories, four others from the uplands, led by a sergeant and *Shumbāshī* Gabremariam.

It was not till the fourth day that we began to find the traces for which we were seeking. Then, in the direction of Motilè, we came upon the remnants of a recent fire and in the scattered ashes there was the imprint of an Abyssinian sandal. My men, who had begun to doubt the presence of the bandits and were becoming irritated and discontented at being asked to look for something that did not appear to exist, took heart at once like hounds. They spread instinctively in all directions, climbing up the slopes, sliding down rocks, following barely visible tracks under the acacia trees, pushing through grass as high as a man and forcing their way among thorn bushes which the rainy season had adorned with large white waxen flowers. At about midday, Lance-Corporal Taddé Bocú returned in a high state of excitement, stuttering, incoherent, and quite unable to relate what he had just discovered. After an effective bout of cursing on the part of Gabremariam and some show of annoyance on mine, Taddé Bocú managed at last to put some sort of order into his tale.

In private life Taddé Bocú was an elephant tracker and this was a day of days, for he had found the tracks of an elephant.

Gabremariam was beside himself, and only my presence prevented him from jumping at the throat of the idiot who had not yet understood that we were looking for bandits and not elephants.

The unfortunate Lance-Corporal tried by gestures to stem the flow of his superior's curses and to beg leave to speak. Finally he was allowed to explain. He no longer stuttered; his musical Cunama speech flowed easily and was illustrated with such pantomime that the services of an interpreter were almost superfluous.

As the elephant tracker began his story Gabremariam became attentive and from time to time nodded his head, his brows drawn together. At intervals he signed to the man to stop and turned to me to interpret the extraordinary tale.

It seemed that after three hours' march to the east of the Shogotah marshland, Taddé Bocú had come upon the tracks of the Abyssinians. There were four of them, but there was also a fifth man who walked barefoot and whose left foot lacked the third toe. This was clearly Anto Alimatú, known in the Laka-takura as a man who prided himself on being an expert tracker, whereas his fellow countrymen, who knew him well, had nick-named him 'tila acoishah' which, in the language of the Cunama means 'the hunter of fleas'. Three of the Abyssinians, according to Taddé Bocú, were of medium height, and one very tall and heavily built because his foot-marks sank into the earth, the left more than the right. The lance-corporal did not wish to commit himself entirely, but he thought that a wound in the leg or foot made him limp, for alongside the foot-marks there was also the mark of a stick on which the bandit probably leaned, particularly in the difficult places – and under a bush the Cunama had found a strip of blood-stained *fūta* which he proceeded to wave under our noses.

There was more to come, however. At this point, Taddé Bocú again became excited and his speech was once more garbled and confused. The Sergeant lost his temper, and having an almost limitless vocabulary of injurious epithets drawn from Tigrinya, Amharic, Baria, Cunama, Arabic and Italian, he gave full vent to his feelings. Overcome, Taddé Bocú composed himself and continued his story.

While looking for the bandits he had also come upon the tracks of an elephant. He described the beast as though he had seen it: an enormous male elephant travelling alone. There was something strange and hurried about him and he did not seem to be making for any precise destination; he was undoubtedly what the Arabs call *el wāhido*, the solitary one.

When the head bull of a herd becomes too old for love-making and too weak to defend his right of selection; when the females no longer obey him and the young males parade their wives under his nose, he leaves the herd and becomes a hermit. No longer disturbed by passion, he resigns himself to solitude, living on the memory of the halcyon days when his virility was tireless and he passed from one love to another; when libidinous rivals fled at his trumpeting, or fell beneath the blows of his trunk and were trodden into the earth. Taddé Bocú was quite certain that the tracks he had found were those of *el wāhido*. He had had some doubts along the pebbly course of the torrent, but on the sandy river bed the marks were large and clear: in the middle of the bed the sand was disturbed and there were deep holes in which water lay: *el wāhido*, driven by thirst, had pushed his trunk into the sand and by blowing had created little wells into which the water slowly rose. The animal had then mounted the opposite bank and entered the wood, leaving an enormous pile of excrement which reached to Taddé Bocú's thigh.

Interspersed between the traces of the hermit elephant there were the marks of Abyssinian sandals and of the naked foot of the flea hunter who, for once in his life, said Taddé Bocú, was actually tracking an elephant.

At the end of the wood he had found a sycamore tree from which a great piece of bark had recently been torn – the sap was still running. *El wāhido* had evidently rubbed himself violently against the tree and his rough, hard skin which the years had covered with warts and callouses, had acted like a hùge file. Whatever was irritating the animal, it had made him furious, for the whole of the surrounding ground was ploughed up with tusk marks. But there was one curious factor: there were no parallel marks, and the elephant evidently had only one tusk.

Taddé Bocú had followed the tracks of the Abyssinians as far as a stream where they had drunk and eaten; from there, he had made his way back to us as swiftly as possible.

Gabremariam, mollified, patted his shoulder as a sign of approval and, overcoming his natural avarice, rewarded him with a minute piece of chewing tobacco.

Taddé Bocú deserved it and more. In the first place he had traced the bandits. This was, of course, the important thing – but by his other discoveries and deductions he had furnished an explanation of the continued presence of the fugitives who, instead of taking refuge with their companions in Abyssinia, were marching in the opposite direction, getting farther and farther into Eritrean territory.

It was obvious that the four had simply lost their heads when they came upon the tracks of the elephant. All their thoughts were concentrated on killing the animal, on acquiring the right to wear a gold ring in the left ear; already they saw themselves returning in triumph to their country carrying the trophies of the hunt; they saw themselves amid the festive fires, drunk with *tech*, stuffed with savoury sun-dried meat; acclaimed by the songs of the men and the ear-splitting notes of the women.

After their first pursuit of the elephant, they must have lost track of him quite soon and then, disorientated by unfamiliar country and incapable by themselves of tracing the animal again, had entered the first village they came to and asked for a tracker. Anto Alimatú, either with a gun in his ribs or moved by a fatuous desire to show his countrymen that he was not only a hunter of lice, had been persuaded to help them. And now the bandits, with their eyes nailed to the ground, followed the elephant like somnambulists, unconscious of danger, insensible to fatigue, unaware of anything that was not a footprint, a pile of excrement, a sign of the animal which roamed through the country without aim or motive.

We ourselves were between the elephant hunters and the point of the river where the rest of the bandits had crossed – so that the farther they penetrated into the territory away from the frontier, the smaller their chances of escaping alive became.

Within all of us there slumbers the executioner; we would all stone the woman taken in adultery; but although it is prudent to refrain from condemning others unless we ourselves are without sin, on this occasion we felt that we were dealing not with ordinary men but with monsters. We could not forget the horrible wounds between the thighs of the Cunama children, their imploring and terrified faces; we still heard the cries of their mothers and remembered the mute desperation of their fathers. 'They are mad dogs,' Gabremariam had cried as I treated the unfortunate children and, sickened, he had turned aside and vomited.

As far as the men were concerned, the desire to reach the bandits was now coupled with the delight of being on the track of an elephant, and their impatience to punish the criminals was joined to their desire to outdo them in bringing down *el wāhido*. Their enthusiasm therefore knew no bounds.

Towards evening we reached the stream where the raiders had bivouacked and began to go carefully, knowing that we were on the track of armed bandits who at any moment might abandon the chase and retrace their steps in order to reach the frontier. This obliged us to restrain the impatience of the men who would have liked to push on in the uncertain light of the stars. We spent the night near the stream, with sentinels posted on the crests of the hills.

From there, for a couple of days, we pursued our prey blindly. The sand and clay had given place to solid rock which preserved no sign of the passage of the elephant, still less of the bandits. The men became silent and bad-tempered. Scattered in all directions, with their eyes fixed on the ground, they went to and fro like shuttles, scrutinising every inch. They worked round the wells and investigated the bushes, seeking the slightest sign we might take for a guide.

On the morning of the third day, we saw through a wet mist a goatherd on a hillock. He was standing on one leg like a crane, with the foot of the other leg resting against his thigh. He stood on the highest point, keeping an eye on a small herd which was scattered over the hillside searching for tufts of grass among the stones. He had not seen the Abyssinians and when he heard of the raid, of the encounter, of the *shifta* who were following the elephant, he was filled with that vicarious fear which people feel for the misfortunes and dangers which a happy fate has spared them. He was from the Condigherà district and was on his way to the lowland pastures. In the early morning of the previous day he had, in fact, heard the furious trumpeting of an elephant and he pointed out the direction from which the voice of the solitary one had come.

If it was the same animal, it was obvious that *el wāhido* had turned back on his tracks and that we had been travelling in the opposite direction, to the east of his route. Perhaps even the bandits had lost sight of him, although in view of the well-known obstinacy of Abyssinians it was very improbable that they had given up the chase; if we could find the route the elephant had taken we were almost certain, sooner or later, to come across the raiders.

The ground sloped slightly in the direction indicated by the goatherd; it became less stony and as we reached the lower slopes the bush became thicker and the heat increased.

After marching a day and a half, a flank patrol came running towards us waving their rifles: they had found the elephant's tracks again and were wild with delight.

There was no doubt about it: they were the marks of our animal. Taddé Bocú pointed out that the foreward edge of the footprint was deeper and that at each step the animal had thrown back the earth he had disturbed so that between the tracks the ground was scattered with loose soil. This, according to Taddé Bocú, was a sign that *el wāhido* was moving at a great pace in an attempt to escape some imminent danger. The men looked around as though seeking that possible threat, but the landscape stretched as far as the eye could see, empty and bare except for a few scattered shrubs, bushes and low, twisted trees with 'umbrella' tops. Within a radius of a mile and more the ground had been combed with the utmost care, and there had been no sign of the recent presence of leopards, lions or men – the only things from which a solitary, tired old elephant, desiring only peace and quiet, would flee.

We followed the tracks of the beast for many hours. There was no sign of any slackening of his pace: in fact, it seemed to have increased, for the marks in the ground became deeper and deeper and the animal had knocked down an acacia tree which had stood in his path. At a certain point, without any apparent reason, *el wāhido* had taken a right turn and, still at a great pace, made off towards a pool which the rain had formed in a basin. Into this he had thrown himself. The mud was still churned up, and the edges of the pool which had been broken down under the elephant's weight, were covered with the marks of his tusk.

The biggest surprise still awaited us, however.

We had entered an area of doum palms. None of them was very tall because the subterranean water level was deep and the roots had a long way to go to reach it, but a good many of them were about thirty to forty feet high, and the whole area was covered with sucker shoots which reached to our chests. Some of these trees had been knocked down or uprooted and much of the robinia had been torn up by the animal in his anxiety to clear a path. At one point there was an open space about forty yards wide. We halted on the edge of it and gazed in astonishment.

It seemed as though a cyclone had passed over the spot or as though it had been devastated by an earthquake. The ground had been stamped down under the sledgehammer feet and then ploughed up to a depth of six inches by the animal's single tusk. The whole space was strewn with uprooted tree trunks and broken branches, some of which, on the edge of the wood, still hung a yard from the ground attached to the mother tree by a few fibres or by splintered bark. Large acacias had been torn up as though they were asparagus, and where the elephant had planted his feet to get a leverage, the marks of his thick, square nails were clearly visible.

Taddé Bocú and the other Cunama trackers ran over the ground lightly on their bare feet, bent double, seeking some sign which would explain the animal's fury: he was old and solitary and therefore there was no question of the madness which takes young males in the mating season. One of the men called us to the trunk of a palm tree which the beast had uprooted and dragged a distance of some yards. The trunk was covered with some substance which was not sap, nor the urine of the animal, but a dense, fetid and sticky liquid – the purulent matter from a suppurating wound.

The trackers consulted together like clinicians round the bed of a patient. As far as they were concerned the symptoms were so clear that there could be no argument. They exchanged very few words but gathered round a fallen tree, a piece of churned-up ground, and made significant gestures. Finally, Taddé Bocú, the most expert and authoritative among them, pronounced the verdict and they all signified their assent by repeatedly nodding their heads. Gabremariam translated their conclusions for me. *El wāhido* was ill, very ill, perhaps on the point of dying. His fury had been caused by the pain he was suffering. He had a gangrenous wound of considerable dimensions on the right side of his head, between the ear and the root of the missing tusk. The unfortunate beast had been fleeing from the lacerating pain in his head, and had relieved himself, when the pain became unbearable, by destroying everything within reach of his trunk, feet and single tusk. The effort to uproot the palm trunk had opened the wound which had begun to discharge its pus; at that moment the pain had been so intense that the poor beast had rolled on the ground – Taddé Bocú pointed with a stick – and had beaten his head against some bushes which were now flattened.

The Cunama had marshalled the symptoms and seemed to expect a diagnosis from me. I was obliged to disappoint them, however, for, apart from the fact that I had never treated an elephant, it is absolutely essential before making a diagnosis to see the patient – and in this case the patient was a long way off. And so were the bandits.

The delirium of the solitary beast had made such an impression on us that for the moment we had completely forgotten our human quarry. They seemed to have vanished into thin air. There was no trace of them in the wood, the forest or the plain. We began to wonder whether they had thought better of it, given up the chase and returned towards the east, making for the Badumà heights and Ethiopia. However, we were too convinced of their stupidity to believe entirely in such an access of wisdom.

We spent that airless night among the broken branches in the open space made by the pain-wracked elephant.

The shadows were filled with a thousand forms of life. We heard the flutter of night birds' wings, the cries of birds of prey, the clap of closing wings as other birds settled on the trees; the guttural croak of the *ngong*, the giant frog; the stealthy footfall, the trotting, the running of animals on the damp ground; the crackle of shrubs as they brushed past them; the constant drip, drip of the sap from climbing plants; the fall of an over-ripe fruit; the rustle of beasts in the rotting undergrowth, and the low hum of a million insects. The hyena, satiated with its carrion meal, laughed its strident laugh; the grunting of the wild boar in the pasture alternated with the belling of the male antelope and the answering call of the female; monkeys broke into a frenzied chattering as from the distance came the raucous cough of a leopard in search of food. The bush seemed to breathe heavily; the trees rustled, and the mist which rose from the wet ground and descended from the overhanging clouds turned to silver in the light of the moon.

The next morning we set out again, following the traces left by our 'solitary one'. After the crisis, he had gone down to the river to drink but had not crossed it: he had retraced his steps for several miles before deciding to resume his journey to the west – almost as though, feeling that death was upon him, he had wished to return to his native region.

On the rain-soaked ground it was easy to follow the foot-marks; the animal had continued to run, but at a less desperate pace and with more frequent halts.

One evening, beside the elephant tracks we found again the marks of the Abyssinian sandals and of the bare foot with the missing third toe. They had come from the north; by pure chance they had found the traces of the elephant and had immediately set off in pursuit again. The bandits' footprints were fresh from the previous day, and we redoubled our watchfulness and pre-cautions.

Three days later, just before dawn, one of the men of the forward patrol left the path and ran up a slope, following a large lizard. Suddenly, in the silence which precedes the rising of the sun, a shot rang out. The report reverberated through the air as the dawn whitened, and echoed back from the hill on the other side.

Thinking that one of the men – in spite of repeated instructions to the contrary – had fired at some wild game, Gabremariam and I made a dash in the direction of the shot. But firing was already becoming general: seeing their comrade fall, the whole patrol had opened fire and the shouts of our men announced that we had finally caught up with the bandits.

The Sergeant disappeared, then reappeared suddenly, followed by three men with rifles at the ready. He ran, bent double, almost on all fours, jumping like a whiskered gnome from one shrub to another, using the cover of every rise and fall in the ground to get to where he could take the bandits in the rear. The bandits, having been under the impression that they had shot an isolated soldier on his way home, had not yet recovered from their surprise at finding themselves in the presence of an armed patrol.

As we passed the dead Askari – who lay spreadeagled on his back, his face in a pool of blood round which the flies were already beginning to buzz – I saw one of the Abyssinians roll down the hillside, hit the trunk of a tree, bounce, and then lie still in the attitude of a marionette when its strings have been slackened.

By the time we reached the crest of the hill it was all over and Gabremariam was wiping his bayonet with a handful of grass. Not a quarter of an hour had passed since the first shot was heard. The four corpses of the *shifta* laid out before us confirmed Taddé Bocú's deductions: three were of medium stature and the third – a colossus – had a great wound in the calf of his left leg. The only missing element was the hunter of fleas, although very recent footmarks proved that he too had been present on the hill.

The earth was already back in the Askari's grave, and the Cunama death chant still hung suspended on the relatively fresh air, when we heard a smothered groan, a cavernous and indistinct shout. We looked round and listened: the voice was near at hand but we could see no place from which it could possibly come.

The Cunama and Baria, awed by the presence of the bodies, and by the smell of blood which still enveloped us, began at once to imagine the presence of the troubled spirits of the unburied dead. Gripping their rifles with trembling hands, they stared about them with wide-open eyes, expecting the appearance of ghosts and phantoms.

The groans and shouts were repeated, louder and longer. This time there was no doubt about it: the voice came from the baobab tree behind us. The men struck the trunk with their rifle butts and the tree spoke again. But this time its voice was feeble and subdued and was greeted with hilarious laughter. For the men had recognised the tremulous accents of Anto Alimatú, the hunter of fleas.

It seemed that at the first shot, terrified and without knowing what he was doing, the unfortunate creature had shinned up a tree; in his hurry he had missed his footing and fallen head first into the hollow trunk. When we mounted the hill and he heard the speech of his own people he realised that the bandits had been annihilated and he had then tried to get out of his prison. But the more he struggled the deeper he wedged himself, until he was held by the tree as in a vice.

Two of his fellow countrymen climbed up the baobab and

pulled him out by the feet, much to everyone's amusement. They let him down like a doll into the arms of the other men, who received him with all kinds of capers.

He was exhausted and covered with scratches and bruises. The Abyssinians had given him nothing to eat because their few provisions were hardly sufficient for themselves; for about twenty days he had lived on nothing but berries, fungi, and doum palm nuts. When he lost track of the elephant the Abyssinians beat him until they drew blood, accusing him of doing it on purpose; when he was tired and slowed down, or when he left the path to look for something edible, they pricked his buttocks with their knives, and at night they tied him by the hands and feet so that he could not run away.

'Ha! Aren't you better off hunting fleas?' asked Tallù Ellana, the philosopher of the group. 'You don't fall into bad company; you sit down to it and all you need is a finger with some spit on it and you can catch as many as you like.'

Anto Alimatú, his mouth full, nodded assent.

The men were delighted to have the hunter of fleas with them: he served as a target for all their pleasantries. 'Now that we have Anto Alimatú among us *el wāhido's* number is up: he is already in our hands, by God's grace.'

In fact, it was the truth. From the moment when Anto Alimatú joined the band the traces of the elephant became fresher and fresher; we found branches he had broken which were still running with sap; scattered leaves and twigs which had not had time to wither; the matter from his wound was still dripping from the trunks on which he had rubbed himself. One evening, as dusk and a veil of rain descended upon the plain, we heard in the distance – or thought we heard – a low and mournful trumpeting. Only those who, in the religious silence of the short, tropical twilight, have heard that voice calling across the primitive wilderness, will understand what I felt at that moment.

We passed the night in the shelter of a crag behind a clump of doum palms. The rain had ceased, but over our heads the sky was leaden, and away in the distance, to the east, the horizon was lit from time to time by flashes of lightning.

I do not know how long I had been sleeping. I was dreaming that I was at the Tiberius baths near the Marina Grande at Capri; I was cushioned on the warm water of the bathing-pool, under a night sky. Suddenly I was awakened by a hand violently shaking my shoulder. It was Gabremariam. 'A flood, a flood!' he cried. 'Quick! We shall drown! Hurry!' He dragged me by the wrist, still half asleep, up the slope to the top of the crag. The continuous roar of thunder filled the air so that we had to shout to make ourselves heard. We called to the men and became anxious when their reply was slow – but they all arrived, stunned and stupid, with their cartridge pouches tied round their heads, and their sandals hanging round their necks. Anto Alimatú was also present, only half awake and shivering, wrapped in a blanket.

Not a drop of rain fell however, and the sky was clear, yet below us, half hidden in the night, lay a landscape we no longer recognised. Where the bush had been there was now a sheet of water as far as the eye could see – only the heads of the doum palms and the 'umbrella' tops of the robinias emerged, like water plants. Above the flood floated a milky mist which shone like mother-of-pearl where the moonlight touched it. In this dead, submerged world only sound survived. The violent thunder which had wakened us now sank to a dull rumble which seemed to rise from the bowels of the earth.

The crest on which we had taken refuge was narrow and not very long and we crowded together in the limited space, seated on the ground with our knees drawn up under our chins, our arms round our legs, gazing at the spectacle before us and waiting for the dawn.

'O Anto Alimatú, wouldn't you like to swim out and find *el wāhido?*' asked one of the men. But no one was in a laughing mood. In fact, bad humour was ready to explode on the slightest pretext and when Gabremariam found that in the confusion of the sudden awakening no one had thought to save the flour, butter, salt or the packet of *berberé;* that there was nothing left from the flood but two days' bread ration, he let loose an astounding stream of invective.

Suddenly, the sun appeared on the horizon, dissolving the mist and making our wet clothes steam.

The water was not as high or as extensive as we had thought under the misleading light of the moon – or else it had had time to subside. The current however – perhaps because we could now see as well as hear it – seemed stronger. Branches and splintered trunks went spinning by, catching themselves in the tops of palm trees which bent to the force of the waters. Corpses of antelopes, gazelles, hyenas and wild boars swept past us, and at one moment the entire roof of a *tukul* floated by, revolving slowly, together with other relics that told their story of destruction and death. There were rags, fragments of rush fences, battered native beds, planks, tubs, a cradle, and a cow on its back, its stiff legs stretched towards heaven and with a kind of marabou perched on its monstrously swollen belly. Later, in the glittering reflection of the sun, we saw in the distance an object we first thought must be the trunk of a tree but as it floated past into the shade of a clump of palms we saw that it was a human corpse.

The flood had caught us unawares in the space of minutes; but it was two days before the bush re-emerged and began to dry itself in the sun. The passage of the waters had swept away the soil and scraped the ground like a gigantic rake: shrubs and bushes, combed by the flood, were bent down to the ground. All footmarks had been washed away and Taddé Bocú and the other trackers looked out disconsolately over the vast area from which every trace had been removed as with a sponge.

Common sense suggested that it would be best to continue in the direction in which we were travelling before the flood had surprised us, but no one could know whether the elephant had changed his course. It might be supposed that he would have moved on to the hills, but it was impossible to decide which direction he would then have taken in his effort to flee the torment he carried with him.

If we were perplexed concerning the movements of *el wāhido*, however, we were still more worried by the problem of food. The flood had decimated the animals in the river area and the rest must have fled to higher ground. In the hope, therefore, of again picking up the tracks of the elephant and of finding some game we might eat, we descended from our crag and began to cross the plain which separated us from the hills.

It was only a few miles, but we took one and a half days to cross it. At every step we went in up to our knees. We walked barefoot so that the mud would cling less, but time and again we had to help each other out of the mire. When, at long last, the ground began to rise and we felt solid earth under our feet again our relief was so great that for a moment we forgot our weariness and hunger.

The ground on the hillside was covered with the tracks of animals, chiefly the heart-shaped marks of the gazelles, accompanied by their excrement which smells of violets. We noted also traces of the ariel, of the *aburuf*, and the horned, deep marks of the *kudu*. But so far there was no sign of the elephant.

We came into the wooded zone, and Gabremariam by a stroke of luck brought down an antelope which suddenly appeared between two trees. We roasted the flesh on an open fire and ate it. Without seasoning of any kind it was nauseating and insipid. At every mouthful Gabremariam renewed his curses on the lazy blackguards, sons of prostitutes, etc., who had been so scared of a little water that they had let our provisions be swept away.

With the flood, the rainy season had had its final fling; now, at the end of September, the good weather settled in and we marched towards the west under a clear sky in which, at night, the stars hung just above our heads.

One day, as we were winding in single file among the spiky bushes, one of the men noticed a small bird and followed it to a tree. It was a large tree like all the others and we should have passed it by without notice, but the bird knew better, and began to knock on the trunk with its beak. Suddenly, a swarm of bees emerged from a gap between two branches and spread out like a shower of golden sparks. The men set to work with their hatchets and soon the trunk lay open like a book, full of dripping honeycomb.

We had a memorable feast. Satiated and disgusted with un-
salted roast meat, we sucked the last drop out of the comb and
then chewed it until all taste of honey had disappeared. It was
a full-flavoured honey with the acrid aroma of forest flowers,
and we fed on it for two days.

In the meantime, Fate had decided to compensate Anto
Alimatú for all the humiliations he had suffered.

The luckless hunter of fleas, although despised by his companions as a poor tracker, was an extremely good shot and
though armed only with an old shot-gun he brought down game
at an incredible range. One day, as he ran down a slope after a
bustard which, wounded in flight, was flapping its way through
the bushes, he suddenly came upon the tracks of el wāhido. It
seemed too good to be true, and he began shouting and dancing
round the tracks, singing a song of triumph.

Anto Alimatú forgot the bustard: the spirits had granted him
a sign of their favour. He, Anto Alimatú, had found the tracks
of the elephant; he was no longer a tracker of fleas; he alone,
Anto Alimatú of Bioccomà in the Lakatakura, had found the
traces of the elephant while the famous trackers, blind and stupid
like owls in the daylight, wandered about the forest expecting
elephants to fall into their hands like doum palm nuts; he, Anto
Alimatú, had discovered the tracks of the solitary elephant.

He scampered back up the slope like a goat and when he
shouted his news to us he was greeted by a chorus of ridicule
and abuse. In the end he had to be believed and we all climbed
down the hillside, grabbing at bushes to keep ourselves from
falling. And there we too found the unmistakable footprints in
the soft earth.

Taddé Bocú walked round them, furious at not being able to
deny the claim of the hunter of fleas. Bending over the marks,
he examined them minutely and touched them with his finger
to test the consistency of the earth and thus decide how long
ago el wāhido had passed that way. Every now and again he
raised his eyes, shook his head and looked with annoyance at
Anto Alimatú who, radiant and puffed out with self-importance,
pretended not to be aware of his presence.

The beast had evidently continued to march towards the west, but instead of going up on to the crest of the hills as we had done, he had gone only half way up – probably because the young plants and shoots for which he had a weakness were more plentiful there. He had been going at a much slower pace, but a tree uprooted here and there spoke of his moments of frenzy: the deep marks of his tusk were visible on the roots of a baobab tree which he had evidently tried to uproot.

Our hunger and weariness were dissipated at once and we stopped shooting at other game so as not to alarm the elephant. Made more venturesome by the undisturbed silence, animals which had certainly never seen hunters before flocked across our path, gazed at us with soft, surprised eyes and followed us like domestic animals. We seemed to be crossing a fairy-tale country in the company of flocks of gazelles, droves of wild boar, and herds of roan antelopes which trotted and galloped beside us through the trees; on the cliff we saw the twisted horns of the great *kudu;* the cynocephalus families came down to drink, and the dawn resounded with the cries of enamoured ariels.

In this strange company, we followed the last tracks of the elephant, speaking little among ourselves but conscious of a curious excitement and some sadness. It had been a long hunt and we had come a long way, our days and nights continuously dominated by the presence of this great beast, this solitary one who, always just out of sight, led us remorselessly with him along his path of torment. We had the feeling now that the last hours of the chase were upon us.

A few days later, as dawn broke clear and transparent as crystal along the edge of the hills, we saw the vultures circling in the sky, and instinctively knew that our search was over.

All day we followed the tracks, and in the late afternoon we arrived at a glen half-hidden among trees from which the carrion-eaters rose heavily at our approach.

And there, on his side against an ancient sycamore tree, his one tusk turned like a scimitar towards the heavens, lay the imposing mass of the solitary one. We made a circle round him and gazed in silence.

He had led us so far, had given us so much trouble, and now there he was, inert and huge as a rock. One wide glazed eye, staring from a labyrinth of furrows, pouches and wrinkles, seemed to mock at us. The other was closed by a great purulent blister and from its socket a thick stream of matter trickled down into the gangrenous cavity which had opened in the jaw and which ran from the root of the missing tusk almost up to the temple. It was a hideous wound and the stench was intolerable.

The men were sad, and their disappointment was plain to see: no one's ears would be adorned with a gold ring to celebrate the death of this elephant; there would be no village festivities and no songs to welcome home the victors. We had tracked and found him, but there was no rejoicing in it.

It was late, and we shook ourselves. As we set about removing his one remaining tusk a monkey's cry broke the silence of the valley.

★ ★ ★

That was not quite the end of the journey, however. We were heading for home, bearing the great tusk of the solitary one between us, and had already come down into the flat country, when we saw across the *dhurra* fields the cone-shaped roofs of the village of Sabatú.

We turned our steps towards it and were no more than a hundred yards away when I felt the onset of one of those sudden, prostrating attacks of malaria to which I was by this time quite accustomed. My knees turned to water so that I could hardly raise my feet from the ground; in my ears a slight buzzing, like the noise of a mosquito, grew in a few moments to a deafening roar; an appalling nausea overtook me and I shivered with cold; I seemed to be falling through a whirl of scintillating sparks into utter blackness. I had just time to call to Gabremariam before I lost consciousness.

When I came to I was lying on a native bed in a darkened *tukul*, naked and running with sweat. I tried to remember, to collect my thoughts, but they escaped me like birds flying from a broken cage: I had not the slightest idea where I was. At a

A Dankali shepherd from Eritrea

The end of the chase

hand's breadth from my face a young negress looked at me with eyes the colour of flax flowers. I assumed that I must still be delirious and that it was the fever which made me see negresses with blue eyes.

But, in fact, the fever had passed. The negress put an arm under my head and tried to lift me so that I could drink from the bowl of frothy milk held in her other hand. I had now become accustomed to the semi-darkness and could see her better. She was naked and her breasts were like polished mahogany and so firm that they were hardly flattened when, in her effort to hold me up, they were pressed against my chest. The *angareb* on which I was lying was too high, and the arm, although robust, could not support a fever-weakened body weighing over twelve stone. The girl therefore raised herself on tiptoe and, placing a knee on the frame of the bed, managed to pull me up. When I was at last in a sitting position I noticed that she was not altogether naked, for round her hips she wore a string of doum palm nuts fastened at the crucial point by a metal disc on which was written in clear print: 'CORNERI & BOGLIASCO, CREMONA — YELLOW PEACH JAM OF THE FINEST QUALITY'.

I fell back on the bed in a paroxysm of laughter. The girl laughed with me without knowing the cause of my amusement and busied herself about the bed, pleased to see that I was better.

Attracted by the laughter, other people entered the *tukul*, including an old woman, two other young women, an elderly man and a few children. A goat also joined the party, together with a couple of sheep — one of which was accompanied by a lamb which looked as if it were made of whipped cream.

The new arrivals crowded round my bed, smiling and showing their wonderful teeth and besieging me with the formal Cunama questions: 'Are you well?' 'Is your body well? Is it at peace?' 'Is your land happy?'

To all these questions the conventional reply is one which is of itself sufficient evidence of the gentle nature of these people: 'Everything is happy, everything is milk.' I began to feel my

G

strength returning and my brain clearing; in fact, as far as I was concerned 'everything was milk'.

But my knowledge of the Cunama tongue went no further than the formal greetings and a little invective – not a very useful vocabulary for sustained conversation, so sitting on the bed I could only reply by nods and smiles to the women, old men and children who crowded around me.

My gentle nurse, proud of my quick recovery, helped me to dress. And it was quite true – her eyes were blue, and they gave an infantile candour to her coal-black face with its flat nose and heavy, prominent lips which were perpetually parted in a smile, showing her dazzling white teeth.

As for the 'peach jam' decoration, it may have been a memento. For during the Abyssinian war, this Cunuma girl, whose name was Mula Mulidi, was the lover of a good-looking Milanese who made gaseous drinks and delivered them by motor-truck to our troops stationed on the Amha Bircutan. This young man, who did not allow the manufacture of aerated drinks to shrivel his heart up, had composed a poem in honour of his Dulcinea which he used to sing to his own guitar accompaniment. I can only remember one verse:

> *Why do you laugh, Mula Mulidi,*
> *Negress with eyes of blue,*
> *There's no one like you, Mula Mulidi,*
> *From Gurma to Cullucu.*

They are not, of course, lines which Petrarch would have written to Laura and they will probably never be found in any anthology: I only quote them to prove my story about the blue-eyed Cunama woman who attended to my needs with so much charity in the village of Sabatú, a little place in the Lakatakura.

By the time I had finished dressing, under the smiling eyes of the villagers, an awful hunger invaded me and I hailed with joy the arrival of Gabremariam who had brought with him a bustard braised in a red pepper sauce in which mysterious aromatic herbs had been slowly dissolved.

I fell upon it, and when I had finished a man from the small hill-post of Antoré arrived to inform me that a lorry would pick us up on the following day and take us all back to Barentú and Agordat.

Our adventure was at an end. So many risks, so much effort, so much water and such a high fever in order to kill four malefactors, take the tusk from a half-putrefied elephant, and make the acquaintance of a negress with china-blue eyes.

And of that man-and-elephant hunt nothing remains now but the great tusk of *el wāhido* which stands on a shelf in my library, pointing heavenward.

Chapter Six

THE SHADOW MERCHANT AND THE
EMPRESS

I T was at Massawa in Eritrea that I first made the acquaintance
of Bughesha *el keddāb,* one of the strangest characters I have
ever known, a mythomaniac of unusual powers of persuasion
and a master trickster even for the Near East. At that time he
was a small boy, but age in those parts is calculated approxi-
mately, and Bughesha's mother informed me that the boy's brain
was unlike that of other children owing to the shock she received
just before his birth when the powder factory at Otumlo
blew up.

I had visited his father, the honest old cobbler, Yàcub ben
Daud, and found him swollen like a bladder of lard, with
nephritis and heart disease. He was a meek creature who accepted
his fate without question, but even he spoke to me with concern
of this odd child of his. When the mother accompanied me to
the door of the house she pointed down the street to a boy who
was running about under the dim and only lamp, waving a rag
in his hand.

'That's my son – chasing moths,' said the woman, shaking her
head in a disconsolate manner.

But Bughesha was not trying to catch moths at all; he was
merely chasing their shadows, which he aimed at with the rag
as they danced on the wall. Each time he struck the wall the
moths disappeared into the night, their shadows with them. The
boy watched them go and waited happily, knowing that the
lamp would soon draw them back again.

His face was thin and on his head he wore a round, white cap.
He had a low and convex forehead, a short nose with wide
nostrils and a soft, full mouth, as red as if it were painted; his
eyes were dark and velvety and shone with the liquid brilliance
seen sometimes in the eyes of antelopes and of saints; the face
had a certain indefinable animal beauty.

192

On hearing his name called, he reluctantly interrupted his game and came towards us, dragging his feet in the dust. He kept his chin on his chest and sucked his under-lip, simulating a shyness which was obviously non-existent. His mother told me in a tearful voice what a burden this strange son was to her. Why did he chase moth shadows? No other boy of his age wasted time in such a foolish way.

'I take them to the sultans,' said the boy.

He spoke, not with a boy's high-pitched voice, but in a deep tone quite out of keeping with his appearance.

The mother sighed and asked him where he had ever seen a sultan; where were these sultans except in his imagination?

'You don't know them, but I do,' said the boy.

I asked him how much he charged for moth shadows, and he looked up at me with a conspiratorial smile which seemed to accept me as someone who could understand his games. He did not sell shadows, he said; he gave them away. But one day he would be vizier; he would have horses harnessed with gold and shod with silver.

The mother held her head in her hands. 'You hear him? You hear him? Already everyone calls him *el keddāb*, the liar, may God have mercy on him.'

A few months later I again met Bughesha, but on this occasion he was not chasing shadows. It was evening and he stopped me in the Moslem quarter of the city and asked me if I wanted a Sudanese girl. As he made the offer he placed his index finger in his cheek to signify that the goods he offered were of first quality.

I gave him a cigarette and asked him if, by acting as procurer, he expected to become vizier more quickly. Offended, he replied that he had never acted as procurer and that, in fact, the Sudanese girl did not exist: he had invented her in order to have the pleasure of speaking to me to tell me that his father, thanks to my treatment, was cured; that he had taken my medicine, had urinated for six hours without stopping, had flooded the whole street and had then gone off for a walk; at present he was in Port Sudan, business was good and he sent home a lot of money.

I knew very well that his father was still chained to his bed even though his kidneys had begun to function again and the œdema had decreased – but I wanted to lead the boy on, so, after having expressed my satisfaction at the restored health of his father, I asked him what he was doing here in such a remote part of the city.

He confided to me with an air of great mystery that, in association with an Armenian friend, he managed a café which was frequented by the most beautiful girls in Massawa and at which one could get the best '*mastica*' (a brandy made from leaves of the mastic tree) in the whole of the Red Sea. He gave me a knowing wink and proposed that I should accompany him to this haunt of delight.

The *fonduq*, which boasted the high-sounding name of 'The Acropolis', was at the end of a sordid cul-de-sac. The impression made by the brothel-like red lamp which hung in the doorway was accentuated by the spectacle presented in the three rooms where about twenty men and a dozen or so women were drinking and smoking, huddled on mats or seated on low, rickety divans which ran round the walls. There were Eritrean Arabs, Arabs from the Negd and from Yemen, pilots of boats that plied across the Red Sea, a *zaptivé* in civilian clothes, a few Greek tradesmen, three gloomy Copts, and two or three negroes.

The women were prostitutes of all ages: veterans emaciated with the years and with disease; florid *sharmoutas* from the coast and from the uplands; young recruits flaunting their beauty in full bloom.

I sat down in a corner at a table about six inches high. The Armenian proprietor, a pot-bellied man as smooth as a eunuch, approached me and I ordered a coffee flavoured with orange-flower. As I drank it, the Armenian's wife – a small woman with fine eyes, a letter-box mouth and a nose like a toucan's beak – led three musicians into the room: a blind man who scraped the *rebāb*, a pipe-player, and a boy who banged on the tambour. The boy was evidently a friend of Bughesha's for the two went into a corner to talk until the music began; Bughesha then slid quietly out of the establishment.

The proprietor, seeing that I was alone, came to talk to me, and having mentioned the drought and the fact that business went from bad to worse, he asked me how I came to know Bughesha. I told him of the father's illness and of my meeting with the boy in the street outside his house.

'Ah – now I understand,' said the landlord. 'It seemed impossible, and my wife also say "but, Mother of God, it cannot be".'

He spoke a peculiar Italian interspersed with French and with the accent of a conjuror in a variety theatre. His name was Dorkoyan, and when I told him that Bughesha had informed me that he was his associate and part-owner of the café, he went purple in the face and put two fingers inside his collar to prevent himself from choking.

'Everyone know that accursed boy world's biggest liar. If he not being with you, he have not enter my door. Ah no! Or I skin his behind, by God!' And sweating with indignation, he called his wife to tell her of this latest outrage.

The players were now doing their best to drown one of the girls who had begun to sing out of tune in a high, ear-splitting voice. Seeing that conversation was impossible in that din, I was led into what Madame Dorkoyan called her boudoir, which was, in fact, a little hole between the lavatory and the storeroom, full of a pungent odour of sewers. Four armchairs were set round a table under the dim light of a lamp.

Here, husband and wife told me of the shameful exploits of Bughesha, interrupting each other, shouting each other down, contradicting and embroidering each other's stories. He was capable of anything, this diabolical boy. He was the friend, confidant and procurer of every prostitute in Massawa; he amused himself by making trouble between these unfortunate creatures and their clients, protectors and exploiters; he repeated gossip and calumnies, altered and added to conversations he had overheard, or invented others – delighted when he managed to provoke a quarrel or a fight. He was hand-in-glove with all the smugglers and thieves of the port; he associated with all the fake beggars with which Taulud pullulated; he was the go-between of every scoundrel in the city. Everyone knew he was a bad lot – but at the same time no one could resist his charm.

A week ago, it seemed, he had sold a packet of cocaine to a Yemenite, saying that he distributed it on behalf of Dorkoyan, and the next day the Arab had rushed into the café shouting like a maniac and demanding his money back because he had discovered that the powder was bicarbonate of soda. And after that, the miscreant had had the audacity to return to the café under my protection!

Then, while Madame Dorkoyan, confused and simulating disgust, whispered to me that the accursed boy was often seen with Greeks who were well known to be pederasts, the door of the café flew open and Fatma, a Somali woman, burst in, followed by Bughesha.

Fatma was still a very fine woman, the colour of milk chocolate. Two years before I had treated her for a skin disease, caused by eating shellfish, from which she had been suffering for many months. Wherever she might be, Fatma had to be noticed; she was only happy when she was the centre of attention and her entrance had to be theatrical, even when it was merely into a miserable Armenian café.

She burst in boisterously with a rustle of silk skirts, a clatter of necklaces and a jingling of bracelets, ear-rings, bangles and armillæ. Her face, surrounded by a gold-spangled veil, expressed delight, surprise and disgust all at the same time. The players and the singer ceased as she entered, and her voice rang through the rooms so that everyone in 'The Acropolis' might know how she, Fatma, with her sensitive nature, was feeling.

In the first place, she was pleased to see me: I was her father, her benefactor, and she invoked Allah's protection for me; I had cured her of the disease which had been eating her skin. She held me in her embrace but addressed her remarks to the four corners of the café as though she were haranguing a vast crowd.

I was in Massawa and no one had told her; I came there every evening to drink 'mastica' and no one had informed her. At this point she shot a glance at Dorkoyan and raised her voice still higher. No one had told her, she said, because Massawa was full of poisonous snakes, of miserable creatures who did not wish her to meet her father, her healer. There were many scoundrels but, fortunately, there were also still a few of God's creatures, a few guileless souls – and she threw a tender look in the direction of Bughesha who stood, humble and self-effacing, in the shadow of a corner, his shoulders against the wall.

She left me and turned to the café proprietor who gazed at her in astonishment and alarm. She shook her fists in his face, saying, 'You go around saying that I am a dirty, foreign prostitute and that the *tebīb* cannot be seen with such filth. I know – the boy has told me everything. You dog! This man touched me when my skin was falling from my body, when I smelt like your breath and when even the negroes who wash the offal at the slaughterhouse would not come near me. Do you understand? Listen, tar face: watch out for your horns and do not slander me, if you value your health. And what's more – stop beating this boy to death when he refuses to go to bed with you.'

While the Armenian furiously denied her accusations, but more by gesture than by word because he was speechless, the woman grabbed Bughesha by the shoulder, pushed him into the middle of the room, turned him round and lifted his shirt to show us the violet, blood-stained weals from two whip strokes (probably self-inflicted) which lay across his back.

'Do you see that, you dog?' she thundered.

She came back to me and embraced me again, assuring me that she would come and see me next day, and then swept out noisily, dragging the little innocent after her and leaving an overpowering wave of perfume behind.

Dorkoyan, overcome by so many insults, had collapsed panting into an armchair; he kept raising his hands to heaven and calling upon God and the blessed Armenian martyrs, while Madame Dorkoyan fussed around him shrieking like a goose that is being plucked.

About a year after that meeting in 'The Acropolis', Bughesha disappeared from Massawa.

Dorkoyan, who was in any case prejudiced, assured me that Bughesha had left with his lover, the pilot of a *sambūq*. Fatma, weeping, told me that the little dear had been kidnapped on account of his beauty, taken to Arabia and sold as a slave. Much later, when I came across him again, Bughesha himself explained that he had left because the Imam of Yemen had sent for him; that he had travelled on a *dhow* made of cedar wood and that he had held a series of high offices at the court of San'a.

It is much more probable that the shadow merchant, chasing the shades of his own fantasy, moved by his irresistible desire for adventure – and possibly in order to avoid a deserved beating – cadged a free passage by telling God knows what kind of story to a *nakuda* who did not know him, or who liked the company of boys with smooth skins.

In any case, the fact is that towards the end of spring this young master of lies was in the Hodeida market, in Southern Arabia. The noisy crowd was composed entirely of men because it is the puritanical custom of the Zaydite sect, which predominates in the Yemen, to keep its women in strict seclusion.

Bughesha had been lounging about the market for a couple of hours when a bearded, elderly man of severe aspect held out to him a bundle and basket and ordered him to follow him. The cobbler's son obeyed, trotting along behind the austere beard through a maze of alleys and side streets. The elderly man stopped at a door in a windowless wall and took the bundle and basket from the boy. Only then did he observe the foreign appearance of his porter, and imprudently asked who he was and whence he came. Bughesha told him that he was the son of a Koran reader who taught in the Moslem schools of Eritrea; that his mother had died three years ago and that his father had immediately contracted another marriage with a girl from the uplands. His young stepmother had never liked him, and since she had given birth to a son of her own she had persecuted him unmercifully in order to force him to leave home and exclude him from his inheritance in favour of her own son; she used her beauty to influence his father against him so that his life had become unbearable. Finally, she had accused him of stealing some gold coins which the learned man his father kept in a box; his father had beaten him so unmercifully that he had been for a month in the Massawa hospital, and from there – in order not to return home – he had embarked on the first *dhow* leaving the port and had arrived at Hodeida.

The merchant of shadows recounted this story without the slightest hesitation, frankly, with his limpid and ingenuous eyes fixed on those of the Yemenite; his story ended, he dropped his eyes to the tips of his sandals and stood, timid and modest, with his hands clasped in front of him.

The pious man shook his head thoughtfully and looked at this son of a man of letters. 'Only God is merciful,' he muttered. How was this stranger, this boy, this poor defenceless orphan, to live among the dangers of an unknown city? God be praised: certainly in his present condition he would agree to act as servant without pay, contenting himself with food and lodging. The old man sighed deeply, opened the door and entered, pushing the son of the Koran reader before him.

When Bughesha was seen in the market each morning with the old woman who was servant to an important local official, Si Abdalla el Yèmeni, and when it was learnt that he was not paid and that he was fed on no more than a couple of onions, everyone admitted that once again old Abdalla had done himself a good turn. But gossip circulates quickly in small centres and is embroidered *en route*, and in a short time Bughesha had become the cousin of Sidi Morghani, the son of the *Cādī* of Port Sudan, as well as the nephew of the Sherifa of Massawa.

The pious and learned Abdalla – an austere man – was unpopular, and so everyone sympathised with the boy who was so humiliated and who, perhaps, had the Prophet's blood in his veins.

In truth, Bughesha did not feel himself at all humiliated, but no one in Hodeida could possibly imagine how unutterably bored he was.

He had been born and brought up in a world of thieves, receivers, procurers, beggars fake and real, smugglers, prostitutes, brothel proprietors and tricksters who lived a colourful life which their many difficulties failed to overshadow; where, in spite of bitter rivalries and savage disputes, each was ready to help the other out; a world in which the days of plenty were enjoyed to the full and where in the lean times you fell back on the mercy of God and disappeared quietly without complaint when difficulties became insuperable.

Upon that strange world and its picturesque characters the merchant of shadows had unconsciously fed his fertile imagination, and now the memory of that kaleidoscopic life made the austerity of Hodeida unbearable. There were no brothels; smoking was prohibited; dancing and singing were not allowed; music – even the gramophone – was considered an invention of the devil. The air of such a virtuous city did not agree with him, and he felt himself suffocating.

Nor was the atmosphere of the house in which he lived less oppressive. Bazarà, the Massawa pearl merchant, told me about Si Abdalla whom he knew well through doing business with him. He was a great gentleman, said Bazarà, but close-fisted to a degree and as boring as a rainy day. He was a misogynist and detested the salacious stories which usually circulate among men: even a faintly licentious word provoked his anger. Bazarà attributed his capacity for being shocked and his gloomy outlook on life to the sect to which the pious man belonged, and also to his palsied senses. It was true he had married late in life, but the pearl merchant was certain he had taken the step out of respect for the Koranic law and not in order to satisfy the remnants of a virility which must in any case have petered out very early.

When he heard that Bughesha was in Si Abdalla's house, Bazarà laughed until he cried.

Si Abdalla discovered that the boy knew his letters and could put them together and so – glad to do a good work which cost him nothing – he began to dictate to him so that he might learn to write quickly, and to teach him arithmetic. But the good work did not stop there: Bughesha was obliged at the same time to listen to interminable discourses on the moral life, on the spirit of self-denial and on the subjugation of fleshly desires, until the unfortunate boy, huddled on his mat, consigned the worthy man to a most inglorious end and swallowed continual yawns.

Finally Si Abdalla would decide to look for his sandals in order to return to his office and, stretching himself like a cat, Bughesha would go in search of the old servant who was by now his staunch ally.

The old woman was grateful to him because he helped her in the kitchen, accompanied her to the market, beat the carpets, washed the floor and tidied those rooms he was allowed to enter. She herself attended to the two rooms in which the master's two wives lived, and from which the boy, of course, was excluded. She admired his intelligence and ready wit, and treated him with a certain consideration, for she too, without being aware of it, had fallen under his spell.

In the evening, when Si Abdalla returned home, he drank a basin of sour milk, recited the evening prayers and then everyone went to bed. But the boy's sleep was light – and he was desperately bored.

Not two weeks after his entry into the austere household of Abdalla el Yèmeni, Bughesha discovered that by removing a grating on the ground floor he could slip out into the street unseen. Bughesha found, however, that even this nightly breakout was not worth the trouble. At night the city was empty: there was not so much as a dog in the streets; not a voice to be heard from the closed houses; no drunkard's brawling broke the awesome silence. Alas, there were none of those cafés which animate a whole district, full of the same people every night and noisy with women's laughter and the sound of singing.

However, although the streets of a virtuous city may be silent and uninteresting at night, there is no knowing what is going on behind the closed shutters.

One morning the old woman awoke to find herself crippled with rheumatism and almost unable to move. In spite of pain and high fever she dragged herself to the women's rooms, but was obliged to return quickly to her bed. In the meantime she was thinking: it seemed to her that a child could perfectly well be allowed to put the prohibited rooms in order. She knew Si Abdalla well and had no affection for him. The fever gave her courage and she decided that it was not a case where authorisation should be requested from a man who attached fanatical importance to the observation of the letter of the law. When the master left for his office, therefore, she grasped Bughesha by the hand and, stopping at each step on account of the pain, took him to the upper floor.

No doubt the servant had already mentioned the son of the Koran reader to the two secluded women, but they must have been more than a little surprised when Bughesha began to talk of countries beyond the sea, of the strange world in which he had grown up, of the extraordinary things that had happened to him. He, of course, transformed reality beyond recognition and abandoned himself with enthusiasm to his inventive genius so that his story would certainly have become more and more highly coloured as the amazement and curiosity of his listeners increased.

No one will ever know the exact effect which Bughesha's lurid fantastications had upon the two women – one a freed slave, the other a Jewess from Taiz. Nor, unfortunately, do we know whether what happened later was due to the excitement provoked by Bughesha's stories or to the initiative of the shadow merchant himself. There is no doubt, however, that from the time when he was first allowed into the women's quarters by the old woman he had many opportunities for spending long hours of the day and night while his master worked or slept, completing his nefarious work of subtle undermining. The servant was unable to stop what she herself had imprudently started; she had so compromised herself by her initial misdemeanour that when the scandalous goings-on became known she was unable to report them to her master and was obliged to become an accomplice.

One morning while the old woman was arguing with a seller of vegetables, Bughesha noticed among the crowd at the market a man named Shamseddin, the *nakuda* of a sailing ship which made long stops at Massawa. He was a man of mature age, but his lean and agile body – which still had robust appetites – and his ready wit made him seem much younger than he was.

'What are you doing in this stinking hole, O father of lies?'
asked the pilot, smiling broadly and showing his excellent teeth.

Bughesha informed him that he was Secretary to the Sharaytic
Tribunal, and Shamseddin roared with laughter.

'Listen, you young liar: in this womanless country I am beginning to develop a liking even for the coppers, if they have curly
hair. Who are you pimping for? The fishes?'

The merchant of shadows became offended. No women,
indeed! Not, perhaps, for creatures like Shamseddin – but
women there were, and beautiful as the full moon.

The man looked at the boy doubtfully, decided that in any
case he could lose nothing by trying, and told him to come and
see him on the *dhow* in the afternoon.

As soon as Si Abdalla had finished his daily discourse on the
virtuous life and left the house to return to his office, Bughesha
also slipped out, ran to the port and boarded Shamseddin's craft.

The four men of the crew were also old acquaintances of
Bughesha's. For some time they had been cruising along the
coast of the Yemen and in the ports of that austere country they
had not set eyes on any woman under sixty years of age.

The boy seated himself on the iron plate used for the baking
of unleavened bread, and the excited, sex-starved men stood
round, staring at him, uncertain whether to believe him.

Bughesha told them that, being employed at the Tribunal, he
saw a great many people because there were many applications
to the judges – on questions of canonical law much too complicated for ignorant sailors to understand.

The fascination of the seller of shadows began to work and
his audience, even although they knew with whom they were
dealing, found themselves hanging on his words.

Bughesha stated that he had the confidence of two widows of
two brothers; they lived together, and found their enforced
abstinence difficult. Naturally, they had to be careful of their
reputations, but he was sure that there would not be too many
difficulties in the case of persons presented by someone in their
confidence – on condition, of course, that such persons were
accompanied by something solid in the way of argument, and

that they were open-handed. These were women of noble birth
– very different from the scum to which *sambūq* and *dhow*
navigators were accustomed; the sailors must, therefore, understand that it was not a case of going into one of those houses
where they left a few shillings on the chest of drawers. After
the meeting – if it took place – they would have to hand a certain
sum to him, Bughesha ben Yacub, and he would in turn buy a
suitable present, a souvenir, for these widowed gentlewomen.

'Remember, son of Satan, you won't get a cent in advance.'

The father of lies lifted his eyes to heaven, snorted with
offence and turned to leave them, but they assured him that they
had only been joking and that they had every confidence in
him. Finally, he allowed himself to be persuaded and promised
that he would go into the matter: he would sound the two
widows on the subject and bring them a reply.

They thought they would see no more of him, but instead he
returned the next day and informed them that he had arranged
everything and that they could rely on him. He explained that
they must present themselves one at a time and that for that
evening it would be the *nakuda*. The appointment was fixed for
two hours after the evening prayer, under the slaughterhouse
arcade.

At the appointed time Bughesha, who was waiting in the
shadow of the arcade, took Shamseddin by the hand and led
him through a labyrinth of alleys and byways until they came
to a broken hedge. Following his guide through the gap, Shamseddin crawled on all fours into a deserted open space; he then
climbed a wall and found himself in a shaft between two houses,
where rats as big as rabbits ran over his bare feet. Bughesha
wriggled through a grating and beckoned to the pilot to follow
him. They were in the house, and the boy dragged him along
a corridor and up two flights of stairs. At the top, a light filtered
from under a closed door.

The boy opened the door very carefully and Shamseddin
found himself in a room in which the only furniture was a carpet.
Here Bughesha left the pilot for a few minutes then reappeared
and led him into another room, which was in semi-darkness. On

a mass of cushions lay an almost white woman, with magnificent eyes and a body as fat as any good Moslem could wish. In fact, when he later described her to me, Shamseddin used the term which, in Arabic, is the highest compliment which a man of his sort can pay to a woman: she was, he said, 'a duck'.

Duck she may have been, but the prowess she displayed was that of a decidedly more vigorous species; Shamseddin assured me he had never encountered her like, either before or since.

'And as you know, I am from Obók,' he said.

The men from Obók in the Gulf of Jibuti are famous for their amatory feats of endurance and they boast of their powers with uninhibited frankness. But on this night Shamseddin met his match; he finally crawled from the house so exhausted that Bughesha was forced to drag him back through the streets like a dead dog, and once arrived at the port he threw himself into the bottom of the boat and lay there insensible, stone deaf to the enquiries of his fellows.

On the following evening it was the turn of the pilot's mate. He was received by a coal-black beauty lying naked on a pile of cushions. She was not a woman, he said, but a spirit, a serpent, a witch, a daughter of the devil, who crushed him between her arms and smothered him with such furious bites and kisses that he was covered with bruises for a week.

No one doubted any longer that the two women were in fact widows – for no mortal husband could have survived such consuming fires.

Bughesha for once, they said, had told the truth: the house was in a fashionable quarter of the town; the widows were obviously well-born; they never asked for any money and the black one in fact had even presented her lover with a silver ring. In order, therefore, not to be considered beggars, the men thought it proper to present Bughesha with a sufficient sum to buy the two ladies a handsome necklace each.

It is improbable that the prince of shadows was able to provide for all the pseudo-widows of the city, but it is possible that the two young wives, incapable of keeping a secret, had foolishly talked to others who complained of absent or impotent husbands, and that, either out of compassion or for fear of being betrayed, they had asked Bughesha to employ his good offices on behalf of their forlorn friends. Whether the whole city was turned into a vast brothel by this resourceful boy is, however, one of those things we shall never know. Nevertheless, his activities in that particular town came to an abrupt end.

One evening when Shamseddin had returned to his 'widow', apparently intent on making another attempt to establish his superiority as a man from Obók, Bughesha rushed into the room and, paying no attention whatever to the fact that the pilot was very much occupied, seized him by the arm and hissed: 'Quick, quick . . . the father . . . run!'

Shamseddin rushed out of the room and ran full tilt into Abdalla el Yèmeni who, covered from head to foot in a white nightshirt, was proceeding slowly along the corridor, a candle in one hand and a Moslem rosary in the other. The impact of the pilot's head in the old man's stomach knocked him reeling against the wall and sent the candle flying. In the darkness the pilot escaped, while the old man, groping for the window, began to call for help.

'Moslems! Moslems!' he cried. 'Come to the aid of a faithful brother!'

As the naked pilot raced for the port, he heard the hue and cry of the neighbours hot on his heels. He quickened his pace, and as he came in sight of the quay he saw his boat lying ready, the sails all set. Bughesha, by some miracle, had arrived before him and roused the crew. Shamseddin took a flying leap, and as he landed on the deck the oarsmen, rowing furiously, pulled away from the quay. As the small craft emerged through the harbour mouth the monsoon caught it and swept it out to sea. At the helm stood the pilot, naked in the rain, shouting with laughter at the wildly gesticulating inhabitants who now crowded the quayside. In the forefront stood Abdalla el Yèmeni, still in his nightshirt, shaking his fists in impotent rage. And in the bottom of the *dhow* lay Bughesha fast asleep, serene and safe, his boats well burned.

★   ★   ★

About a year after these events I left Massawa for Italy. At Aden, Dr Spiro Photiadès, who for ten years had been practising as a physician in that furnace, boarded the same ship. We had known each other many years before, at Florence University, and we passed most of the voyage together, talking of the old days.

One day, Spiro brought out a packet of photographs in order to show me pictures of his house in Aden and of the dispensary, infirmary and operating theatre he had there. In many of these photographs I noticed a young native tied up in an enormous overall. At first I paid no particular attention to him but on looking more closely I became quite certain that this was none other than Bughesha.

I asked who he was, and Spiro told me that his name was Mohamed – or rather, Hajj Mohamed, because he had made the pilgrimage to Mecca, where plague had killed his parents. He was born in the Yemen and had been in his service for nearly a year; he spoke fluent English, kept the dispensary records and the inventory of drugs in order, and was very useful in both the day-clinic and the operating theatre – a veritable Godsend, in fact. The doctor had left him behind in Aden where, in accordance with instructions, he was to continue treating the regular patients until he, Spiro, returned.

My stay in Italy was short and I was soon in Eritrea again. At the end of the year a letter reached me from Photiadès. He informed me that on his return to Aden he had found no trace of Hajj Mohamed, and that with him had disappeared the pharmaceutical chest, the poison chest and all the surgical equipment.

My indignant colleague gave me particulars of the young man so that I could inform the police in case he should take refuge in Eritrea. Among the identification marks mentioned was a star-shaped scar on the neck – and the shadow merchant had an exactly similar scar as the result of an incision I had made in a boil he had when he was the Benjamin of Fatma, the Somali woman.

I reported the matter as my colleague wished, although I was certain that after the Aden exploit Bughesha was not likely to show himself in a country where he was so well known.

I thought no more about him, convinced that that was the end of him as far as I was concerned.

However, only a few months later I again heard talk of *el keddāb*. A Greek exporter of mother-of-pearl spoke of him first, but I did not imagine that his story referred to Bughesha. But Bazarà, the pearl merchant, also had strange stories to tell and in this case there was no doubt at all that the person concerned was our friend. The stories were confirmed by others and finally the pilot of a *dhow* from the Dalak Islands insisted that he had seen *el keddāb* with his own eyes.

On the coast of Arabia, washed by the Indian Ocean, stands the little town of Bet-et-Tassàur. Seen from the sea it appears to be little more than a group of fishermen's huts, but what a stranger would not know is that in this town no one fishes and everybody is rolling in money.

In those days a great many *dhows* and *sambūqs* crowded into this little bay which the ordinary atlas does not record and which the seaport register gives only as an indentation in a rocky coast.

Craft arrived from everywhere and left again heading north, south, east or west, loaded with contraband which had reached the sea by very circuitous routes 'because man's foot is chained to the path, but the prow opens its way where it will'.

It was the pilot and crew of the Dalak Island *dhow*, newly arrived in Massawa, who told me they had seen Bughesha at Bet-et-Tassàur. Bughesha was no longer 'Bughesha' of course and when they had addressed him by that name he had looked at them, surprised, and asked who Bughesha might be. The seafarers knew him well, however, and although some years had passed since they had last seen him, they were quite sure they were not mistaken.

The story was as follows – and the men in telling it seemed unable quite to believe it.

They had disembarked their merchandise at Bet-et-Tassàur, and were already loading rolls of Indian silk, intending to set sail in two days' time, when the pilot sat down on a knife and made a six-inch gash in his thigh. The people who ran to his aid lifted their hands and thanked God that he had wounded himself in a country where there was a true physician, one who, under Allah's guidance, worked miracles: to patch up a wound in the leg was child's play to this wonder worker.

On hearing this, the men wasted no time: they laid the *nakuda* on a sail and took him, bleeding profusely, to the physician's house. It was a handsome house and the portico was crowded with patients. Most of them were men and women from the township but there were also seamen who happened to be in the port, and patients who had been brought from coastal centres and from the interior. Two enormous negroes kept order, and when one of the boys from the *dhow* began to protest at the length of time the injured man was kept waiting, they threatened to throw him down the hillside.

They had to wait three hours, during which time they not only lost their patience, but also exhausted their very extensive vocabulary. Towards evening, however, the physician received them – and he was, most certainly, Bughesha.

He had grown up. He had a moustache and his cheeks were dark where his beard had been cut with the point of the scissors. This disguise, however, was not sufficient, and his way of looking sideways with a diffident air betrayed him at once to anyone who had known him.

After a brief discussion regarding his identity, and after he had coldly informed them that they were mistaken, that he had never been in Massawa, that he came from an old family of Bassora which he had left for political reasons, he carefully examined the thigh of the *nakuda*, disinfected it, sewed it up and bandaged it with astonishing deftness.

They saw him again several times in the fifteen days during which they were obliged to remain in the port, and they were able to confirm beyond any doubt that 'Jàfar el Hakim' and 'Bughesha *el Keddāb*' were one and the same person.

During the treatment, the eminent doctor asked what merchandise they were carrying and when he was told that it was silk he smiled into his moustache. Such a lot of trouble for so little money? He spoke in a low voice, bent over the *nakuda's* wound. Such a lot of trouble, and yet with no further effort sixty times as much could be earned. He rebandaged the leg without pursuing the argument.

That same evening, two unknown men presented themselves on the *dhow* and offered to buy the silk they had on board and to replace it with a consignment of hashish. They mentioned associates in the ports, unwatched points along the coast where there was no danger and where the 'money of the horse' – golden sovereigns with St George and the Dragon on them – would be paid for the consignment.

The mariners gradually learned that Bughesha was not only a physician, but also the organiser of all the contraband operations at Bet-et-Tassàur.

Opium and hashish arrived from India; from Europe, by a roundabout route across Turkey, cocaine was carried to the Persian Gulf, thence to the hideouts on the Arabian coast where it waited for transfer to Egypt at an opportune moment. It was only necessary to pass a few kilos in contraband and you could look forward to a comfortable old age. Also, from India in the famine periods, and from Ethiopia and Somaliland all the year round – singly or in small groups or in hordes – slaves were disembarked. Castrated children were worth their weight in gold throughout Arabia and Iran; strong men were sold for work in the fields, and young and good-looking women went into the houses of the rich, who did not quibble over the price when it was a Galla girl with a golden skin, or a perfectly made young woman from Somaliland.

Was Bughesha worth a lot of money? The seafaring men blew out their cheeks and made gestures indicating stacks and piles of money. He made money on everything. They had concrete proof of this when, they having asked how much they owed him, and he having replied that he did not take money from poor seafaring folk, he ended by allowing himself to be presented with a piece of silk worth forty rupees.

To relieve my conscience, I wrote to Spiro Photiadès to tell him that his Yemenite pearl was practising medicine at Bet-et-Tassàur. Spiro, who was at that time director of the Greek hospital in Cairo, replied that he now had other fish to fry and if there were people so foolish as to allow themselves to be murdered by Hajj Mohamed, he saw no reason why he should deprive them of that privilege.

All that was a long time ago; years passed, the war came and went, and during that period of tragic and grotesque events it is not surprising that the king of invention passed entirely out of my mind.

A few months ago, however, as I opened an illustrated paper, the memory of him leaped from the subconscious as fresh as though it had never been absent.

The paper contained an account of an international dispute and there was a photograph showing a Commission which had just been set up in an attempt to settle the matter. In the front row sat the Secretary to the Commission. And he was none other than Bughesha *el Keddāb*. He was not so named in the caption, of course, but so far as I was concerned there was not a shadow of doubt about it. The picture showed him smiling urbanely at another member of the Commission. What kind of story was he selling him, I wonder?

With the picture in my hand I thought of the first time I had met Bughesha, when he was chasing moth shadows on the lamp-lit wall. Perhaps that was the secret of his success: he had always left his imagination free and sold its shadow to whoever liked to buy. He did not become a vizier, and certainly he had no horses shod with silver – but it was obvious that he had success-fully sold a great many shadows to innumerable sultans.

★ ★ ★

When I returned from my leave in 1934 I was, to my chagrin, assigned to Asmara. I have never liked colonial capitals. I dislike intensely the small provincial towns of Italy with their malicious gossip and tittle-tattle; their respectable traditions which have crystallised good and evil into something absolute and static; their drawing rooms which set the social 'tone'; their cafés where the young man who thinks he is a wit is always to be found in company with the girl who is 'not quite nice'; their virtuous matrons who spend their time giving advice to young wives.

But at least in Italy it is possible, by sitting in a train for a couple of hours, to escape from these small towns with their burden of ancient glory and present boredom, and to lose oneself in the anonymous crowd of a big city. Asmara did not offer even this consolation, because a two hours' journey could take you only to Massawa or Keren – where little relief was to be found.

I had lived too long in fascinating natural surroundings and was unable to free myself from the nostalgia which often, even today, assails me. The dull uniformity of the upland Copts was certainly not calculated to help me forget the kaleidoscopic array of peoples with whom I had lived: the Beni Amer with their geometrical hair-dressing; the Hadendowa, descendants of the ancient Egyptians; the Cunama python-hunters; the Rashahida with their henna-tinted beards.

Instead of wide, noisy rivers, the chatter of families of monkeys, forests where at dawn spectral giraffes stretched their necks up to the tops of the highest trees; instead of hillsides on which one might see the massive forms of elephants outlined against the moon-bathed landscape, or troops of antelopes galloping up a grassy slope – instead of all this, I had the unsuccessfully ambitious streets of Asmara to look upon.

However, since there is nothing so sterile and useless as hankering after the past, I put aside my nostalgia and endeavoured to organise my life in Asmara in the best way possible. The house and garden which were placed at my disposal were more than adequate for my needs: the garden was large and full of flowers, and in front of the door there was a vanilla tree which, in the evening, gave off a perfume so strong that it went to the head.

A town house creates a whole series of problems. As far as the service was concerned, Jemberié assured me that only a cook was needed because he would see to the rest. Jemberié was convinced that Asmara was a den of thieves intent on robbing me.

Thus it was that Tabhatú, a widow of uncertain age – a Coptic Christian turned Catholic – entered my service. She was an excellent woman and a first-class cook who could hold her own with any European *cordon bleu*. As far as her religion was concerned, she was fanatical like all converts, and she had certain curious manias. She always recited the rosary before starting to prepare a new dish. She also dedicated dishes to particular saints, based on a system which I was unable to grasp; it may have been some assonance which had struck her ear that caused her, for instance, to place her *spaghetti alla matriciana* under the protection of the Mother of God. Whenever I went down with an attack of malaria, she filled my bed with pictures of saints and sacred talismen: I would wake, exhausted and soaked with sweat, to find St Ignatius on my stomach, St Cecilia the Martyr under my arm, and the Holy Family on my chest.

For some time we managed with Tabhatú only, but when, to Jemberié's consternation, I began to entertain people to tea and to dinner I had to promote Jemberié to major-domo and find someone to help him. So Tesemmà arrived on the scene – young, timid and frankly and engagingly stupid. With the patience of a saint, Jemberié taught him to hold a plate in his gloved hands without letting it fall, to fill glasses without wetting the table-cloth, and to serve at table without pouring soup over the guests. That period of servitude under the yoke of the oppressors evidently stood Tesemmà in good stead for, with the advent of democracy, he has become an authoritative exponent of an Eritrean political party.

After a few weeks, my staff was still further increased, because I was unable to refuse a friend who desired to bequeath to me Omar, a silent, colossal Mussulman from Assaorta. His functions were somewhat vague and ill-defined: he made canes into whistles, set traps for rats, weeded the garden paths and roasted the coffee. He had no qualifications; but on the other hand he had a lady friend from his own country who, two or three times a month, sent me a dish of *zighini* cooked as they cook them in Assaorta – a masterpiece, stewed with red pepper and aromatic herbs and surrounded with vegetables simmered gently in the piquant and fragrant sauce.

Unfortunately, this young artist – whose acquaintance I never made – poisoned Omar's life with her faithlessness. Every so often the unhappy man would come and throw himself at my feet, sobbing out noisily that she had deceived him again. I always found it difficult to conceal my amusement at the sight of this giant, shedding tears like a cut vine over the obviously unworthy object of his affections, but the memory of the delicious *zighini* always suggested to me so many excuses for her and so many subtle arguments in her favour that poor Omar, who asked nothing better than to be convinced, always ended by believing that there was no foundation for his jealousy.

Although in those days I had no time to occupy myself with medicine, it happened that I was called upon to treat a lioness.

I have always envied veterinary surgeons. They can treat their patients without having to listen to their stories; they are not tormented by the morbid scruples of psycho-asthenics or bewildered by the inventions of psychopathic liars; they are spared the sight of man's pitiless egoism and cowardice. More-over, they are not persecuted by the ignorant verbosity of anxious relatives – and they are certain that their prescriptions will be followed. And finally – since man does not live by bread alone – they may occasionally come across a quadruped who is grateful to them for their care.

But much as I fancied the animal doctor's life, I did not imagine, when a lioness arrived unexpectedly at my house, that I was about to put it to the test.

That morning I was certainly not thinking of lions but of the next day's dinner guests – important people, 'people with big stomachs', as Jemberié called them – and worrying about the expense.

All the servants were with me, going over their respective responsibilities and receiving confirmation of the decisions taken. In view of the number of guests, two would have to serve at table: Jemberié and Tesemmà. I urged Tesemmà to do his utmost not to pour anything over the lady on my right and to avoid getting mayonnaise on the general's new uniform. Tesemmà cast his eyes heavenward and laid his hand on his heart. Omar was to open the door and bow the guests in. Had Omar practised his bow? The native of Assaorta stepped forward into the centre of the room and proceeded to bow to each of the cardinal points with such solemnity that Tabhatú burst into a laugh like the whinnying of a horse. Before I could reprove her, the door opened and Eleonora entered.

Eleonora, who had been my guide and prompter at Jemberié's wedding, was the eldest of five half-caste sisters known throughout Eritrea for their beauty. When very young, she had married an Italian settler who, when she met him, ran a small general store in the Corso del Re, and also managed a tannery in the Gajjiret district. This little man was from the Italian Province of Marche, and was Jewish; he had the quick intelligence and caustic, ready wit of his race, but he had a generosity of soul I have rarely found, not only in Jews, but in any other human being. He was the first Italian assassinated by the bandits in Eritrea after the arrival of the liberators.

Eleonora entered with the springy and undulating step which years in a college in Venice had not managed to Europeanise, and announced that in the garden there were three Abyssinians and a cat.

The Abyssinians were caravaneers I had known during my long stay on the Ethiopian frontier, and the 'cat' was a lion cub. They had brought it to me because they knew that I liked animals and remembered that my garden at Agordat had been like Noah's ark. They had encountered a lioness near Um-Hajer and had killed her. Of the two cubs, one had died *en route*, and this was the other. Unfortunately, in getting hold of the animal they had broken one of its legs.

When the caravaneers left, I carried the cub into the garden and, sitting on the steps, I placed it on my knees to see how badly it was hurt.

It was a female not much bigger than a tabby cat. The right thigh bone was broken in the lower third, and when I tried to bring the ends together the cub jumped round and bit a piece out of my shirt.

Jemberié recommended me to drown the ferocious beast at once, but I ignored him. With the aid of two sticks, a bandage and a packet of cotton wool I managed to immobilise the fractured limb in a primitive but sufficiently solid splint.

The lion cub lay on its back on the grass with its injured leg, packed round with cotton wool and bandages, stretched straight upwards. It looked at Eleonora and at me with great, green eyes in which the pupils were only tiny slits, and every now and again it yawned, opening a rose-pink mouth full of milk teeth. It was tawny coloured and curly, with a white stomach and disproportionately large paws.

'Shall you keep it?' asked Eleonora – adding immediately some appropriate words in Tigrinya for the benefit of Jemberié, who continued to insist on the advisability of drowning the animal.

'Of course you must keep it. Imagine the fun of going walking with a lioness and scaring the whole town! Lovely!'

We began to discuss the question of a name for the new arrival but failed to come to any decision. The cub, as though it thought it should have some say in these proceedings, turned on its stomach and tried to get on to its feet, but the splint prevented it. It raised its head, gazed at us with a worried expression and attempted a roar, but in spite of repeated efforts it produced no more than a feeble little falsetto squeak; it seemed annoyed at this result and shook its head furiously, scraping the ground with its two front paws.

'Do you see how her eyes shine?' asked Eleonora. 'Look at her proud expression – like a queen. You must call her "Neghesti".'

And so the young lioness was named 'Neghesti' which, in Tigrinya, means 'Empress'.

People who have never had a young lion with a fractured femur in the house will be unable to imagine how unsettling it can be. In the first place, someone had to take care of the beast. Tabhatú's work was too delicate and important to permit of further responsibilities. Tesemmà was too stupid to have charge of such an intelligent animal. I sounded Jemberié and when, appealing to his religious sense, I mentioned that Neghesti was also one of God's creatures, he agreed, but observed gravely that God had placed lions in the forest and not in men's houses. Thus, the task finally fell to Omar: he was appointed dry nurse to the cub and he took on his new duties with enthusiasm and delight. He accepted his charge immediately, picking the little beast up with a tenderness unsuspected in those great hands, and when the cub licked him with its rough tongue he was moved almost to tears.

When Neghesti began to mee . . . ow desperately we came to the conclusion that she must be hungry, and a long discussion took place as to whether a lion of that size had already been weaned. Eleonora, for whom the cub was an orphaned babe, flew home and returned with four pints of milk. During her absence, however, I had asked Tabhatú for a slice of raw meat from the kitchen, and this the lion cub had swallowed at one gulp. But Eleonora was not to be denied, and poured the milk into a salad bowl. The cub plunged her nose into it and lapped it up at such a rate that the bowl was empty in a trice, whereupon she licked it with such enthusiasm that it overturned and smashed on the stone steps. Obviously, a mixed diet and metal dishes were indicated.

The next morning I took Neghesti to the hospital and a radiograph reassured me with regard to the reduction of the fracture. In the afternoon I called in my veterinary colleagues attached to the Vaccine Production Service and we discussed housing and feeding arrangements for the cub, who sat combing her whiskers with two great paws.

The mixed diet was approved and the amount fixed at six pints of milk and four pounds of donkey meat a day: the latter the Vaccine Service offered to supply to me at cost price.

On this diet Neghesti every day grew bigger, heavier and more beautiful. In a month the leg had healed so well that the most careful observer, watching her run and jump, could not say which of the two femurs had been broken. But Neghesti had not forgotten the pain or her doctor: I had only to sit down near her and immediately she would lie on her back and offer me her paws so that I could feel the thickened bone which was the result of the fracture.

She was by now too big to sleep in a basket in Omar's room, so I had a large cage constructed at the end of the garden in which she could pass the night. I had to be firm to prevent Omar, who never left her, from also taking up his residence in the cage.

One morning Omar rushed into my room as I was dressing:

the lioness was ill and her guardian wept as though she were already dead. I found Neghesti unrecognisable: her fur was staring, she was listless and she moved with difficulty about the cage, dragging her feet on the ground. When I called to her she looked at me with dull eyes and then flopped heavily on the ground.

By a process of eliminating one hypothesis after another, we arrived at the cause of the trouble: fearing that raw meat might make her savage, we had been boiling it, and the unfortunate animal presented all the symptoms of acute avitaminosis. The daily ration of meat had now been increased to three kilos, and after she had again had it raw for a week she recovered completely.

She was very fond of Omar, who devoted his entire time to her: he fed her, brushed and combed her, and passed the day playing with her.

She knew very well that Tabhatú was terrified of her and amused herself every morning when the poor woman returned from the market by following at her heels across the garden. The cook, terrified, would begin to run, and the animal would lollop playfully after her right into the kitchen. Here Tabhatú would climb on to the stove, invoking the Madonna and all the saints, while Neghesti – seated in the middle of the room – looked on with immense satisfaction, waving her tail furiously.

With Tesemmà she adopted another system: when she heard his voice she would make her way silently, on her belly, to where he was and spring out at him suddenly so that he jumped into the air, his eyes nearly out of their sockets.

But I was her great love.

When Omar brought my coffee in the morning, Neghesti came with him and sat down at the head of my bed. Keeping her claws carefully sheathed, she caressed my face with her front paws, smoothed my hair and pushed her face into my neck, licking my face and purring like a giant cat. I was required to return these caresses by rubbing her behind the ears and talking to her as one talks to a child, to which she replied with deep, short roars that sounded like a blacksmith's bellows.

When I left the house in the morning, she came with me as far as the gate, and standing on her hind legs, her front paws on the railing, she followed me with her eyes until I disappeared at the end of the road. Only then did she allow Omar to lead her back to the house where breakfast awaited her.

When I returned at mid-day, Omar had to run to open the cage because she leapt and threw herself against the iron bars in an effort to reach me. She raised herself on her hind legs, her front paws on my shoulders, looking into my eyes with her own half-closed and a fainting expression which was really absurd on the face of a lioness. From that moment she never left me until I returned to the office again: she accompanied me to the sitting-room, came with me to the bathroom, followed me into the dining-room and sat down beside my chair without ever taking her eyes off me. Even while I was eating I had to take notice of her. If I seemed to have forgotten her, she nudged my elbow with her head with increasing violence until I turned to talk to her or offered her a little piece of meat, or a piece of orange – for which latter delicacy she had a special liking. One day I had taken some office papers to the table and was absorbed in reading them when, annoyed at her insistence, I gave her a slap. She took the table-cloth between her teeth and pulled everything – plates, knives and forks, bottles, glasses – on to the floor, leaving me with the papers in one hand and a fork in the other, sitting before an empty table.

She did not hide her ill humour when I had visitors, and although she just managed to be civil to the men guests she had great difficulty in curbing her feelings with regard to my lady visitors. The only exceptions were Eleonora and her little girls who, on their way to school, came to me for a cup of coffee and milk.

If I forgot to have Neghesti shut up when a lady visitor arrived, she would think of the most subtle jokes to play on the poor woman. If, while she was free in the garden, she heard a female voice in the ground-floor sitting-room, she would leap through the window, plant herself squarely in the middle of the room and – a thing she never did otherwise – open her mouth in a roar which showed all her teeth. Omar would arrive at the run, and lead her away prancing with satisfaction, while I supported the fainting lady.

During a luncheon to which I had invited a couple of men friends and a lady who was on her way through Asmara, Neghesti, piqued because she had been excluded from the dining room and furious at the intrusion of the female guest, took the latter's hat into the garden and reduced it to pieces the size of postage stamps.

One summer afternoon, the wife of a colleague, seeing me at the window, called to ask if she might gather some flowers from the garden. I told her to cut as many flowers as she liked and to come in and take a cup of coffee. I did not think about Neghesti who, unseen by me, had crawled under the divan on which the young woman sat down; I only became aware of the lioness's presence when I saw flowers and coffee cup fall on the carpet and my guest, the colour of chalk, slip senseless to the floor, while Neghesti trotted out of the room holding in her mouth the remnants of the stocking which, with extraordinary delicacy, she had removed from the lady's calf.

Jemberié had disapproved when I adopted Neghesti, and he watched her installation in the house with ill-concealed displeasure; he saw the cub become a robust and lively lioness and watched her manifestations of affection towards me with distaste and suspicion.

'Lion is lion and Christian is Christian,' he announced with deep disgust on one occasion when he found Neghesti lying on my bed.

One morning, his curiosity having been aroused by Omar's description of the lioness's behaviour when I awoke in the morning, he came to see what happened, watching through the half-closed door. From that day he never failed to accompany Omar and Neghesti at a respectful distance, his nose and brow wrinkled in perplexity at our dialogue and her show of affection.

He was now puzzled as well as displeased for, in addition to being an element of disorder in the house, Neghesti had become a strange phenomenon which he could not understand.

Neghesti

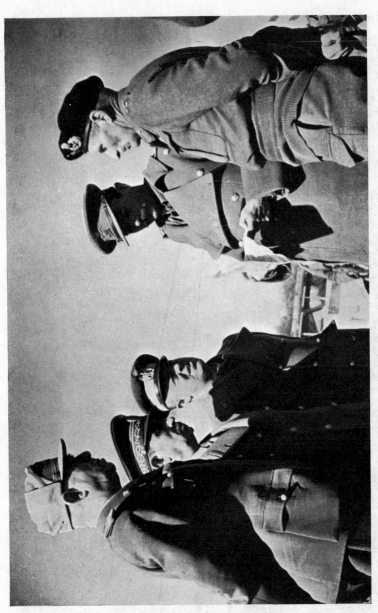

Surrender of Tripoli: the author (*left*) with General Montgomery

One afternoon, while I was reading in the sitting room, Jemberié called me and led me on tiptoe to the door of my bedroom, signalling me to keep quiet. Neghesti was sitting in front of the long mirror: she bent her head over her shoulder, studied her profile, looked at herself full-face, and then, sitting on her haunches, her eyes half-closed, carefully combed her whiskers.

On another occasion, Omar summoned Jemberié to see what the lioness was doing in my room. She was sitting facing a wall, gazing with a rapt expression at a portrait of my mother which hung beside my bed. She barely turned her head at their approach, and returned to her ecstatic contemplation of the photograph.

When he told me of this, Jemberié could no longer keep his thoughts to himself. With many a roundabout phrase he confided to me that he did not believe Neghesti was really a lioness at all: he was sure that she was an earthly form my mother had taken in order to return and protect her son.

He had watched her day after day, he said, and had come to the conclusion that there was no other explanation of her behaviour. Certainly, he said, no such *ambessa* had ever been seen before. Even a child knew that the *ambessa* was a wild, ferocious and evil-smelling animal which sprang at men and devoured them. And there was Neghesti, serious, dignified, moving about the house like a great lady, and with never the slightest smell of the wild beast about her. Jemberié had noticed other things too: not only had Neghesti clearly defined ideas with regard to the social position of the people around her, but she made other perspicacious distinctions between them. She loved to frighten Tabhatú, said Jemberié, because she realised that she was just a timid, silly woman; she played jokes on Tesemmà, and frollicked with Omar because the giant had remained a child and did not know how to do anything else. While Jemberié had looked upon her as just a lioness, Neghesti had never taken the slightest notice of him: she passed him by as though she did not see him, and if he entered a room in which she was, she did not even lift her head. But since he had begun

H

to suspect the truth, said Jemberié, Neghesti's attitude had changed, and now she looked him in the eye, watched him as he moved about the room, and more than once he had had the impression that she was about to speak to him.

He had given a great deal of thought to these portents, but, knowing himself to be too ignorant to get to the bottom of the question, he had consulted a *cashi*, a Coptic priest, who had a profound knowledge of the mysteries of life and death; and this learned man had removed all shadow of doubt. Neghesti's morning greetings could be no other than manifestations of a mother's joy on her son's awakening – her son as an infant, of course, because sons are always infants to their mothers, even if they have grey hair. The worthy priest had an explanation for all Neghesti's prodigious doings. It was natural, he said, that Neghesti should look at herself in the mirror: even butchers' and plumbers' wives looked at themselves in the mirror, and therefore a great lady would certainly wish to do so. Neither was there anything surprising in the fact that the lioness had remained in ecstasy before the portrait in my bedroom. Of course she had taken no notice when Jemberié and Omar had entered: great ladies did not notice servants – and in any case, at that moment she was far away from them, far away in time and space: she was in her own country; she saw again her human form, lived again the days when her son was small and at her side. Even the distaste for women visitors was understandable, since the lioness reincarnated the mother who wished to stay always with her son: these women were frivolous, young and thoughtless and might be dangerous for her son, to whom the years had not given overmuch wisdom . . . Jemberié stumbled, tried to pass this off, apologised and explained that that, of course, was what the *priest* had said.

Jemberié was convinced that from the moment he had believed her to be the incarnation of a woman Neghesti had altered her behaviour towards him, and he was unable to see that the real change was in his own attitude. He was no longer suspicious of her, and began to treat her with the utmost respect; he placed a mirror in her cage and sprayed her every day with my hair lotion, and when she wished to make her exit from a room he opened the door for her with great deference.

Neghesti was already full grown when one morning I awoke with my tonsils swollen and inflamed. After two days the germs were circulating nicely and the thermometer showed a hundred and four. As the fever rose and I began to shiver from head to foot, Neghesti sprang on to my bed and refused to leave it. Omar called her, entreated her and tried to force her out of the room, but he might as well have talked to the wall: Neghesti seemed to be unaware of his presence, and when he tried to push her off the bed she looked at him indignantly with scintillating eyes and showed her teeth with such a savage growl that the poor creature was quite upset. Jemberié, who was present at the scene, led Omar away and sent him to tell Eleonora that I was ill.

As soon as Eleonora entered the room, Neghesti ran to her and looked at her with an expression of such desperate anxiety that Eleonora took her in her arms and whispered words of comfort and reassurance to her. Neghesti licked her face two or three times and then returned to the bed, resting her nose on my shoulder.

There were a number of physicians in Eritrea at that time, some of them very capable, but my physician was a vet – a young biologist of wide culture and great modesty who was at that time directing the Eritrea vaccine-producing Institute and who is now teaching in an Italian university.

When he came to see me, he stopped dead on the threshold. Neghesti, deciding that I needed protection, had lain down on top of me, with my head between her paws, and was glaring at those around me in a threatening manner.

'How do you feel?' asked the doctor tentatively.

'I feel awful,' I said. 'I've got a fever.'

'Well what d'you expect me to do . . . with a lion on your bed?'

But Neghesti would not budge. Omar's calls, Eleonora's entreaties, Jemberié's respectful exhortations left her unmoved: she fixed her eyes on the doctor, and when any of them tried to insist that she remove herself, she emitted a low roar which reverberated through my chest.

Eventually, hardly able to stand on account of the fever, I was obliged to put on a dressing-gown and slippers and go out into the garden. Neghesti followed me like a dog, allowed herself to be shut in the cage, and let out a desperate wail as I left her. The next day, however, they had to bring her back to my room because she refused to eat, and only when she was beside my bed, having reassured herself that I was still alive, did she decide to put her nose into her dish of raw meat and eat.

I was in bed a week, and during the whole of that time Neghesti lived, slept and ate at my bedside; when the doctor arrived, I took her back to the cage, where she watched impatiently for his departure, roaring furiously if they did not then bring her back to my room immediately.

Months passed. The light rains had fallen and ceased, and the dry, red earth, cracked by the sun and reduced to a fine dust, was covered by green shoots. The great rains had followed and were now drawing to a close and the season of damp heat and swollen rivers was upon us.

It was afternoon and I was alone in my sitting-room with Neghesti. I had returned from the office and was sitting at the window, looking at the rain which fell from the heavens in great sheets: the garden was water-logged and visible only through a diaphanous vapour; rain poured from every leaf, and rivulets and waterfalls cascaded in all directions.

Since the days of Herodotus all travellers' tales have been received with a certain amount of scepticism; Marco Polo's compatriots were so unbelieving of his wonderful adventures that his book was given the title of *Il Milione* – meaning, the million tall stories which they refused to swallow. My experiences *in partibus infidelium* have nothing of the prodigious about them, and anyone who refuses to believe the following story about Neghesti has my full sympathy, for I have myself no explanation to offer.

On this particular afternoon I was sitting looking at the rain with Neghesti at my feet. Jemberié entered, bringing the day's letters: on the tray were a newspaper, a post-card signed by a group of friends who had thought of me when they were dining together, and a letter.

The letter came from far away, and it was written in large handwriting on blue notepaper: it announced that someone dear to me had committed suicide.

When we suddenly hear of the death of someone who has been near to us, whose life and affections we have shared, it seems in that moment that a part of ourselves has ceased to be. If the friend who has preceded us into the next world is younger than we are, the whole thing seems incongruous and we have the impression of having lived too long. When, in addition, the death has been self-inflicted, we are shocked by it as by an injustice: there is a sense of betrayal.

It was this tumult of feelings, this comfortless bitterness of heart, that prevented me from noticing Neghesti's furious nudges. Finding me so absorbed in my thoughts, she stood up at the side of my armchair and began to ruffle my hair with her nose and paws. I pushed her away roughly, reread the letter and remained with my elbows on my knees, looking into space.

I do not know how long I stayed like that, but at a certain point I heard the door of the sitting-room open and, raising my eyes, I found a small group in the doorway. Jemberié was there, and Tesemmà with a terrified expression and one hand still inside the shoe he had been polishing, Tabhatú, ashen, with her fingers in her mouth, and over the heads of the others Omar peered at me, awestruck and apprehensive.

For a moment no one said anything. Then Jemberié, seeing the letter which had fallen to the floor, asked: 'Bad news?'

I nodded automatically and then after a moment, surprised, I asked him how he knew.

The sound of my voice broke the spell and they all came forward together talking and gesticulating in the direction of Neghesti who had entered behind them and who now lay beside me, watching the group of servants and sweeping the floor with rhythmic movements of her tail.

It seemed that while they were all in the pantry adjoining the kitchen, each about his business, Neghesti had leapt in through the window and, lashing her tail like one possessed, had thrust them all with her head and her shoulders towards the door. She preceded them across the dining room but, seeing that they were hesitating, she returned and again pushed and hustled them towards the door which led to the sitting room.

Jemberié recounted the details in a low, respectful tone and the others confirmed his statements with awestruck pantomime, rolling their eyes and opening and closing their mouths in astonished assent.

When we were alone, Jemberié came close to me and re-marked in a hushed voice that obviously the 'Signora' had suffered unbearably at the sight of her son's distress; she had not known what to do to console him and had, therefore, called the servants. Jemberié then left the room, bowing his head respectfully as he passed in front of the lioness.

By this time, everyone was convinced that Neghesti was an animal only in outward aspect. Tesemmà did not dare dispute Jemberié's interpretation and when he retired from a room in which the lioness was, he moved backwards to the door and made his exit without turning his back, keeping his eye on Neghesti who thoroughly enjoyed the spectacle of Tesemmà walking like a crab. Tabhatú was a Catholic and the idea of a Christian incarnated in an animal shocked her deeply; neverthe-less, Neghesti's conduct was so extraordinary that in spite of herself she could not help admitting that there was something human in the lioness; moreover, the miracles of the saints as narrated by the good sisters at the Mission led her to accept marvels without argument. One thing was certain, however: she no longer feared the lioness, she no longer ran away from her, and often she passed a timid hand over her head. Omar was of a different opinion because, as a good Moslem, he did not believe that a human soul could enter the body of an animal — but he did believe Neghesti was more than an animal: he thought it very probable that she was a jinniyah, a female spirit from the lower regions which had taken on the form of a lioness in order to be near me. Was I sure I had never been loved by a jinniyah?

The colony was changing: it was being prepared as a jumping-off ground for our advance into Ethiopia, and the civilian element – which was thought to be unadapted to what became known as the *clima eroica* – was swamped by the military.

In the preparation for the conflict, the Information Services were naturally of vital importance. We are, however, a naturally exuberant, Latin people and we could not be content with one Information Service: we had six.

There were the military Information Service, the Information Office, the Counter-Espionage Service, the Carabinieri Service, the Customs Officers' Service, and the Service attached to the Department of Foreign Affairs. Each of these organisations was hermetically closed against all the others: each worked on its own account to collect information from beyond the frontier, and each was obsessed with the idea that the information so obtained might fall into the hands of the other Services. The man who brought the news of the presence of three Galla goatherds at the Cuddago wells might so easily pass this invaluable information to someone else and thus another Information Service would learn that three Galla goatherds, armed with two lances and a Mauser gun, had spent the night at the Cuddago wells. Naturally, in spite of the threats which were supposed to seal the lips of informers, they took the same useless tales – or the same lies – to all six Information Services, cashed in on all of them, and departed over the frontier to inform the local Abyssinian chief about the real or invented movements of our troops.

But this was not confusion enough. Men well known for the ability with which they had organised the military Information Services on our Alpine frontier were brought to Eritrea, and the authorities thought they might as well make use, too, of colonial officers who had for some time directed regional Commissariats on the Abyssinian frontier or acted as consuls at Adowa, so these were also called in.

These two measures were the last straw. The new arrivals

from the Alpine frontier had for the most part never been in
Africa before and made up for their lack of experience by the
disconcerting originality of their methods. It was difficult to
make them understand that methods which had given excellent
results in Europe were not advisable on the Ethiopean border,
but when at last they were convinced that they must change
their ways, their ingenuity knew no bounds.

When I heard that one of the counter-espionage aces from
the Ventimiglia-Modane frontier in Italy intended sending a
Chinese, whom he had discovered in Massawa to Abyssinia to
collect news of the movements of the Negus's bands in the
Tigray, and that the man was to go on the pretext of selling ties
to the natives, I felt that, after five years in Eritrea, the moment
had come to ask for repatriation.

To go back to Italy was a simple matter. I had only to go
down to Massawa and take ship. But what about Neghesti?

I could not leave her in Asmara, and even though the journey
did not present any difficulty, I did not see how I could keep
a full-grown lioness in an Italian hotel or in a flat without a
garden, nor could I see myself taking her for daily walks in the
Villa Borghese. Neither did the idea of presenting her to the
Zoological Gardens attract me – with the prospect of paying
her a visit every Sunday surrounded by admiring maidservants
out with their corporals.

Neghesti was in the room when I told Jemberié that I would
be leaving the Colony next month and that I did not know what
to do with her. She laid her head on my knees and looked into
my face with eyes the like of which I have never seen in any
other animal. Jemberié threw me a significant glance, but said
nothing. Later, when we were alone, he remarked very seriously,
'Not speaking when *Signora* listening: yesterday Omar saying
bad word and she hitting so hard his middle with her head so
he falling down.'

The days slipped by. Open trunks stood about in the hall and
lent a depressing air of imminent departure. Good-bye visits;
farewell dinners; my successor already in my office, criticising
my work and itching to change everything; requests from ladies

to take letters and messages to their friends; natives stopping me in the market to say, 'I hear you leaving . . .' All these things made me feel I had nothing to do with the person I had been for so many years of my life. All at once that life lost its interest for me and in thought I was already back in Italy. I had already returned in imagination to the old haunts, found old friends; I began to call to mind faces dear to me which had become indistinct with the passage of time.

But what about Neghesti?

One morning I awoke and realised that in five days' time I must leave. Sitting up in bed, I smoked and turned over in my mind every possible solution to the problem of the lioness. Suddenly Omar burst into my room and threw himself on his knees at the bedside, weeping loudly and knuckling his head. I immediately imagined that his faithless girl friend had deceived him for the hundredth time – and now that I was no longer interested in the *zighini* I decided that perhaps it was the moment to reveal to him the dreadful truth about that black-skinned Messalina. But it had nothing to do with the woman. Neghesti was dead.

The news was so unexpected that I was struck dumb and sat looking at Omar who was huddled on the ground, sobbing. Jemberié arrived followed by Tessemà, and Tabhatú in tears put her head in at the door. Neghesti was dead.

She had been in excellent health the evening before. She had stayed in the kitchen until ten o'clock; Omar had given her a nice piece of raw meat together with the bones of the previous day's beefsteaks which Tabhatú had kept for her; she had eaten with excellent appetite and after a short run in the garden had gone to her cage and had fallen asleep immediately, under Omar's eyes. He had found her in exactly the same position in the morning – but dead.

An hour later my friends from the Vaccine Institute were in the cage with me, bending over Neghesti's body. We put forward many arguments and discussed many possibilities but did not succeed in making any diagnosis. What was the use?

In Neghesti's passing there was a definite breaking of links

which transcended the mere fact of her death: her end closed a
chapter of my life and it did not seem important to know what
had killed her; when one of the doctors suggested an autopsy
I shook my head.

At the foot of the pepper tree which opened its umbrella
over the flower-bed in front of the house Omar dug a deep pit,
while Tabhatú wrapped a white sheet round Neghesti's body
and sewed it up with an interminable row of neat, even stitches.
In the evening, Tesemmà and Omar laid the body of the lioness
in the grave and Jemberié covered it with earth, flattened the
soil with his spade and replanted the flowers which Omar had
taken up carefully before beginning to dig.

Before he began putting the earth back, I saw Jemberié throw
a silver Coptic crucifix down into the grave. Tabhatú saw it too,
and with her thumb she made the sign of the Cross.

Chapter Seven

THE ROAD TO TRIPOLI

IT HAS often been said that the mission of the doctor and the mission of the priest have much in common, and that the art of healing is a priestly function. There is, of course, some foundation for this. Physicians and priests are both called upon to succour those who turn to them in time of crisis; both prescribe certain rules for living, and predict trouble later if the prescribed rules are not kept; both receive confessions and promise salvation – one in this world, the other in the next. But there is another and less often remarked affinity : a priest always remains a priest and a physician always remains a physician. The priest may put aside his habit and the physician may find himself occupied in an entirely different field, but '*Semel abbas, semper abbas*'.

It was therefore not surprising – although I was at this time *chef de cabinet* to the Viceroy in Addis Ababa – that on receiving an urgent call from a sick man I answered the summons at once. But I must admit that it turned out to have been a very imprudent move, for never did any patient so harass me with tenacious affection and esteem, or so torment me with remorseless gratitude.

The patient in question was a bronze-skinned Abyssinian prince, son of the king who had reigned over the country where Jemberié was born. He was almost illiterate and averse to soap and water, but it was quite obvious, without consulting his family tree, that he came of royal stock. He was tall, lean and of a most stern countenance; and when his eyes fell upon the colourful rabble that formed his court his people automatically lowered their own.

When I made his acquaintance he must have been over seventy. His movements were lithe and quick; his hair, moustache and goatee beard were dyed a prodigious black; and when he smiled he displayed a dazzling set of false teeth, which had been supplied by a Swiss dentist. He was courteous, violent, overbearing, or obsequious, according to the circumstances and company; his swift changes of attitude and expression were those of a descendant of a long line of autocrats.

I had already met him on several occasions at official ceremonies or when he had called at my office to obtain facilities of one kind or another. We had to converse through an interpreter because I do not speak Amharic and the *ras* knew no Italian, nor any other of the few languages I possess. His interpreter – as round as a barrel and with tightly curling hair – wore a perennial smile and sweated profusely in all seasons.

Once, when they were both in my office, this engaging young man explained to his master that I was also a doctor. The *ras's* enthusiasm knew no bounds: he insisted on embracing me and I had no choice but to submit, for the delicate political situation made a certain flexibility desirable in dealing with a chieftain possessed of so much authority and such a strong following.

A month later, looking up from the sea of papers in which I was immersed, I again met the eyes of the perspiring interpreter. With the most joyful of smiles he told me that his master was dying and wished to see me before he breathed his last.

In the *ras's* room, as I entered, the smells of civet, incense, stale air and dried sweat on dirty skin vied with each other for the upper hand. There was very little light and I had to accustom myself to the smoky semi-darkness before I could distinguish people and objects. A decrepit old man in a gold-embroidered cloak took me by the hand and led me to a bed from which came the sound of laboured breathing through catarrh-choked bronchial tubes.

The *ras* was naked except for a *fūta* over his legs; he was half-sitting and was supported by a girl who, curled up on the bed, served as a bolster for him; another girl held his head up, while a third and fourth massaged his forearms vigorously, as though they were kneading bread.

The *ras* was the colour of lead. Without the false teeth his face was no bigger than a fist. It was a network of wrinkles, and great drops of sweat ran slowly down his cheeks; the girl he was leaning against wiped them continuously with a cloth. On the whitening hairs of his chest a large, gold filigree cross hung from a greasy ribbon, rising and falling with the painful breathing.

I heard the sound of invisible people moving about in the dark corners of the room – a woman's sobbing, a cough, a mumbled prayer. An infant with a pear-shaped head appeared for an instant at my feet, gave me a meaningless smile and disappeared under the bed.

The old man in the gold embroidered cloak, who until that moment had not said a word, told me in excellent French that the *ras* had been ill for some days, that he had pains, a violent cough and a high fever.

I persuaded the patient to lie down and substituted a couple of cushions for the Shoan girl, but the masseuses transferred their attentions from their master's arms to his legs and feet and continued their manipulations during the entire examination. It was a clear case of lobar pneumonia at the stage of resolution and half an hour later we were in an ambulance, on our way to hospital, the *ras* wrapped snugly in half a dozen blankets.

My official duties kept me extremely busy at that time and I was not able to follow up my occasional patients as closely as I should have liked. The *ras* was in good hands, however, and every now and again a colleague telephoned to give me the latest news of his progress. I felt, therefore, that I need not worry and that I could leave the old man to his fate.

He was certainly far from my thoughts when, one morning, I was again confronted by the sweaty, smiling interpreter together with the decrepit old man in the gold-embroidered cloak. While the former mopped his forehead, the old man informed me that the *ras* had recovered and would go home next day. He, the *ras*, begged that I would accompany him: I had brought him good fortune on the outward journey and my company on the way home could not fail to have a beneficent influence. It was obviously impossible to refuse an invitation couched in these terms, and I was punctual at the appointment.

The personage who received me at the hospital bore no resemblance whatever to the sick man whom I had found propped up on his bed with a Shoan girl for a bolster. He held court in the corridor, dressed in an immaculate *shamma* bordered with red like a Roman senator's toga. The false teeth, back in their place, flashed smiles at the doctors, assistants, nurses and native servants, the latter gazing with awe on the great man who was known and feared throughout Ethiopia.

When he caught sight of me he ran to embrace me, proclaiming through the interpreter that without my intervention he would certainly now be dead, and declaring that he loved me like a blood relation; he called upon the Trinity to witness his words and again took me to his bosom.

A cortege accompanied us down the stairs and crowded on to the steps to see us depart.

In a dilapidated Ford the *ras* and I sat together, facing the interpreter and a Coptic priest who was the *ras's* personal confessor. This humble servant of God, whom the hair-raising confessions of his penitent seemed to have reduced to a stunned condition, sat bolt upright on the seat, his eyes fast closed. At regular intervals, perhaps in order to assert his spiritual authority, he unwrapped from an excessively greasy red cloth a large gilt crucifix, polished it and passed it to us to kiss; this done, he gave it another rub, wrapped it up again in its dirty cloth and placed it on his knee, where it remained until the next exactly similar rite.

The courtyard of the prince's residence was full of cheering people. Zealous janissaries opened a path for us with kicks and blows in all directions. Deafened by the shrill cries of the women, we passed through the inner court, up wooden staircases flanked by genuflecting dignitaries in full rig, and through squalid, dusty apartments, until we reached a room so long and narrow that I took it for a corridor. A Persian carpet which would have brought water to the mouth of any collector was spread over the uneven floor tiles. Against the wall stood an eighteenth-century writing table of inlaid rosewood ornamented with bronze to which time had given a pleasant patina. On the writing table a large photograph of the Viceroy was propped against a glass case which protected a bottle containing a pirate ship in full sail. On the opposite wall, under photographs of the King and of Mussolini, was a long shelf filled with a strange assortment of books, clocks of all kinds, alabaster statuettes, saucerless cups without handles, a few odd silver spoons and forks, a stuffed owl half eaten by moths, and images of Abyssinian saints with round eyes like hard-boiled eggs. Near the door, Marlene Dietrich in a bathing costume exhibited her legs on the colourful cover of a French magazine which was stuck on the wall. A layer of dust toned down the colours, softened the outlines and threw a veil of melancholy over the whole scene.

The *ras* installed himself in an armchair and the march-past began. There were men of all ages, although for the most part they were getting on in years: some were white-haired but there were a few young men and adolescents and even a few children clinging, frightened, to their mothers' skirts, awaiting their turn. Some were dressed in velvet or silk and gold; others wore their everyday clothes and some were covered with rags. All went barefoot.

There appeared to be no order in the procession, nor any question of precedence. The only indication of rank, or degree of relationship to the *ras*, seemed to be the measure of the warmth of his greeting, and the expression – imperious, distant, condescending, affable, affectionate – with which he received the homage.

Some who prostrated themselves to kiss his foot failed to move a muscle of his face; but others were raised and embraced even before they could bow before him. Some bent to kiss the master's knee while he passed a hand absent-mindedly over their heads in a gesture of benediction. One old man, whose beard was so white in contrast to his dark skin that it did not seem possible that it could be real, placed a kiss upon the august shoulder and in return was kissed on the forehead. Many kissed his hands, and there were just a few who made the first move towards an embrace; these friends he strained to his heart, speaking a few words into their ears. Two small boys who threw themselves at his feet were raised, placed on his knee and caressed with a tenderness so at variance with the *ras's* stern expression that they were obviously more scared than gratified. There was one man of Herculean build who burst into tears and cried like a child in his master's embrace.

When the ceremony was over and I was free to withdraw, I assumed that my relations with the *ras* thenceforward would be no longer those of physician and patient, but would revert to those I maintained in my official capacity with all the other native chiefs living in the capital. Little did I know how tenacious gratitude can be in a generous heart and what unexpected forms it may assume.

A week after the ceremony in the palace I was invited to a banquet given by the *ras* to celebrate his recovery. It began at midday and took place in marquees set up on the open space behind the palace. After three hours of it the guests, seated round long tables, were eating with less appetite; some were on the point of falling asleep, overcome by the spring heat and by too much food and *tech*, the strong native beer. To wake things up, a troupe of dancers entered. There were about thirty of them, slim and lithe, with small regular features, their bodies bound from neck to ankles in fine white linen so that they looked like Tanagra statuettes. In single file, with small steps and without raising their feet from the ground, they wound slowly back and forth, serpenting to and fro to the accompaniment of harsh, twanging music and an intermittent dull beating of drums. Their bodies responded to the savage rhythm with a shudder that started at the hips and was accentuated at the shoulders. To my European eyes there was nothing lascivious in the dance, but possibly the motions had some erotic significance for the other guests, conjuring up no end of disturbing images in their excited brains. They followed every movement with smouldering eyes, and showed their appreciation by uproarious shouting and thunderous applause as the dancers made their exit, leaving behind them a trail of perfume mingled with the smell of the rancid butter with which their hair was dressed.

After a lull, during which a speech in honour of the *ras* was made by some pompous dignitary covered with gold and with a lion's mane on his head, the servants rushed in under the tent flaps and·ran round the tables refilling plates and glasses. As they withdrew, the singers entered. They were dressed exactly like the dancers and moved about from table to table, singing short verses in subdued voices with occasional bursts into high trills and cadenzas.

I did not, of course, understand a word and the singing was too strange for me to be able to judge its merits. From time to time a guest threw a handful of coins or a banknote to the girls, and every now and again someone rose to announce that he was giving such and such a sum in honour of the *ras* or of some other notability present at the feast; applause greeted each offer and the singer, having pocketed the money, placed herself in front of the person named and improvised a few couplets in his honour. It was clear that the lines often made fun of some feature of the banquet and contained topical allusions; the guests swayed with noisy laughter and made the plates and glasses bounce as they banged the tables with their hands.

At the head of one of the tables was an important merchant from Massawa whom I had at one time treated for severe syphilis. He shouted over the heads of the others that he offered twenty thalers in my honour.

As a special guest, I was seated on a small raised platform, at a separate table protected by a canopy. Two servants were assigned to me and as soon as my plate was empty they refilled it with the dexterity of conjurors. I have always had an excellent stomach of considerable capacity and I have a special weakness for *zighini*, the Abyssinian stew made with red pepper. I have no idea how many plates I had polished off on that occasion but it must have been an imposing number.

At the moment when the merchant from Massawa called my name my mouth was full and I was chewing with gusto. Suddenly I found the *ras's* interpreter at my side, and in front of me, a few paces away, a singing girl who watched me furtively and smiled with one side of her mouth. She was young and beautiful, tall and coffee-coloured with liquid eyes; her hair was arranged in tiara fashion above her forehead. For a few moments she remained silent, her chin on her breast – then she raised her head and sang. The interpreter translated the lines for me as the girl improvised them.

The beautiful creature declared herself to be terrified; she trembled, so she affirmed, from head to foot, her teeth chattered, she could hardly speak and a cold perspiration ran down her body. For a moment she held her audience in suspense, tickling their curiosity, and then explained that she was terrified because she found herself face to face with a lion.

I assumed a modest air and smiled my most benign smile. The young woman covered her face with her hands and continued her song: she could see the lion – he was tall and large-limbed, with a silver mane, and he crouched in the shade looking at her with eyes of fire. I began to be embarrassed. Hundreds of eyes were fixed on me and I wondered what sort of figure I cut as a lion. Yes, the girl insisted, she saw the lion, the *ambessa*, and she recognised him not because he roared, for in fact he smiled at her; not because he was ferocious, for in fact he was kindly. How did she recognise him? 'I recognise you, O *ambessa*, because you have been eating for four hours without a pause!'

The guests rose to their feet and yelled their approval. The *ras* smiled and waved to me. The Massawa merchant, shouting down the others, invoked God's blessing on me in Arabic. The interpreter mopped himself and offered congratulations and good wishes.

In primitive communities the big eater or drinker is always a popular figure: a large appetite is taken as an indication of strength which demands respect and inspires admiration. At that particular moment, however, I would have been glad to disappear into the earth; instead of which I had to rise and thank the company. There was further applause as, through the interpreter, I praised the beauty of the singer and the melody of her song and put some thalers into her hand.

The next day, when Jemberié opened the door to me on my return from the office, he announced that a man and woman were awaiting me in the drawing room. The man was the *ras's*

interpreter and the woman was the singer who had professed
herself terrified at the sight of the lion.

The rotund and jovial interpreter became eloquent. The *ras*
loved me and even venerated me, for to me he owed his life;
the *ras* thought of me continually: he admired my capacity for
work and was often sad when he spoke of my solitary life, passed
between the four walls of an office or in a house in which there
was no one to bear me company. When he was with me, the
interpreter continued, the *ras* had no eyes for anyone else: he
followed my every movement, hung upon my words and almost
divined my thoughts. He had been happy to see me laugh at
the singer's improvisations. The girl was of noble family and I
had myself praised her beauty and her singing. Very well then –
the *ras* begged me to keep her: when I was sad she would smile
at me; when I was tired she would sing for me; when I was
lonely she would bear me company – in fact, there was no limit
to what the charming girl would do for me.

The small villa in which I lived was part of the same property
as the Viceregal residence and this situation saved me. I feigned
extreme disappointment as I explained that the Viceroy did not
allow women to live within the precincts of his residence; it
was for this reason, I said, that my staff was all male – valet,
cook and chauffeur. I expressed sincere regret at being thus
obliged to refuse the generous offer made by the *ras*.

The interpreter was completely nonplussed and scratched his
head seeking, but not finding, a solution to this knotty problem.
His Highness did not permit? He blinked his eyes, pushed out
his lips, perplexed in the face of such an unexpected obstacle.
Of course, if His Highness did not permit there was nothing
to be done. Almost as though he expected the Viceroy to appear
in the doorway at any moment, he hurried the singer out of the
room, out of the house, and pushed her into the dilapidated Ford.
With a sigh of relief I watched them drive away.

Two days later I found the *ras* waiting for me in my office.
He did not mention the singer, but invited me to go and live
with him. I could take my servants with me and if I desired
he would supply me with others. The cook whose ability I had

so much appreciated should be placed at my disposal, and a garage was ready for my car. He was ill, he said, and I would be doing him a favour if I would live near him. With the greatest difficulty I managed to make him understand that my functions did not permit me to leave the Viceroy, that I could not for any reason be absent. I promised him that if he called me by telephone I would run to his bedside at any hour of the day or night. With protestations of eternal friendship and undying affection I managed to avoid hurting his feelings and to pack him off, disappointed but not offended.

About three weeks of relative tranquillity followed – not taking into account, that is, the sporadic arrival of monumental dishes of chicken, guinea fowl, bustard, goat and mutton swimming in fiery sauces. These masterpieces of Abyssinian culinary art were a continual threat to my excellent digestion and I should certainly have succumbed to them if my faithful henchmen had not come to my aid by consuming large quantities of birds and goats with an appreciation even greater than my own.

But where the *ras* was concerned peace was short-lived. On my return from the office one night I found Jemberié and the cook on the steps leading to the house. The cook – even blacker than usual – informed me that he was leaving and would like a reference. Jemberié was extremely glum and said that matters were 'not good' – words that, on his lips, were equivalent to the announcement of a major catastrophe. Annoyed, I collared him and ordered him inside. The cook assured me that he would not enter even if I covered him with gold, and Jemberié tried to excuse him by saying, 'Him poor fish very frightened.' Before I had time to ask for explanations a low roar came from inside the house, so powerful that the window-panes still vibrated some seconds after the sound had died away.

In the lounge a very healthy leopard greeted me with the stupid and villainous grimace which is peculiar to its kind, and displayed a set of what seemed to me unnecessarily large claws. There was an iron collar round its neck and two stalwart keepers held the ends of two chains soldered to the collar.

The keepers bowed deeply and the leopard, which seemed

to be in an uncomfortably playful mood, jumped from side to side and pawed the air as though it wished to shake hands with me. One of the keepers handed me a letter bearing the seal of the *ras*, as large as a saucer.

The letter said that the *ras* sent me the leopard so that it could cheer my solitude. It was positively morbid the way my solitude seemed to worry the noble prince.

It was now past midnight. I had a leopard in the house and the truck on which it had arrived had gone again. The cook had also gone. Jemberié, with a gun in his hand, was keeping an eye on me through the half-open door. I struggled to keep calm and to think.

I decided to telephone to a friend in the police. After several unsuccessful attempts, I managed to find him; he was dancing at the Imperial Hotel. He advised me to have the leopard stuffed and send it to a natural history museum. When at last I made him understand that I was not joking he agreed to come at once and concoct a plan of defence, although he did not consider that the affair came within his functions as a police official. With the arrival of the police some order returned to my devastated home. It was arranged that for the time being the beast and its keepers should be housed in an empty shed and that the army mess would provide half a goat for the animal's supper. Next day we found a valiant native battalion which was delighted to adopt the leopard as its mascot and so they took it away.

I have already mentioned that the *ras* was the son of a king and that he wielded more authority and enjoyed greater prestige than any of the other chiefs. I have also said that the political situation at that time demanded that any high-ranking dignitary should be treated with particular consideration. It will therefore be realised that there was every reason for me to control myself and not to let my feelings get the better of me. The effort I made to this end was so great, however, and the resulting nervous tension so severe, that I began to suffer from all the phobias and obsessions that afflict the psychoasthenic. I developed the habit of telephoning home before leaving the office, to see if anything had happened. I tried to persuade myself that this was a perfectly natural thing to do but the fact was that I lived in a continual panic, trying to guess – to foresee – what diabolical idea would next occur to the *ras* as a way of showing his gratitude.

One day, towards two o'clock, the morning's work being done, I put my papers in order, locked the drawers and telephoned home. In answer to my enquiry Jemberié replied in an unusually cheerful tone of voice, 'Little one come, make laughing everybody.'

Shaking with agitation, imagining that the *ras* had made me a present of a son, I asked if the 'little one' was a child and Jemberié, laughing, said it was not and that the 'little one' had a tail and sang. Relieved, I replaced the receiver: evidently it was a bird, I thought – perhaps a parrot.

When he opened the door to me, Jemberié was not alone. At his side, reaching no higher than his elbow, stood a hideous little monster making faces at me.

It was certainly not a child. Black, tough hairs grew out of its chin and upper lip, under a flat nose. It – he – was dressed all in green; at the back his tunic reached to his buttocks and then stood out like the eaves of a roof, draped over a bunch of bulrushes which he wore like a tail. Waddling about on his short, crooked legs, with an obscene movement of the hips, the horrible little monster wagged this outgrowth from side to side. As though his disgusting deformity were not enough, he sang in a shrill and at the same time croaking voice which made my flesh creep. Whatever obscenities he sang about appeared at least to be amusing because the normally impassive Jemberié could hardly restrain his laughter and the cook was doubled up in the doorway, wiping his eyes on his apron. Still singing, the repulsive little abortion hung on to my jacket with his horrible, monkey-like hands, and pulled me here and there in an attempt to make me dance with him.

He was the *ras's* jester. The letter which had come with him was categoric: the little monstrosity was to keep me company and cheer my solitude. His name, I was informed, was Tellaé – which in Amharic means 'My joy'.

I sat down, all the spirit gone out of me, and resigned myself to my fate. 'My joy' turned cartwheels and somersaults all over the room. My resistance was broken: I had no alternative but to keep the creature, much to the *ras's* satisfaction.

But although it was necessary to keep him, I was determined never to set eyes on him. I gave strict orders: he was to be treated well and watched to see that he played no tricks; he was not to go beyond the servants' quarters – he could disport himself in the courtyard; on no account was he ever to be permitted in the sitting room, dining room or in my bedroom; and above all he was to be kept out of my sight.

Unfortunately, the rumour spread that I had a jester and whenever I had guests there was certain to be a lady who, her eyes bright with curiosity, would ask if she might not see him. So 'My Joy' had to be sent for and would arrive, wagging his ignoble hindquarters. He made faces at everyone, imitated the noise made by a hen laying an egg, climbed on the furniture, ran on all-fours under the table snapping at the legs of my guests, and performing any other devilish trick that occurred to him.

If anyone danced after dinner, Tellaé followed them skipping and jumping at their heels and tugging at the lady's skirt. Sometimes he sang at the top of his hair-raising voice, and at others, sitting on the knee of some attractive woman, he would drone out sentimental airs, gaze wistfully into her eyes, and run his hand up and down her bare arm. Men usually found him repulsive, but I was surprised – and mystified – to find that women were almost always interested in 'My Joy'. He was allowed to kiss their hands and they took him on their laps without repugnance, laughing at his caresses, finding his tricks amusing, combing his curling mop of hair with their fingers or pulling his beard playfully as they might have pulled the beard of a goat.

The wife of an American engineer begged me to let her have him. In return she offered me a refrigerator.

My ignorance of the monster's language made it impossible for me to discover whether the creature was really an idiot or whether he was intelligent and astute enough to pretend idiocy and make the most of it. Jemberié was always evasive on this point; he was too much of a peasant to betray Tellaé, who came from his own country. Once, being hard pressed for an answer, he announced that even idiots have heads – and, in fact, this aphorism might explain much of the little monster's behaviour.

In the meantime, the *ras's* debt of gratitude, according to him, became incalculable. He came to my house one day and called for Jemberié who, hearing himself addressed by the son of the former king of his country, lost his head completely. It seemed that what the *ras* had to say to me was extremely confidential and knowing Jemberié's attachment to me, he trusted him more than his own interpreter.

We were all in a nervous condition: the *ras* on account of what he had to tell me; Jemberié on account of the incredible honour done to him, and I myself because I already foresaw further misfortunes as a result of this interview. Jemberié held his breath while the *ras* talked. It is a pity I cannot reproduce the conversation word for word. Jemberié's Italian was always more or less of his own invention but on this occasion the awe inspired in him by the *ras*, as well as the delicacy of the subject, caused him to mix his metaphors in the most astounding manner and to light upon the most unheard-of comparisons.

The gist of the matter was this: the *ras* was no longer young and his desires outran his performance. Was it true that there were medicines which renewed youth in old men? Although hardly prepared to play Mephistopheles to this unfortunate Faust, I felt that it would be cruel to deny him the pleasure of an illusion. Having ascertained that his kidneys and heart were in good order, I sent him a preparation which I discovered tucked away in the stockroom of the Swedish hospital. The extraordinary thing is that – according to the *ras* – this preparation worked a miracle. It was a compound of vegetable extracts, often advertised on the back pages of German newspapers, and well-known in medical circles for its absolute inefficacy, and I have never found any explanation of the fact that it appeared to restore to the *ras* some semblance of his lost youth. If he had been a young man suffering from what, for want of a better term, is called sexual neurasthenia, it might be supposed to have been the result of auto-suggestion – but on the dust and ashes of seventy years, suggestion has as much effect as a poultice on a wooden leg. Nevertheless, the *ras* was exultant and his gratitude became almost frenzied and positively dangerous.

One evening as he served at table, Jemberié informed me that the hunchback's sister was in the courtyard, having come to pass a couple of hours with her brother. My jaw fell and I sat with my fork in mid-air, between plate and mouth, struck dumb with terror: in my mind I saw my peaceful little house transformed into a shelter for all the abortions of nature, full of whole families of monsters.

But Tellaé's sister was not deformed: she was tall and beautifully built, and she smiled at me timidly as though excusing herself for the subterfuge her master had forced her to adopt. I recognised her at once: she was the Shoan girl who had served as a leaning-post for the *ras* when he was ill.

It was the last attempt. Twenty days later I left for Asmara on my way to Massawa where I was to embark for Italy. The *ras* was among the group of friends who gathered to bid me farewell. As he strained me to his heart in a suffocating embrace, the hunchback jumped round us wagging his tail, and the interpreter, almost completely dissolved in perspiration, gabbled panting interpretations of the blessings and good wishes and salutations and thanks which the *ras* showered upon me.

I never saw my fantastic patient again but I have not forgotten him. With his glowering, unprepossessing countenance that could nevertheless smile so graciously, he was not a type to be easily forgotten. Though he plagued and tormented me I bear him no grudge. In my life as a doctor in Africa he occupies a place apart: the barbaric prince of a fabulous country in which I once lived.

★ ★ ★

Eighteen months later I was back again in Africa and the world had changed. The war had come, and Libya was a battlefield;

meanwhile, I had been sent out to Tripoli to assume the
Governorship of that city. I arrived during the retreat from Sidi
Barrani, while our Headquarters were wondering why the
British were such a long time in coming. They were expected
any day. In fact they did not reach Tripoli until two years
later.

But the advancing and retreating armies did not pass through
my dispensary and I am, therefore, not obliged to talk about
them. In the city we kept order, while the bombs sank the ships
in the harbour, cleared vast open spaces in the crowded native
districts of the town, and killed many women and children. In
the meantime Rommel had arrived – that extraordinary Teuton
from the fields of Germany, who passed untouched through the
fires of battle almost as though the Gods of Valhalla had made
him invulnerable. *Rommel, Rommel, portami via con te*, sang
the Italian soldiers. But the song was not officially encouraged.

After their early successes, the British troops had to withdraw
beyond the Egyptian frontier, but the Royal Navy retaliated
by besieging Libya and cutting off its supplies. Simultaneously,
interminable British convoys carried into Egypt, up the Red Sea,
men and equipment whose vastly superior strength could not
fail in time to break through from el Alamein to Quattara. The
dam had finally broken and the flood swept towards us.

Italian units, beaten but in good order, passed in a continuous
stream, sad and silent, through the streets of Tripoli towards the
Tunisian frontier. The great mass of the German troops passed
by on the outskirts of the town, and for several nights we heard
the rumbling of their tanks and the scraping and creaking of the
caterpillars on the broken asphalt.

Finally we were left alone – to wait.

We waited three days. Then, with Lucio Pagnutti, who was
mayor of Tripoli, I passed the whole of the third night driving
up and down the Gasr Garabulli road in the hope of meeting
some British patrol through which we could inform the British
Command that the town was now undefended, without army
or arms, and that there was therefore no further justification for
continuing the bombardments. We met no one but stragglers

from the Italian divisions making their way painfully on foot.

Being ingenuous civilians, we had thought that the enemy would arrive from the east. Instead, while we ran up and down the coast road, Tripoli had been outflanked and the advance troops of the Eighth Army, marching over the lowlands, entered the city by the Porta Gargaresc. Neither Pagnutti nor I had had any training in military strategy.

Dawn was breaking when we re-entered the city, and as the mist rose we saw in the pale morning light a great, formless mass of armoured vehicles and tanks drawn up along the sea front from the Belvedere to the Castello.

Round the armoured vehicles moved men whose faces, hair and uniforms were all the colour of sand. Here and there a redcap broke the monotony of the colour and a shout from time to time broke the silence. It was a silence that seemed uncanny and inhuman – not a voice, not a laugh, not a song. Perhaps in that silence lay the secret of their victory.

On the camp stoves scattered along the roadside, the water was boiling for tea. Groups of men were eating standing up, chewing slowly, their eyes fixed on the waters of the port, on the masts of the sunken ships, the tangle of ironwork, the disembowelled shops, the shattered quays. Some of them, stripped to the waist, were washing at tubs full of water; others stood leaning against a wall or the trunk of a palm tree, gazing fixedly at nothing. The smoke from their cigarettes and pipes hung in the air.

Every now and again a dispatch-rider tore along the road, his motor-cycle sounding like a machine-gun, and the silence he left behind seemed more ominous than ever.

I had not slept for two nights and when I got back to my office I found it difficult to keep my eyes open. On my desk lay a note, three days old, in which the Command informed me that 'for strategic reasons' they were withdrawing to the west. I laughed as I read it, thinking of its authors who were following the course of the sun, and then I tore the thin paper very slowly into small pieces.

Now that it was all over, I was suddenly weary. After two years, the vain labour, the futile risks, the unprofitable anxiety weighed unutterably upon me.

In order to overcome the temptation to put my head down on my desk and sleep, I got up and went to the window. Opposite was the bishop's house, peppered with white spots where the plaster had been blow away; on the asphalt in the middle of the road was a large white patch where an incendiary bomb had fallen. The cathedral square was deserted except for a dog which lay asleep in the central flower-bed.

A friar came out of the church, paused an instant on the steps blinking his eyes in the strong light of the winter morning and then, with quick, short steps, made his way towards the Shara Azizia arcade. As he reached the end of the road, a great mastodon of a British tank came round the corner and a boy dressed in leather leaned out of the top and saluted the monk with a wide, ironic sweep of his arm. The humble friar stopped, astonished, and stood staring after the machine until it disappeared behind the Social Insurance building.

I heard the door open behind me and Marchesi, my Deputy Governor, came in holding the side of his face. I thought he had toothache until he began to excuse himself for not having shaved. Before I could make any suitable rejoinder, the door opened again to admit a British captain. He was lean, of medium height, with a rather yellow, melancholy face, close-set eyes and drooping moustache and shoulders. On his arm he wore a white band with some cabalistic signs on it, and at his belt hung an enormous revolver in a white canvas pouch. He looked at us through sleepy lids and in a rather squeaky voice asked if we could tell him where he could lodge the military police. I pointed through the window to the Royal Carabinieri barracks on the other side of the road, empty and at the disposal of anyone who cared to occupy them.

When we were alone once more, Marchesi and I looked at each other. This was our first meeting with the British forces. We had imagined that it would be a solemn, probably a dramatic moment; we had expected the arrogance of the victor and had prepared ourselves to be firm and dignified. Instead, here was a meek man, certainly suffering from his liver, courteously asking us where he could lodge his men. I must admit that we were rather disappointed.

The ring of the telephone made us jump . . . but the message was brief and simple. Together with my Deputy Governor and the mayor, I was required to go to Porta Benito to hand over the city to General Montgomery.

Before I had time to analyse my feelings, the mayor rushed into the room to say that he had received the same instructions. Pagnutti could not keep still. He was thick-set but very agile and he walked up and down and round and round the office. He paused a moment and pointed to the calendar on the wall which had not been changed since 31st December 1942; he talked, without stopping for breath, of the weather, of the people who had invaded his air-raid shelter, of the cook who would not go out and do the shopping for fear of the British. From time to time his features contracted in a nervous tic and he looked at me with his head on one side, one eye half closed, as though entreating me to interrupt his monologue.

In front of Government House my Deputy Governor was talking to a tall, slim British captain who some years before had been vice-consul in Tripoli and who spoke Italian like a native. Next to him stood an irate and self-important brigadier-general who shouted orders and curses, both in Arabic and English, at sentries, motor-cyclists and passers-by.

The Deputy Governor and I got into a car and the captain squeezed in beside the driver. In perfect Italian, with a Florentine accent inherited from his Tuscan mother, the captain (whose loyalty as a British officer at no time prevented him from behaving like a gentleman) informed us that Montgomery was an extraordinary man and that when he said something had to be done, it had to be done and that was all there was to it. As I gazed out of the window on to the streets of the city that no longer belonged to me I asked myself if this remark was meant to intimidate us. Did he expect us to be impressed, I wondered? We knew very well that we were going to hand over Tripoli and that, sooner or later, they would put us behind barbed wire. It was inevitable.

At Porta Benito we found the square lined with trucks full of military police, their machine-guns at the ready. Other red-caps were posted at regular intervals, their revolvers in their hands. It was really rather funny, but we were not in a mood for laughter.

A car arrived from the direction of the sea and General Bernard L. Montgomery stepped from it. With the brigadier-general on one side of us and the captain on the other we moved towards him. Out of the corner of my eye I was watching my Deputy Governor. His face was ashen, of that particular hue which is characteristic of heart cases, and for a moment I thought he would not have the strength to cross the square. But his will was stronger than the disease which a year later caused his sudden death behind the barbed-wire barrier of the Nanyuki camp. He walked slowly, his head high, his face turned to stone, his eyes seeing nothing. He had been ordered to hand over the undefended city to the invader and he fulfilled his last task as administrator with the same sense of duty that had characterised his whole life. Everyone had gone – the leaders who had sworn to defend the city to the last stone, the '*di qui non si passa*' authorities – all had left. The last hospital ship making for Zuara had been crammed, not with the wounded, but with gold braid, and chests covered with ribbons and medals; he, a civilian, with no medals, stayed on.

The mayor's nervous tic had become worse and he kept one eye closed as if he were taking aim. Fortunately, I was not able to see what sort of show I myself was putting up.

At twenty paces from Montgomery, the brigadier-general stepped briskly forward and intoned our respective functions and titles. In the presence of his chief he was much less self-important: he was red to the roots of his hair and his shoulders seemed to me to droop in a most unmilitary manner. He hurriedly presented us, as though anxious to end his part in the ceremony. His brief words of introduction ended, he took up a position two paces behind and to the left of Montgomery, lifted his head very high, threw out his chest and cast a ferocious look at the three of us.

The Commander of the Eighth Army had saluted by touching his beret with two fingers, and at a sign from him the captain went to his side to act as interpreter.

With his back to the radiator of his car and his head drawn down into his collar, the British commander spoke in an abrupt, nasal voice, emphasising his short, sharp sentences with brief gestures of the hand. To avoid looking at us, he kept his eyes on the ground; the bone structure of his lean face was clearly visible under his tan; at the end of each sentence he lifted his eyes, with a flash of blue, to the captain's face; in the intervals for interpretation he remained with his head bent, looking at the ground.

While Montgomery was speaking, I kept my eyes on his face – and the face of the enemy is never beautiful. In all probability, the people conquered by Alexander the Great found even the beauty of the divine Macedonian repugnant.

Troops were to abstain from acts of violence, he said, and to respect private property; the population was to refrain from provoking disturbances and from hostile acts; the Italian colonial officials were to remain at their posts because, in conformity with the laws of war, the functions of local administration must go on; no political collaboration would be requested but, in the interests of the population, the normal administrative activities must continue under the control of the occupation authorities. If they carried out these instructions loyally, said Montgomery, the Italian civilian officials would have nothing to fear.

The British commander's car moved off and disappeared from sight.

The police remained in their trucks, stiff, immobile, with machine-guns and pistols at the ready. Except for them, the square was deserted as we re-crossed it to the waiting cars.

Although the British may have been surprised to find the Italian colonial administration still functioning, they were not slow in deciding to make the fullest possible use of it. It has always been the far-sighted policy of the British in other countries to evaluate and then make use of existing systems of government. On this occasion·they realised that they would be able to operate the administrative machinery of the country very much more rapidly if they first watched the Italian staff at work, than they would if they had to start at the beginning on their own and feel their way. In fact, we were allowed to work un-molested, as we had been promised – until we were no longer needed.

The heat arrived suddenly that June and was excessive even for Tripoli. I had finished luncheon and was seated on the divan in the alcove that served as a sitting-room. The windows were wide open to the stifling air, and a bird chirruped in the distance.

My man Mohamed had placed a cup of coffee on the table. As he stood waiting for me to finish drinking it he gave me the latest news and local gossip in his mixture of Italian and Arabic – the search of Engineer So-and-So's house; the watch stolen from the employee at the municipal offices; the arrest of Mahmud el Gader; the sudden transfer of the military police lieutenant who thought he should receive his meat gratis; the confidences of the beautiful Jewess who was always in a certain colonel's car ('she say he stink like dead dog, curse his mother, but my God he full of lire like sand, and cigarettes and jam, and when he drunk calling sergeant for unbutton').

Suddenly Mohamed broke off and his shiny, black, Fezzanese face took on the greenish hue of a country priest's robe. Leaning on the corner of the table, he swivelled his eyes towards the window and, in a strangled voice, said, 'English in garden: redhat with gun.'

I put down my cup. Although I had been expecting this moment for four months, I noticed with annoyance that at Mohamed's words my heart had jumped into my mouth. I stood up, hoping I had not changed colour.

A major of the military police and a captain entered with business-like steps. A sergeant remained in the doorway, barring the exit. The major was embarrassed.

'I'm frightfully sorry about this ... it's a bad show ...'

I had now regained control of myself: my heart was in its right place and I was sure I was the right colour.

'Do sit down,' I said. 'Have a cup of coffee. My things are almost packed and I can be ready in a few minutes. A cup of coffee for the sergeant?'

I was astonished now at my own composure. For the first time in four months of unceasing tension, of moral discomfort, of unspeakable bitterness, I felt calm and serene. The absurd and paradoxical thought occurred to me that these men who had come to arrest me had, in fact, brought me liberation.

To pack the last few things into my bag was a matter of moments only. When I returned to the sitting room the captain was examining a jug and basin of cast copper – the work of Arab artisans. I invited him to keep it as a souvenir. Blushing profusely, the young man replied that he would look after it until my return.

'Of course,' added the major, 'you mustn't consider yourself a prisoner; it's only a temporary measure – a passing phase – and then everything will be as before.'

I laughed loudly and he gave me a pained look without speaking.

We left the house and climbed into a jeep. The vehicle started up and as we drove away I heard the clang of ironwork behind us. It was probably Mohamed shutting the gates, but it sounded to me like the shutters closing on my African dispensary for the last time.

GLOSSARY

Ar.–Arabic. Amh.–Amharic. Heb.–Hebrew. Tig.–Tigrinya.
Tam.–Tamahàk. Turk.–Turkish. Cun.–Cunama.

aburuf (Ar.): roan antelope
alif (Ar.): first letter of Arabic alphabet
'ālim (Ar.): wise man
ambessa (Amh.): lion
amenokhâl (Tam.): king
angareb (Amh.): native bed
asri (Tam.): sexual freedom

baglāwa (Turk.): kind of sweetmeat
bakkūsh (Ar.): deaf-mute
bakshish (Ar.-Per.): tip, gratuity
ba-n'amuk (Tam.): suspension of prayer
baraka (Ar.): blessing
bashi-bazouk (Turk.): irregular soldier of the Ottoman Empire;
    brave but rapacious
bazina (Ar.): kind of porridge: oats cooked with oil and pepper
bembaka (Ghadames dialect): prostitute
berberé (Amh.): red pepper (see *filfil*)
bhur (Ar.): scented seeds
blād el asrar (Ar.): the country of mysteries
bölük-bashi (Turk): corporal
brīk (Am.): Tunisian sweetmeat

Cādī (Ar.): judge administering holy law of Islam (see *Nà'ib*)
cashi (Tig.): Coptic priest
cumin (Heb.): seed of a plant resembling fennel, used for
    seasoning
cuscus (Ar.): North African dish: groats and vegetables, some-
    times meat

255

dhow (Ar.): Arab sailing vessel, lateen-rigged
dhurra (Amh.-Tig.): durra, millet
Dīvān (Turk.): Ottoman State Council

faqīh (Ar.): Islamic lawyer
fatha (Ar.): first chapter of the Koran
filfil (Ar.): pepper
fiqh (Ar.): jurisprudence
fonduq (Ar.): inn, tavern
frangi (Ar.): foreigner, European
fūta (Ar.): cloth, rag

gandurra (Ar.): tunic
ghebi (Amh.): palace, large house

habībī (Ar.): 'My friend'
hāik (Ar.): Arab outer garment
Hajj (Ar.): title of one who has made the pilgrimage to Mecca
hammâl (Ar.): goat's hair mat
hāwīya (Ar.): the lowest pit of Hell
holy (Ar.): *hāik* (q.v.) worn by women

ihaggaren (Tam.): patricians
iklan (Tam.): negro slaves
Imām (Ar.): prayer leader, leader of Islamic community
imghad (Tam.): vassals

jinn (Ar.): supernatural being, good or evil; Mohammedans
  believe they can assume various forms
jinniyah (Ar.): female jinn (q.v.)

Kāymakām (Turk.): Turkish title
keddāb (Ar.): liar
khālkhāl (Ar.): heavy silver anklets
kharâymi (Heb.): Jewish dish: fish cooked in red pepper sauce
kohl (Ar.): antimony, used by Arabs as eye cosmetic
kudu (Amh.-Tig.): large African antelope
kumiss (Tatar): sour fermented mare's milk

lālla (Ar.): Berber equivalent of 'Mrs'
lām (Ar.): letter 'l' in Arabic alphabet
legbi (Ar.): palm wine
lubān (Ar.): seeds burnt as incense

Maghreb (Ar.): West: in general, Arab-speaking countries of North Africa (West of Tunisia)
mehari (Ar.): dromedaries, for riding (not pack animals)
meze (Turk.): tray of assorted delicacies
mrabba (Ar.): large red woollen tassel
mràbet (Ar.): Holy man, Moslem hermit
Mudīr (Ar.): District chief
mugyas (Ar.): bracelet
mumtāz (Ar.): lance-corporal

Nà'ib (Ar.): *Cādī* (q.v.) or Deputy-*Cādī*
nakuda (Ar.): pilot
ngong (Cun.): giant frog

okka (Ar.): Arab measure of weight

Padishah (Per.): Persian title given to Sultan of Turkey

qibla (Ar.): direction of Mecca, to which Moslems turn to pray

Ramadān (Ar.): ninth month of the Moslem calendar, during which Moslems fast from sunrise to sunset
ras (Amh.): chief, prince
rdā (Ar.): type of *holy* (q.v.); garment worn by women
rebāb (Ar.): kind of violin
rebaza (Ar.): four-stringed mandolin

sa'lūk (Ar.): Moroccan pilgrims to Mecca
sambūq (Ar.): kind of *dhow* (q.v.)
sanduq (Ar.): coffer, chest
Sanhedrin (Heb.): highest court of justice and supreme council in Jerusalem

Saqar (Ar.): one of the pits of Hell

sawārī (Pers.): regular cavalry

shamma (Amh.): white outer garment, like a Roman toga

sharmouta (Ar.): prostitute

shekka (Ar.): woman chief of a tribe or camp

shifta (Amh.): brigands

Sharī'a (Ar.): brigands

shumbāshī (Ar.): sergeant

sīdī (Ar.): 'My lord'; '*Monsieur*'; 'Sir'

simoom (Ar.): hot, dust-laden wind

sīn (Ar.): letter 's' in Arabic alphabet

sirwāl (Ar.): long trousers worn with Arab dress

spahis (Turk.): irregular cavalry, originally Turkish, now Algerian

stambulina (Turk.): long jacket reaching to the knees

sūra (Ar.): chapter of the Koran; most of the chapters have traditional names, e.g. the 57th is known as the *Sura* of Iron

surīya (Ar.): chemise worn by women

Tab'a (Ar.): name of a jinniyah (q.v.)

takuba (Tam.): sword

Tamahàk: language of the Tuaregs

tanfust (Tam.): service, favour

tarbūsh (Ar.): fez, formerly worn by Turks and still by other inhabitants of the East

tebīb (Ar.): physician

tech (Tig.): Abyssinian native beer: a kind of mead

teswîra (Ar.): photograph

tifinar (Tam.): written Tamahàh

tukul (Amh.): hut

uàsra (Ar.): outer garment worn by Berber men, made of goat's hair

'ud (Ar.): lute

ukhaytī (Ar.): 'My little sister'

umzad (Tam.): lute

undufoonay (Cun.): wood mushrooms

wādī (Ar.): river valley or dry watercourse

Wāhhabī (Ar.): puritanical Islamic fraternity founded in the eighteenth century

Wāhido (*el-*) (Ar.): The Solitary One: God

wallàhi (Ar.): exclamation: By God!

yummī (Ar.): 'Mother mine'

zaghārīt (Ar.): battle-cries and cries of greeting with which women hail returning warriors

zâmel (Ar.): pederast

zaptivé (Turk.): native policeman

zāwiya (Ar.): religious school

zighini (Tig.): Abyssinian dish

Zikir (Ar.): religious ceremony in which mystical fraternities attempt to achieve ecstasy by dancing, singing and other means

Zintan: village in Western Tripolitania, known for beauty of its women

INDEX

A VISIT TO DON OTAVIO

SYBILLE BEDFORD
A Mexican Journey

I am convinced that, once this wonderful book becomes better known, it will seem incredible that it could ever have gone out of print.
Bruce Chatwin, Vogue

This book can be recommended as vastly enjoyable. Here is a book radiant with comedy and colour.
Raymond Mortimer, Sunday Times

Perceptive, lively, aware of the significance of trifles, and a fine writer. Applied to a beautiful, various, and still inscrutable country, these talents yield a singularly delightful result.
The Times

This book has that ageless quality which is what most people mean when they describe a book as classical. From the moment that the train leaves New York. . .it is certain that this journey will be rewarding. When one finally leaves Mrs Bedford on the point of departure, it is with the double regret of leaving Mexico and her company, and one cannot say more than that.
Elizabeth Jane Howard

Malicious, friendly, entertaining and witty.
Evening Standard

This edition is not for sale in the USA

*If you wish to receive details of forthcoming publications,
please send your address to
Eland Books, 53 Eland Road, London SW11 5JX*

THE DEVIL DRIVES

A Life of Sir Richard Burton.

FAWN M. BRODIE

Richard Burton searched for the source of the Nile,
discovered Lake Tanganyika, and, at great risk,
penetrated the sacred cities of Medina and Mecca.
But he was much more than an explorer:
he was also an amateur botanist, swordsman,
zoologist and geologist. He wrote forty-three books,
translated erotica, and spoke forty languages and
dialects. His life is probably the most fascinating
and outlandish of all the Victorians.

A model of what a life of Burton should be.
Philip Toynbee, Observer

No one could fail to write a good life of Sir Richard
Burton (not even his wife), but Fawn Brodie has
written a brilliant one. Her scholarship is wide and
searching, and her understanding of Burton and
his wife both deep and wide. She writes with clarity
and zest. The result is a first class biography of an
exceptional man…Buy it, steal it, read it.
J. H. Plumb, New York Times

*If you wish to receive details of forthcoming publications,
please send your address to
Eland Books, 53 Eland Road, London SW11 5JX*

VIVA MEXICO!

CHARLES MACOMB FLANDRAU
A traveller's account of life in Mexico

With a new preface by Nicholas Shakespeare

His lightness of touch is deceiving, for one reads *Viva Mexico!* under the impression that one is only being amused, but comes to realise in the end that Mr Flandrau has presented a truer, more graphic and comprehensive picture of the Mexican character than could be obtained from a shelful of more serious and scientific tomes.
New York Times

The best book I have come upon which attempts the alluring but difficult task of introducing the tricks and manners of one country to the people of another.
Alexander Woollcott

Probably the best travel book I have ever read.
Miles Kington, Times

His impressions are deep, sympathetic and judicious. In addition, he is a marvellous writer, with something of Mark Twain's high spirits and Henry James's suavity ... as witty as he is observant.
Geoffrey Smith, Country Life

Previously published by
ELAND BOOKS

TRAVELS WITH MYSELF AND ANOTHER

MARTHA GELLHORN

Must surely be ranked as one of the funniest travel
books of our time — second only to *A Short Walk in the
Hindu Kush* . . . It doesn't matter whether this author
is experiencing marrow-freezing misadventures in
war-ravaged China, or driving a Landrover through
East African game-parks, or conversing with hippies
in Israel, or spending a week in a Moscow Intourist
Hotel. Martha Gellhorn's reactions are what count
and one enjoys equally her blistering scorn of
humbug, her hilarious eccentricities, her unsen-
timental compassion.
Dervla Murphy, Irish Times

Spun with a fine blend of irony and epigram. She is
incapable of writing a dull sentence.
The Times

Miss Gellhorn has a novelist's eye, a flair for black
comedy and a short fuse . . . there is not a boring
word in her humane and often funny book.
The New York Times

Among the funniest and best written books I have
ever read.
Byron Rogers, Evening Standard

*If you wish to receive details of forthcoming publications,
please send your address to
Eland Books, 53 Eland Road, London SW11 5JX*

A STATE OF FEAR

ANDREW GRAHAM-YOOLL
Memories of Argentina's nightmare

For ten hair-raising years Andrew Graham-Yooll
was the news editor for the Buenos Aires Herald.
All around him friends and acquaintances were
'disappearing'; and as an honest and brave
reporter he was under constant suspicion from all
sides in Argentina's war of fear.

Because of the author's obvious honesty and
level-headedness, we get an especially frightening
picture of life in a society where the slightest
deviation may cause you to disappear for ever.

'I have never read any book that so conveys what it
is to live in a state of permanent fear...'
Graham Greene, Observer

'Will become a classic document about 20th
century Argentina ... It is a small masterpiece.'
Hugh O'Shaugnessy, Financial Times

If you wish to receive details of forthcoming publications,
please send your address to
Eland Books, 53 Eland Road, London SW11 5JX

Previously published by
ELAND BOOKS

HOLDING ON

A Novel by

MERVYN JONES

This is the story of a street in London's dockland and of a family who lived in it. The street was built in the 1880s, and the Wheelwright family (originally dockers) lived there until its tragic demolition in the 1960s, when it was replaced by tower blocks.

As a social document, the book rings with truth, but it is much more than that: its compelling narrative brings the reader right into the life of the Wheelright family and their neighbours.

Moving, intelligent, thoroughly readable…
it deserves a lot of readers.
Julian Symons, Sunday Times

A remarkable evocation of life in the East End of London… Mr Jones fakes nothing and blurs little… It is truthful and moving.
Guardian

Has a classic quality, for the reader feels himself not an observer but a sharer in the life of the Wheelwrights and their neighbours.
Daily Telegraph

*If you wish to receive details of forthcoming publications,
please send your address to
Eland Books, 53 Eland Road, London SW11 5JX*

THREE CAME HOME

AGNES KEITH
A woman's ordeal in a Japanese prison camp

Three Came Home should rank with the great imprisonment
stories of all times.
New York Herald Tribune

No one who reads her unforgettable narrative of the years she
passed in Borneo during the war years can fail to share her
emotions with something very like the intensity of a personal
experience.
Times Literary Supplement

This book sets a standard which will be difficult to surpass.
The Listener

It is one of the most remarkable books you will ever read.
John Carey, Sunday Times

Previously published by
ELAND BOOKS

A VIEW
OF THE WORLD

NORMAN LEWIS
Selected Journalism

Here is the selected journalism of Norman Lewis,
collected from a period of over thirty years. The
selection includes ten of the best articles from *The
Changing Sky*, eight more which have never been
collected within a book, and two which have
never previously been published.

From reviews of *The Changing Sky*:

He really goes in deep like a sharp polished
knife. I have never travelled in my armchair so
fast, variously and well.
V. S. Pritchett, New Statesman

He has compressed into these always
entertaining and sophisticated sketches material
that a duller man would have hoarded for half a
dozen books.
The Times

Outstandingly the best travel writer of our age, if
not the best since Marco Polo.
Auberon Waugh, Business Traveller

If you wish to receive details of forthcoming publications,
please send your address to
Eland Books, 53 Eland Road, London SW11 5JX

Previously published by
ELAND BOOKS

LIGHTHOUSE

TONY PARKER

What is it that leads a man to make lighthouse-keeping his life's occupation? Why does he select a monotonous, lonely job which takes him away from his family for months at a stretch, leaving him in a cramped, narrow tower with two other men not of his own choosing?

Lighthouse-keepers and their families have opened their souls to Tony Parker, and his portrait of their lives is as compelling as any novel, and gives us an exceptional insight into the British character.

A very human book; and a pleasure to read.
John Fowles

Immediate, vivid, and absorbing... one of the most fascinating social documents I have ever read.
William Golding

A splendid book which has enriched my understanding of human nature.
Anthony Storr, The Sunday Times

*If you wish to receive details of forthcoming publications,
please send your address to
Eland Books, 53 Eland Road, London SW11 5JX*

Previously published by
ELAND BOOKS

NUNAGA

DUNCAN PRYDE

Ten years among the Eskimos

Duncan Pryde, an eighteen-year-old orphan, an ex-merchant-seaman, and disgruntled factory worker left Glasgow for Canada to try his hand at fur-trading.

He became so absorbed in this new life that his next ten years were spent living with the Eskimos. He became part of their life even in its most intimate manifestations: hunting, shamanism, wife-exchange and blood feuds.

This record of these years is not only an astonishing adventure, but an unrivalled record of a way of life which, along with the igloo, has vanished altogether.

He tells us stories, which he seems to have been born to do.
Time

One of the best books about Arctic life ever written . . . A marvellous story, well told.
Sunday Times

If you wish to receive details of forthcoming publications,
please send your address to
Eland Books, 53 Eland Road, London SW11 5JX

Previously published by
ELAND BOOKS

THE LAW

A novel by
ROGER VAILLAND

With a new preface by Jonathan Keates

The Law is a cruel game that was played in the taverns of Southern Italy. It reflects the game of life in which the whole population of Manacore is engaged. Everyone from the feudal landowner, Don Cesare, to the landless day-labourers are participants in the never-ending contest.

Every paragraph and every section of this novel has been carefully cast and seems to be locked into position, creating a structure which is solid and formal, yet always lively. . .while we are reading the novel its world has an absolute validity. . . *The Law* is an experience I will not easily forget.
V. S. Naipaul, New Statesman

The Law deserves every reading it will have. It is and does all that a novel should – amuses, absorbs, excites and illuminates not only its chosen patch of ground but much more of life and character as well.
New York Times

One feels one knows everyone in the district. . .every page has the texture of living flesh.
New York Herald Tribune

A full rich book teeming with ambition, effort and desire as well as with ideas.
Times Literary Supplement

If you wish to receive details of forthcoming publications,
please send your address to
Eland Books, 53 Eland Road, London SW11 5JX